TRACEY TRUSSELL

D1556593

life lines

WHAT YOUR HANDWRITING
SAYS ABOUT YOU

UNICORN

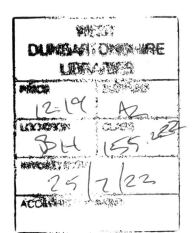

'You've got to know yourself,
So you can at last be yourself.'

D.H. Lawrence

Part Three

Looking forwards

Part Four

Appendix

Part One

A compilation of personal, intimate and professional case study stories

CHAPTER 1

Graphology explained

Introduction

Usually my work as a graphologist flies under the radar. I work behind the scenes, quietly unravelling handwriting in order to piece together broken hearts, fragmented minds and unfulfilled dreams. I reveal the authenticity of paper people and unpick their real lives. My commissions are strictly private and confidential, which means I cannot share the empowering insights of the meaning behind handwritten symbols, nor how they uncover the truths of what may be lurking in the depths of people's minds. *Until now.* Now I have been given the green light to tell some deeply personal and often raw human-interest stories.

One of the strangest facts about my line of work is that although my clients give me permission to delve into the most intimate apparatus of their psyche, I rarely get to meet any of them in person. The closest I usually get to any kind of introduction and engagement is on paper. That is, once the inner self has been revealed and the writer, figuratively speaking, comes to life and steps off the page.

My work is non-gender specific and therefore unprejudiced. This is because the timely limitation of handwriting analysis is that it uncovers the writer's innermost self but is unable to see the physical body – the shape or form the writer inhabits. I have none of the usual physiological details waiting to blind me, or trip me up – no beautiful face, no designer stubble, no skin colour nor toned physique, no warts or wrinkles, no grey-blue eyes, nor any mannerisms or superficial props, no camouflage or fashion labels, no proxy selves. No clues at all, beyond the prosaic knowledge of which hand the writer used (their right or left), their gender (because I am looking at a person's soul and would not know for sure if someone is male or female) and their chronological age (so I am aware of their maturity and evolution).

The whole procedure, from start to finish, is entirely non-invasive and physically painless. The only bodily function involved in the production of a sample (so my work can be carried out), is the natural movement of a right or left hand producing a scribble or a handwritten note. The mental insights gained may prove more painful and intrusive, although the endpoint is always valuable, in some shape or form enlightening and empowering, when the writer gets to know themselves better.

The other remarkable fact is that although the practice of graphology has been around for donkey's years (it can be traced back to antiquity to 3000 BC), it is relatively unknown and unexplored today.

These are the three most common questions I get asked about my work as a graphologist:

'What's graphology?' is the first one. Or sometimes just: *'What's that?'*

'It's handwriting analysis,' I reply.

'Oh! So what can that do?' is the second question.

I explain that it is a way of revealing people's personalities, and that it can uncover pretty much everything – someone's character, behaviour, skill sets, values, aspirations and proclivities, core motivation and potential, and many other things, depending on exactly what the client wants to know. In fact (although I do not say this at the time, simply because it is too much information), your handwriting is the unique pattern of your whole psychology expressed in symbols on the page, and as a fully trained graphologist, I am the person who is able to interpret these symbols.

'Mmm,' they reply. There is usually some headshaking going on at this stage. *'So, how does that work?'*

This third question is invariably asked in a sceptical tone.

I wonder if it is because I have exceeded the eight second rule (the rule that says that by eight seconds people have lost attention and the ability to concentrate) or, because they are truly baffled, my explanation simply does not compute.

I admit, the name graphology does not sound very sexy and it is quite old-fashioned, but that is because it dates back to the time of Confucius. It did not just rock up in the twentieth century. It is not the latest fad. Plus, the concept of what it does – what it can tell you – sounds highly suspect and implausible. However, my goodness, is it effective!

So I do not give up, and I confidently and patiently explain further. I describe the premise of graphology. How it all begins in the classroom when we are taught to write in a specific way and how few people carry on writing in exactly the same way they were taught, and that is why everyone's handwriting looks different and why everyone's handwriting contains the story of themselves. However, I find people are rarely convinced, so usually I end up saying:

'Why don't you try it for yourself? You don't have to take my word for it. The best way of proving if something works or not, is by trying it out.'

Occasionally, I get the opposite response. Sometimes people's faces light up and they say: *'Oooh, really? Can I give you a bit of handwriting?'* And without even waiting for an answer, they are scrabbling around, desperately trying to find a scrap of paper and pen. After all, who does not love knowing more or talking about themselves?

There is one other scenario. Another common theme is the number of people who are afraid to let me see their handwriting and refuse to show it to me; especially when they discover (usually after I've finished analysing someone else's writing they know) just how revealing graphology can be. It can be unsettling, but this is a repercussion of a job done well!

However, the people who are now looking at you as if you are half insane, try to close off the conversation by saying: *'I don't believe in that.'*

So then I am forced to explain that it is not a religion or a faith – it is not something you have to believe in subjectively. I point out that it is an empirical process that has been developed and finely honed over hundreds of years, tried and tested countless times throughout many countries in the world and generally, depending on the expertise and experience of the graphologist who is doing the analysis, it works. And not only that, the system works exceptionally well, with a high degree of accuracy, and it helps people (that is the best bit) for a whole raft of different reasons, every day of their lives. Sometimes it helps in constructive ways that can be quite surprising and life changing.

You may think you know someone inside out, but do you? Really? Appearances can be deceptive. The smart woman with the nice smiley face at a job interview, the chivalrous man on his first date, your leaders, your heroes, your friends and even your enemies are so much more through their handwriting.

It is a whole different story when I actually 'do' the analysis. Then there is a completely different question, and it is the same one virtually every time: *'How could you possibly know that?'* Followed by an emphatic: *'No-one knows that about me!'*

As I say, I do understand. I scoffed and was cynical myself to begin with. In fact, I spent a year doing my own research and observing from a safe distance before I decided to wet my feet and plunge in wholeheartedly. People often ask me how I got into graphology, so I tell them that it was a moment of serendipity. It all began a couple of days after my father died in 2002. My mother had booked to attend a one-day workshop on graphology in Great Missenden and asked me to go along for moral support. Observing graphology first-hand for the first time, it seemed like a magic trick (believe me when I say it is not – there are years of study and hard work involved to become a fully qualified expert graphologist). However, because the 'magic trick' kept on working every single time, I was hooked. I was bursting to understand more – fascinated and hungry for information – because I wanted to perform this magic trick myself. In fact, I wanted to learn everything I could about handwriting analysis. I could see the value of having insight into people's personalities, and I was sold.

Life does not come with directions or a map, but the answers you seek are closer than you think – they are literally at your fingertips. Handwriting (which incidentally begins in the brain, not in the hand) reveals the essence of character. Ergo, graphology is an accurate tool for giving you 'inside' information about yourself (of which you may not even be aware), as well as uncovering personal knowledge about other people too. Who would not want to know about that? Who is not interested in other people's private lives?

One thing about being a graphologist is that I get asked some pretty awkward questions. On one occasion, a client asked if I could tell if her husband was having an affair. She suspected he was, but did not know what to do, so she was looking for evidence. I explained that as a graphologist, I could not know if someone was having an affair, any more than I could predict what would happen in the future, but what I could reveal was a person's character and their propensity or likelihood to behave in a certain way, given a particular set of circumstances at the time. And what I could divulge in this particular instance was his proclivities and sexual preferences, and I could tell almost immediately that he was a heterosexual and repressed homosexual. The suppression of his feelings was palpable; the pent-up tension and anger pumped to bursting. This was one very angry man, who was ready to snap. My concern was for my client, because I could see in her handwriting that she was likely to be devastated by the news. And, of course, she was entrenched in the situation – the reality and facts pounding ad nauseam in her head, intruding on her everyday life. It was one of the hardest reports I have ever had to write.

So imagine, for one moment, having to break the news to a woman you have never met that you believe her husband may be having a secret fling, just from looking at his innocuous handwritten notes on a partially tea-stained, considerably creased and pre-lined A4 sheet of notepaper. Imagine having to explain that whilst you can only advise on the likelihood of someone having an affair, given a certain set of circumstances, you *can* confirm the man she married several decades ago, spent the best part of her life with, was sharing a bed and with whom she was rearing two children, is, in fact, bisexual. I know this just from the way he composes his letters; just by the way he innocently spills his DNA, leaving traces of his whole psychological profile in symbols on the page. Not, you must understand, from the humdrum content of the shopping list, but by analysing the handwriting itself and 'reading' the insight accidentally provided in the flow, the rhythm, the pressure patterns, the spacing and layout, and the formation of his letters.

In any piece of handwriting, the relationship of the author's character to their pen strokes forms an insightful subtext. Every swirl and mark on the paper, irrespective of language, time or location, offers up profound clues to the writer, telling their unique story. Revealing secrets. It may sound unbelievable, but it is true. This is my job.

Imagine also having to explain to a woman what her husband was thinking and how he was feeling, on the day he decided to end his own life – just by interpreting the handwritten contents of a suicide note. Or trying to describe to a young woman what her departed aunt was really like (behind the blissful smile in the decrepit tatty photo), and why her partner might have murdered her in cold blood before taking his own – just by exploring their intimate love letters and dated postcards. Or being asked to construct an in-depth personality profile for a spooked client – just by deciphering an anonymously written poison pen letter and giving clues as to the type of person who wrote it. Or being responsible for the break-up of a fresh relationship – just because the couple's handwritten samples revealed utter incompatibility. It may have taken months after the initial lust had worn off for the unpalatable truths to emerge. The point is, I am dealing with people's lives, with their hearts.

It is not all bad news. Mostly, I have the opportunity to unravel people's personalities by tapping into their handwriting like a gold-digger revealing hidden potential and life-enhancing benefits. I arrive at a psychologically in-depth portrait of the writer by synthesising all the dynamic components of the handwriting (a collaboration of movement, form and space), until they all slot into place, like a multi-dimensional jigsaw. It would be erroneous and potentially inaccurate to focus purely on one handwriting movement in isolation. It is not just a singular loop, angle or flamboyant swirl of the pen that offers up meaning, it is the number of other collaborating handwriting movements that all contribute to verify an interpretation.

I shine a light on issues that confront us every day, helping my clients to understand themselves or someone else just that little bit better, so that they can make informed decisions and therefore make the very best of their lives. I have advised parents selecting the most suitable school for their children. I have helped people in the throes of a midlife crisis explore and confront their thoughts, feelings and anxieties, so they can look at themselves objectively, see who they really are and identify any areas they would like to change. I have supported couples building and strengthening relationships, and I regularly assist companies sourcing the best talent. The list goes on. Every commission is different, and the versatility of graphology cannot be overestimated.

It is all in the script, and that is why I can never resist the urge to analyse a piece of unique handwriting and meet someone new on paper. Every time I hear the tell-tale thud of post landing on the doormat, I always get an excited feeling in the pit of my stomach. The letters are just waiting for me to slit open their envelopes and discover the secrets our handwriting gives up, and the tell-tale clues in the marks we leave behind.

The best part for me is that the study of decoding inky marks and symbols does not discriminate against the visual appearance of the script, but rather champions and treasures these genuine marks on the page. Remember that line in *Bridget Jones's Diary* when Mark Darcy says he likes her just the way she is? Well, that is how I like handwriting – just the way it is. Just the way it naturally spools out on to the paper.

I can circumvent the persona in super-quick time and see exactly what a company is getting for their money, what a man or a woman is dealing with in a spouse, what a young child may be hiding in their heart.

CHAPTER 2

Getting under the surface

Handwriting is intrinsically and unequivocally linked to the brain, inadvertently supplying a direct line to the human mind. So, let us roll out a very broad topic by taking a deep dive into some personal case studies, to find out what this all means and discover what the writing says about the individual.

Can you hide your true character?

Unravelling the inner self

Can you spot if someone is faking it?

On the next page is the handwriting of Wendy.

Now, here's the thing. Wendy's handwriting is mostly legible and therefore fairly easy to read, but try to resist the temptation and habit of digesting the content. Go back to it again and this time imagine instead that the letter has been penned in a foreign language, so it does not mean anything at all to you and the subject matter is irrelevant. Then try to adjust your eye and zoom out, letting the letters almost blur over, so you are observing a sweeping overview of the piece, as if you might be assessing a work of art. Pretend you are looking at a Magic Eye painting, where you have to shift the focus of your attention so you can see a hidden picture in the depth. There is a whole sub-text going on here. If it helps, hold this book at arm's length, just out of clear vision, so you are forced to look at the handwriting from another perspective. Try not to be impressed or prejudiced about your personal judgment of what you think looks beautiful or shocking, or unpractised writing. None of these perceptions will give you true insight into the writer's inner self. Now, you should be able to see other features emerging, particularly ones that stick out like a sore thumb: it may be the style, size, shapes and curves, layout, spacing and structures, thickness or thinness of pen strokes, or even the ebb and flow and 'beat' of the handwriting as it moves across the page. Only now can you begin to see what this living form of enduring expression is telling you about Wendy's character,

très posh/oon lady answered the door, complete
with black Labrador. She had no idea,
hardly surprising, since she sounded as though
she was fresh out of Kensington, but she
pointed me to a cottage further down the road,
where she said an elderly lady, who had lived
in the village forever, resided. I trogged back
down the road and knocked on my second
door [2] (The lady invited me in (Test of a 'real'
Yorkshire person). She knew Lane (Top Farm;
it was immediately opposite her, but the
farmer's name was not Wade.
At that moment, she spotted the postman
driving past & said he would stop near my
car at the top of the hill, so I set off in
hasty pursuit.

I was just in time to catch him —
well I had to yell at the top of my
voice actually. He turned out to come
from Heath in Wales, but he could at
confirm that the people in Lane (Top Farm [3]
had a different name. He the ran through
all the Lane — something farms he visits,

Wendy, 60s, right-handed
Persona style. Medium—heavy and variable pressure.

just by translating the composite or collective movements and symbols that are prevalent on the page.

On first impression, the script looks quite stylish and as if it has been stretched taut across the paper canvas. The handwriting also seems restrained, controlled and contrived, slightly reclining. The main parts of the letters residing on the baseline are unjoined and look somewhat flattened and compressed, whilst the great sweeping downstrokes are huge by comparison – so long, in fact, that they occasionally bump into the sentence below. The writing is accessorised with some long t and H-bars and what appear to be flying *arabesques* dotted around, embellishing the overall fairly lean piece. On closer inspection, some of the t-bars also shoot up diagonally from the baseline and the small r's are unusual because they *jump up* too, vying for attention. We can dissect what this all means, piece by piece.

Any attempt at formulating a superficial or affected style (however well-practised and fluently it is composed) is known as *persona* and handwriting penned in a *persona* style is equivalent to an actor adopting a character and role-playing, or like someone dressing up or putting on a mask. As you can imagine, it takes some conscious effort on the part of the writer to achieve a style that diverts from their natural organic hand. So there is always some degree of control going on and some deliberate attempt to appear sophisticated and stand apart from the crowd, but it is usually a sign that the writer is hiding something or faking it.

People who write in this way are cultured masters of smokescreens and often impose impossibly high standards (on themselves, as well as other people). These people are chiefly concerned with projecting an image and are motivated to present themselves in the best possible light. The reason for this is because there is some aspect of their personality they do not like, so they will go to great pains to hide anything about themselves they believe to be flawed or faulty. In Wendy's case, she feels inadequate and does not want people to see her vulnerabilities, so she tucks them away discretely behind the suit of armour. She is 80 per cent emotion and 20 per cent front. The latter façade inadequately protects the former, hence the *persona*. In other words, Wendy is very sensitive and emotional, so she does her best to cover this up. However, her one-dimensional *persona* is not 100 per cent effective. If it were, the unpicking of her true personality would be limited and harder to crack.

Invariably, an overdeveloped *persona* is equivalent to an underdeveloped personality and then it is just a question of looking at the extent or scale of the artificiality, so the handwriting movements will need interpreting accordingly. Here the paradigm is subtle and can be seen in the arrested or slightly *slow speed* of her writing, the *rigid tension*, *stilted rhythm*, *disconnected letters*, *carefully constructed forms* and finally, in the way Wendy *adorns* and *embellishes* her handwriting. All these movements have an impact on the natural style and flow of the script. When you write quickly, there is no time to disguise your handwriting.

So we can see that the affected script is not overly contrived because Wendy's personality shines through the artifice. There is something about her unique penmanship that leads me to believe she is a flamboyant, eccentric character who revels in a sense of the dramatic. Although I have never met her, in my mind she comes across like a vivid cartoon that enriches and brightens people's lives. Wendy is not of course a cartoon – she is much too dignified (her large upper case letters confirm that), but she is also incredibly delicate and insecure, not a totally 'together' person. These feelings of inadequacy can be seen not only in the *variable pressure* patterns, but also in the way the small parts of her letters in the *middle zone* go up and down size-wise on the baseline, fluctuating greatly (in size) – look, for example, at the word 'people'[3], third line up from the bottom: the oval parts of the p's are visibly larger than the vowels. This means she is all human – very real and authentic beneath the mask.

The fast track to revealing emotion is by examining these small *middle zone* letters (a, c, e, i, m, n, o, r, s, u, v, w and x) sitting on the baseline, because this is the ego area that relates to everything happening daily. A *small* and *weak middle zone*, as we have here (compared with the other zones) pinpoints a personality under strain – it is the classic inferiority complex. We can spot changing moods and social sensitivity by measuring the amount of fluctuation seen in these letters. You would expect everybody's *middle zone* to seesaw to some degree, just because we all have feelings and mood swings that vary from day to day. It is that question of degree or *how much* that is so important. A little variation is considered normal, but letters bobbing around and fluctuating *greatly* is a sign of someone who is feeling highly emotional, moody and temperamental. The more variation in *middle zone* size, the grumpier the writer!

There is another reason Wendy needs to protect herself. The *broad*, stretched-out forms and widely spaced letters tell us that she is highly intuitive and like a sponge. She is taking it all in, soaking up everything, charitably allowing atmosphere, ambience and the quirks of human nature to seep (sometimes insidiously) into her soul, affecting her deeply (*medium–heavy* and *variable pressure*).

You cannot miss those long, bold, frequently high transmitter *t-bars*, which are also replicated on the horizontal gate crossing of the upper case letters H. This tells us that Wendy likes to control the narrative. She can be bossy, persuasive and keen to dominate her environment. This desire for assertiveness is strongly backed up by the *heavier pressure* seen on her downstrokes in the vertical axis. The upper case letters, accessorised by *elaborate arabesques* – see the 'flying curves' in the initial upper case letter T of 'The' in line 9[2] – reveal that she is the grand eloquent and raconteur (never a dull conversationalist) prone to a bit of hyperbole who rarely lets the truth get in the way of a good story. This interpretation is perennially supported by a smattering of open *ovals*, which like little mouths are symbolic of how gossipy, chatty and talkative a person can be. The dramatic *lower zone* also makes its entrance, uncovering an inflated imagination, and the big *arcade*-shaped letters (the humps in the n's and the m's) reveal creativity. There is no doubt Wendy overreacts and exaggerates things that happen, frequently distorting the facts and happy to let fantasy overtake reality. She can come across as quite a drama queen, but actually needs much more reassurance than she shows or to which she would ever admit. This is the root of unexpected moments of childish petulance, which is where the unprescribed* *jumped up* letter r's[1] (extending from the *middle* to the *upper zone*) make their repeated appearance. It is noteworthy that these elevated letters are only ever seen on the r's (which is the letter associated with a bad temper, particularly when it is seen as a *misplaced* upper case letter‡), so it follows that Wendy has a contentious streak. This is a woman who loves an animated discussion, putting the world to rights and will not baulk at arguing or playing devil's advocate.

---

* The *prescription* refers to the benchmark copybook model most of us were taught in school and by which we should all aspire to continue to write. This template would generally be described as *medium-sized* and slightly tilting forwards. The writing should give an overall impression of *balance, rhythm* and *regularity* throughout, and with no distinctive noticeable jarring or excessive movements. Some letters should be joined together, some left unjoined, and all applied by not pressing too forcefully, but hard enough to make a slight indentation on the back of the paper.

‡ *Misplaced upper case letters* are *capital letters* where you would expect lower case only, such as in the middle of a word. They reveal people whose judgment is suspect, as they often get their priorities wrong by attaching importance to things of little consequence, or to the wrong things. They can behave inappropriately with undue self-importance and are also prone to fly off the handle without warning, which means their behaviour is unpredictable. It should, however, be noted that writers who have been taught the Irish copybook are prescribed n's and r's to be written as upper case letters. So care must be taken to ensure the writer was not taught to write in Eire, before assigning a negative meaning! Please also note that Wendy is not guilty of printing this movement – I am just explaining a point.

People who create exclusively arched *arcade* formations in the letters n, m and h are invariably careful, cautious and calculating in their manners and behaviour. They also make steadfast, loyal friends. However, I am left wondering whether these 'friends' are true allies or just acquaintances who are happy to engage in vital conversation, because the writer who *disconnects* or leaves letters unjoined rarely connects with other people in a deep or meaningful way. I also doubt that Wendy shares her secrets with other people, because there is a defensive *left slant* and, of course, a *persona* writer always holds something back!

Do you give out mixed messages?
Talent Resourcing

One of the beauties of graphology is that when it comes to talent selection it cuts right across appearances and slithers beneath the veneer of professionalism, revealing the things people most want to conceal. Some companies use graphology as a tool for recruitment just because it circumvents the *persona* in super-quick time. Sometimes an initial scepticism is an overwhelming factor – it can be hard to get your head around how accurate and far-reaching the technique can be – until the system is tried and tested, and minds are put to rest. The guinea pig is invariably the owner, proprietor or person responsible for paying the bills, who wants to know exactly what they will be getting for their money.

On one such occasion, Amanda Wigzell – director of a franchise of children's nurseries – who was wary of hiring the wrong talent, approached me, following a recommendation. Given her dissidence, we agreed that the most sensible course of action was for me to analyse her own handwriting, so she could test drive the skill first hand. I was confident that the utilitarian evidence would impress and lead to an arrangement. This is my client's handwriting:

I am delayed in getting this handwriting sample written as I have just returned from a fantastic family trip to Lapland! We flew out from Gatwick airport on Thursday morning and arrived to minus 12 degrees! Thankfully snowboots and skis were provided very soon after landing and I was actually really surprised that I wasn't cold at all during the time we were there. My kids, Ellie and Dayje, had the most magical time seeing reindeers and huskies and looking for Santas village. It was an experience none of us will ever forget.

Amanda, age 36, right-handed
Heavy–very heavy and slightly irregular pressure.
Very wide word spacing and strong avoidance
of the edge of the right margin.

A *left slant* often uncovers a desire for personal autonomy, so I could immediately see that Amanda was a strong self-sufficient woman, and this interpretation was supported by her *wide word spacing* and the oversized *defiant letter k*. She comes across outwardly as a nonchalant, cool character, but the *heavy–very heavy pressure* discloses vast energy reserves and deep passions bubbling away just beneath the surface. When you factor the *irregularity* (of her *pressure*) into the equation, it adds another dimension and shows just how much Amanda was struggling to manage this power.

Amanda's disproportionately *large* and *greatly fluctuating downstrokes* – i.e. the *long stems* beneath the baseline, which is the location of the *lower zone* – reveals that boredom is not an option. Amanda is super-restless, always on the go and cannot sit still for two seconds. She works hard and needs a busy, productive schedule (*rising baselines* and *angular forms*), and it seems she is not afraid to try new approaches or embrace new ideas and viewpoints, because the outstretched, *broad, thready* letters and tall yo-yo-ing stems in the *upper zone* all uncover her liberal curiosity. In fact, Amanda enjoys being challenged in this way (*angles,* some *mixed slant, large* and *marked right slanting signature* with *vertical emphasis*).

Amanda needs to see tangible results, and she does not mind working alone in a demanding, practical field. She is a classic hands-on manager, preferring to do things herself, rather than delegating. We know this because the *absolute size* of her handwriting is *small*, the spacing between her words is *wide*, and she closely dots her i's and crosses her t-bars. Her modus operandi is dealing in no-nonsense practicalities and applying a fun, creative twist (*simplified, broad, small* with *arcades*).

Amanda likes to play her cards close to her chest (*left slant*), and whilst she may not want to be the centre of attention (*small size*), she *does* want to stand apart from the crowd and be seen as a businesswoman who transmits a professional goal-orientated attitude and is going places (*large* and *strong right slanting signature,* with *angles* and *vertical emphasis*). An emphasis on the vertical axis always discloses how much a person cares what other people think of them. The *vertical axis* is all about how the writer presents and asserts themselves – the *'Who I am'* – and the more their rank and status matters and the more they need to make their mark, the more prominence and intensity will be applied to the downstroke direction of the pen. The fact that Amanda's signature is completely different to her 'normal' script is also telling.

Part of the enigma is created here because there are paradoxes in Amanda's make-up. When you go inside the mind of any ordinary person, one of the biggest stumbling blocks tends to crop up where you have opposing features, hence mixed messages. These are known as *counter-dominants*, in graphology-speak. This is where you have two very different handwriting movements coexisting side by side within the same script and yet whose interpretations seem to contradict each other. At first sight, it would appear to be a conundrum, just because they do not gel, but look again and you will see that enormous value can be gleaned by amalgamating the two opposing poles. Recognising *counter-dominants* is a quick shortcut way of getting a handle on the contradictory nature of people's personalities.

Let us face it, people are complex and rarely straightforward, so it is not surprising when you come up against conflicting evidence within the same person. Actually, it is these very polarities that make people so intriguing. These mixed messages highlight the paradoxes of personality, brilliantly pinpointing any unresolved issues, friction or stresses all fizzing away beneath the shiny veneer. You just have to work out how these opposing movements interact and then integrate both interpretations, always remembering that one does not automatically cancel out the other.

For example, Amanda's handwriting slopes to the left most of the time, but her signature is directed forwards to the right. This means there is a marked difference between her public and private representation of herself. Her signature projects a typically strong businesswoman *persona* whilst her ordinary handwriting tells a different story.

Naturally we only ever give the version of ourselves we want to project, and this is revealed most lucidly in our signature. The signature is a form of identity, a very personal statement reflecting our public image or trademark, and simultaneously revealing our inner desires and how we wish to be perceived by other people. You could say the signature is the writer's 'shop front', giving a quick snapshot peek at the window dressing. It does not tell us much about the true character nor what is really going on behind closed doors – you would need to look at the writer's usual handwriting to know that. Even the phrase *signature-look* alludes to a manufactured attempt to create something representative of a person's essence. A signature that is congruent with the text means you are dealing with someone who is genuine and upfront with nothing to hide. These individuals project transparency as they face the world with equanimity. The fact that Amanda's signature contrasts with the rest of her writing means that we are provided with symbolic images of the 'real' woman compared with a posed snapshot version of the Amanda she would like everyone else to see. Some people have different signatures in the workplaces and sign themselves off much more informally elsewhere.

When *counter-dominants* are treated carelessly, the end result can give the impression that you are contradicting yourself. However, if you can blend conflicting movements skilfully, you will be able to highlight the humanness of people's inscrutabilities. There is a world of difference, and appreciating what people are wrestling with internally can be the key to understanding what makes them tick.

Sometimes the ambivalence seen reveals the person who is unable to make up their mind and feels pulled in different directions. You may see many clashes within the same sample seeming to make a nonsense of graphology, when in fact they are gifting you an accelerated insight into the writer's unresolved inner struggles. The trick is to merge the two opposing meanings into a final blend, with the stronger element given more importance and emphasis over the less prominent one.

There are some more discrepancies in this script.

Amanda's *left slant* reveals she is the type of woman who wants to make up her own mind and is not the sort of person to be persuaded of anything unless she decides it is right. However, at the same time some of the letters n and m are *overly broad*, which also means she can be easily persuaded.

She dislikes rules and conventionality, yet embraces tradition and has a great love of family – home is where she finds her sanctuary (*broad, left slant varying, defiant k,* some *missing letters* and *downstrokes,* versus a *narrow left margin (LM), arcades* and *cradles*).

There is deep feeling, but it is not shown (*heavy–very heavy pressure* combined with *left slant varying* and *wide word, letter* and *line spacing*).

She is a good communicator and adept at managing her interpersonal skills, yet can be evasive (*part connected* with *clear letter spacing, mixed letter structures* and *broad width,* combined with *wide word* and *line spacing, illegibility*).

Amanda is hard-working, persevering, competent and tough – 100 per cent committed to her cause – but given half a chance, she has a tendency to avoid obligations and responsibilities (*heavy–very heavy pressure, angles, rising baselines, tee-pee d's,* combined with *overly broad, avoidance of right-hand margin,* some *neglect, quite slow* and *50-50 speed*).

She is a broadminded, opportunistic entrepreneur, but equally wary and mistrusting (*broad* and *thready,* combined with *left slant, 50-50 speed, wide word spacing*). She believes that a healthy dose of cynicism aligns her with the straight and narrow and keeps things real.

Amanda's impartiality is difficult for her to deal with because she does not know what to do with all the various thoughts and options rattling around in her headspace, or where next to direct her immense physical energies and enthusiasm. This makes her indecisive. We see the symbolism of her struggling to make decisions in the *greatly fluctuating upper zone* and the *50-50 speed* of her handwriting.

What is more, she suffers from isolation (*wide word spacing*) but knows how easily influenced and indiscriminate she can be in relationships (*overly broad, greatly fluctuating upper zone*) and that there is a propensity to get involved with the wrong people. And so she finds that she often gets hurt or feels let down by discovering she has chosen the wrong friends, colleagues or employees. She has already learnt the hard way that she can relinquish autonomy and be overly accommodating, sometimes to her detriment. So she forces herself not to be instantly reactive to everyone and everything going on around her, and this is why she puts up a defensive stance and keeps people at a distance. In other words, Amanda copes by shutting out the world (*left slant varying, wide word spacing, wide right margin*). There is a battle going on between wanting so much and knowing how easily swayed she can be, so she puts all her muscle into promoting positivity (*angles, rising baselines, heavy–very heavy pressure*). Amanda is intent on submerging her own feelings for the sake of her business (*small size* with a *small, weak* and *greatly fluctuating middle zone, different styles of personal pronoun I, wide word spacing,* and *left slant varying*).

There was a 'should I, shouldn't I?' syndrome going on. Amanda was anxious and scared of what lay ahead and did not know whether to hold back or surge ahead. She was afraid of making the wrong decision, doing the wrong thing and failing. It was as if she had one foot on the brake and one foot on the accelerator. She acted on the spur of the moment one minute and then had second thoughts the next (*50-50 speed* and *avoidance of the right-hand margin*). It did not help that she felt stuck in a rut and was going round and round in circles (*small size* with *greatly fluctuating middle zone*). She needed to gain a sense of perspective and to come up with an organised plan and strategy (hence the *wide line spacing* and some attempts to write slightly larger).

I could see that Amanda was struggling to blend her ideals with practical considerations. Her inability to make decisions was having an impact on everything she did and everything she felt. She needed someone else to give her direction and to help her find a solution, particularly since the current uncertainty was undermining her self-confidence (*weak* and *greatly fluctuating middle zone, irregular pressure, mixed personal pronoun I's, elliptical ovals*).

Once Amanda had eliminated all the suspicions and distrust lurking ominously in the back of her mind, she was progressive enough to take on board my insights and recommendations and implement resolutions. It was agreed that I would assess prospective franchisees before their meeting. That way, candidates may have been on their best behaviour in an interview situation but my client already had insider knowledge – she had had a sneak peek behind the window dressing.

Does your handwriting ever change?
The evolution of Jenny

Handwriting, like personality, is made up of thousands of variables. So the shelf life of a piece of script is indeterminable. Our penmanship naturally changes daily to a lesser extent because we are not robots and we are prone to mood swings, and sometimes to a greater extent just because life happens – and everything that happens in our lives is reflected in our handwriting – but how much would you expect your writing to change over the years? You might expect your core character to remain the same, and any deviations are most likely to be seen in your fluid behaviour and shifting motivating factors.

Adulthood, for most people, continues to be an ever-evolving process of development and maturity. Naturally, everybody's life is different, and people develop and mature at varying speeds. Some people's handwriting rarely changes during their lifetime, while others' alters dramatically. Transformation will depend not only on personal circumstance but also on global evolution, because we are all collectively part of a bigger picture.

You only have to compare the handwriting of all the different people you know in your own personal circle of friends to appreciate that each and every one of them has different handwriting – handwriting that is specific to them. This fact is the premise upon which graphology is based. It is the graphologist's barometer of gauging, quantifying and assessing just *how* and *how much* an adult has departed from the copybook model taught to them in school, that uncovers how far an individual has come and exactly what twists and turns their personality has taken. Graphology does not try to 'flatten' personality, like so many typologies and types which attempt to put people's characters into boxes. It is very individual, pinpointing the uniqueness of a person's psyche in an insightful and far-reaching way that transcends any other type of practice. It is an undeniably rich pattern that reflects the unique story of each writer.

One of my clients emailed, saying: *'You wrote a report for me back in 2009 that was so scarily accurate I wondered if you had been stalking me for most of my life!'* She asked me to revisit her handwriting a decade after her first analysis, to see if she had changed at all with the passing of the years. This is a story about the evolution of Jenny (a fabricated name).

I imagine you are looking at the samples overleaf and going from one to the other and then back again, wondering what the differences are. In Jenny's eyes, her handwriting has changed, but to you, the reader, the basic structure and overall picture looks exactly the same as it did ten years ago. To be fair, even looking through a magnifying glass, the variables are minimal – merely whispers. It seems it does not matter if it is your handwriting or your hairstyle, it is the same old story: we are always more self-conscious and critical of ourselves. When we look in the mirror, we may notice a hair out of place, a few lines or wrinkles appearing, or the odd small spot or blemish on our face, but they are tiny things that other people are unlikely to see. Others generally miss the miniscule detail and are only interested in the outline silhouette. My job is to seek out the disparities within the similarities and evaluate their impact on a shifting personality.

The weather is dreadful today which is an awful shame as we were planning a spending the day in Morpeth on saturday. A little bit of a walk and a potter followed by a pub lunch. Nonetheless I am sure we will find plenty with which to occupy ourselves. It is going to be quite a busy day particularly at the beginning and end. Although Beatrice and Susannah are away all weekend on a WRAX activity weekend, I have to get up to Busy Bees for 10.00. This will mean dropping Chloe at Jane & Victoria's around 9.30. Fairly quiet after that until the evening when Stuart will have to pick up Tom from the bus stop at 6pm. Meanwhile I shall toddle over to Ferryhill to collect Kate from her rehearsal and stay for an hour parents' meeting. It surely can't take a whole hour to tell us about parking outside the theatre! Race home and quick change so that we can go out to dinner with the Morningtons. I think I shall come back to work for a rest next week. Content very dull I can't imagine that you are all that interested in our weekend, but hope this gives you enough material.

Jenny, 40s, right-handed

[Handwritten text:]

Despite outward appearances it is almost the end of April and thus the beginning of spring. I cannot speak for the rest of the country but here in the north of England it seems to have reverted to winter. As I write it is tipping it down with rain. Yesterday I was in London and despite a cold start it remained warm and sunny for both days. So you can imagine my dismay when, on the train journey home we encountered rain and sleet, and on my arrival, snow.

I long for the sunshine, for the ability to get up in the morning and only have to think of one or two items to wear and for there to be no need for socks, tights or coats. Given the choice I don't bother with a coat even when the weather is foul, preferring a cardigan/wrap or brolly. Which is ironic when I consider how many coats I own!

Jenny, 50s, right-handed

31

Let me put you in the picture. Mostly it is true, Jenny's handwriting movements are much the same now as they were a decade ago, and so her fundamental character remains the same, but with two interesting exceptions. First, her handwriting is now more pronounced in every way. It is bigger, heavier, more elaborate, flamboyant and 'loopy', and also more compact (hence more *interlinear tangling*). Even her signature is larger (although this has been edited from final copy for the sake of confidentiality). This means that my previous interpretations can be accentuated. She is fundamentally the same Jenny as before – her core character remains unchanged – but now everything is magnified, so all her colours are more enhanced. They are bigger, bolder and brighter. She is more impassioned, intense and determined; more instinctual, more dramatic and keener to impress. She is even larger than life. It is as if someone has turned up the volume on her personality. You could say that age has endowed Jenny with confidence. She is sassy, spiked with ebullience – the ubiquitous crowd pleaser – and now she would make an excellent leader or a formidable adversary. That is the new flavour of Jenny.

How do I know all this? The *large size* handwriting has become larger, the *light–medium pressure* has become *medium–heavy* and therefore heavier, joined-up words have become uber-cursive or *over-connected*, the *close word* and *line spacing* is even more compact and invasive, there is more *illegibility*, hence more bluffing going on, the *slant* is still inclined, but now it is *right slant varying*, the *t-bars* are still *concave*, but now they swoop down before they dip, and high *arrogance arcades* have appeared, the *ovals* were closed and knotted, but now a few a's are gaping, wide open ...

However, I mentioned *two* exceptions. There is one less conspicuous, almost imperceptible deviation. One more almost invisible but potentially significant development that deserves a mention. If you look very closely at the recent sample penned when Jenny was in her sixth decade, you may be able to see that the pigment in the ink is beginning to blur slightly around the edges. (See the ends of the letters p in 'tipping' and the base of the t-stem in 'the', highlighted in the magnifying glasses). In her forties her pen strokes had a clear-cut outline, but now they are starting to appear slightly frayed and a little *ragged*, as if they are *bleeding*. It is such a subtle deterioration that you may not be able to see it with the naked eye. These tiny details are always so much clearer in the original version – sometimes copies can distort or contribute to the blurriness, however good the reproduction – and therefore you may need to view this mutation under magnification. This impairment is known graphologically as *currency*, which headlines the calibre of the script. The quality of the handwriting is associated with the health of the writer. Blurry edges can indicate the onset of a health problem, although it may be something less sinister and mean that the writer was feeling tired at the time, or simply enjoying the good life and indulging in a tipple or two!

It is all about training the eye to zoom in on the minutiae – the tiny traces, the finer details and the nuances – and then evaluating the variations. Your starting point would be to look at the deviation from the copybook model learnt in school, and then (at a later date) you would be examining, comparing and contrasting any handwriting modifications witnessed over the passage of time. Sometimes the differences will be obvious, sometimes more subtle, but unless the writer has accomplished nothing in their life and stopped evolving, there will be change.

What motivates you in life?
What is the key to your happiness?
Seeking a side hustle

Jessica Martin is a seasoned entertainer with a career spanning thirty years performing in theatre, comedy, television and radio (she was a voice in the 1980s TV comedy *Spitting Image* and appeared as a guest star in the cult *Doctor Who*, amongst other things). Several years ago she was looking to broaden her horizons and expand her repertoire by re-visiting and exploring her career options, so she came to me for help with suggesting a side hustle.

When Jessica approached me initially by email, I knew nothing of her or her background. All I had was a long sample of handwriting – the content of which did not give anything away – a name (which meant nothing to me at the time), her age and the knowledge that she wrote with her right hand. I did not question what type of work she was already doing, as if that would somehow demean my ability as a graphologist or spoil the surprise (for myself) or perhaps make my work look too easy. Jessica did not volunteer any further information and I did not ask. I was working 'blind'. So I realised from the outset that it was imperative I should get some kind of grasp on what she might already be doing, before I could even begin to investigate what else she could do going forwards or how she might expand her established enterprise.

The two main criteria you would be looking to evaluate in such an 'open' situation would be the individual's potential (the 'whats') and motivation (the 'whys'). Getting a handle on someone's potential revolves around uncovering the essence of personality and understanding the writer's core mindset and talent. Then once you have discovered their key motivation, you will know what ignites the heart and gets a person out of bed in the morning.

The majority of us work most days of the week, through the longest hours of the day and for most of our lives, so there needs to be some element of job satisfaction. Money, as well as ability, frequently conspire against personal desire. It is fairly common that practical obstacles dictate type of work, but a job without either passion or motive undermines a person's self-esteem, confidence and sense of worth. Obviously not everyone has the luxury of being able to do something they truly love in life, which leaves motive as a headline requirement. However, if you address potential and motivation synchronously, it is a good starting point.

Let us look at the data (opposite page) and consider Jessica's potential first.

Jessica has an interesting demeanour. She is a socially poised individual living in the moment and absorbed by her everyday experiences – someone who is strongly in tune with the here and now and everything that impinges on her daily life. Jessica is self-possessed yet understated and modest, with a certain pizzazz and frisson about her. She epitomises pragmatism with no nonsense frills and exudes low-key sassiness. Jessica is also delightfully upbeat, brimming with cheerful enthusiasm. She is astute and ingenious, good at improvising and easily bored. She is hands-on and likes doing her own thing, but with plenty of animated company buzzing around her. Jessica knows when to turn on the charm, and oh, she can talk for England, readily hogging airtime. She is shot through with honesty and reliability – a real people pleaser.

The overall *high form standard* (i.e. the quality of her handwriting) only reflects the excellent

Opposite

Jessica Martin, age 47, right-handed

Positively stylish, lively, fluid rhythm with fast speed, high form standard (FS), medium and distinct pressure, small size with dominant, full and rounded regular medium zone (MZ) and fluctuating lower zone (LZ), mixed slant. Compact yet clear and aesthetic layout (with the exception of left margin greatly widening and some avoidance of right-hand margin). Close word and line spacing with no interlinear tangling (apart from one word 'playing' near the end of the script – line 4 from the end). Part connected, clear letter spacing, rising baselines, angles and garlands, closely dotted i's and many crucifix t-bars, regularity (except in LZ and slant). Ovals clear, rounded and closed. Hooks in LZ and personal pronoun I's (PPIs). Impatience ticks. Angles in LZ y's. Pointed upper zonal (UZ) d's. Vanity loops (also seen in her signature).

34

To fulfil the requirements for my handwriting analysis I have been asked to fill out a sheet with as much writing as possible. This I am doing at this precise moment in the comfort of my kitchen on this particularly bleak, snowy day. I don't want to describe my surroundings in case that reveals something of my personality. As I understand it, every stroke, dot, shape, spacing of my script should give an analysis that Sherlock Holmes himself could not surpass.

I am starting a new paragraph (aha, does that as well contain any arcane information). The scribbling of this endless piffle comes easily and is almost like a meditation. The subject of the meditation is what to cook for dinner tonight. We had chicken for dinner last night. I have sausages sitting at the bottom of the fridge. I am always in a turmoil as to whether it is a good idea to consume meat two days in a row. The old days rule was that one only had meat perhaps twice a week it being such a scarce and expensive commodity. Now of course we have all the supermarkets vying with their cheap goods. Sainsbury's prices are cheaper than Asda's. Asda's prices are cheaper than Morrisons. And after Morrisons you've probably got Lidls and Aldis. Not that I am going to get out to any of these shops before the end of the week. I keep looking out of the window each morning to see if there is some break in the white out that we have had since Christmas. I know I could shovel out the snow in the driveway and get the car out but last February, when we had a similar snowfall, I foolishly indulged in a car trip to the corner shops. On my way home I collided with a teenage driver who had lost control of his car. It did a perfect glide into the side of my car. The driver didn't look old enough to be driving. I blamed him entirely of course but secretly I took it to be some kind of divine punishment for me because I'd been too lazy to go out to the shops. So, flash forward to this January, I am housebound, I am playing it safe and have the necessary stocks at hand to keep me from risking my car in this inclement weather.

This is the end of my writing sample.

Age 47

calibre of Jessica's personality and reveals that she is operating and expressing herself from a powerful level of intellect and creative competence. Jessica's considerable resources and talent, together with her agile, versatile mind would need something commensurate with her abilities. I weighed up various possibilities, sifting ideas carefully, meticulously and empirically through my mind:

☛ Just because her writing was neat and legible throughout, and her carefully *closely dotted i's* and *crucifix t-bars* suggested that her attention to detail was sound, it did not necessarily follow that she would find fulfilment functioning in a typically conventional office job.

☛ Just because the *size* of the writing was *small* and there were umpteen *angles*, it did not mean she would relish rolling up her sleeves and knuckling down in a highly focused analytical or research backroom position either.

☛ Just because her *baselines* were *stable,* the *pressure* was *medium/firm* and her *middle zone* was *regular* (with minimal variation), all underlining her sensible 'together' nature and consistent personal self-discipline, it did not mean she would not want or could make do without plenty of stimulation and variety.

☛ Just because she had excellent interpersonal skills (seen in the *lively rhythm* and *mixed forms of connection,* the *clear letter spacing, legibility* and *part connectedness*), it did not mean she wanted to listen to other people and give of herself emotionally all the time.

☛ And just because the *middle zone* was *large* and *dominant, full* and *rounded*, with copious *right tends* and *garland connecting strokes* (uncovering her distinct personable skills, which were tuned into the practicalities of the here and now), it also did not mean she was a bleeding heart who would enjoy dishing out selfless and benevolent care (although I must admit I did toss around the idea of her getting involved in charity work or organising events and bringing people together to raise money or awareness for a cause).

There were other elements and stand out features that needed to be considered and factored into the whole broader, deeper picture. For example, the *large signature* (compared to the size of the main body of script), the *wide* and *significantly widening left-hand margin*, the *greatly fluctuating lower zone*, the tell-tale sign of the *pointed d loops*, the *mixed slant, fast speed* and *stylish* genre, all exposed her potential dissatisfaction with a humdrum run-of-the-mill type of 'ordinary' job. Jessica needed some razzle-dazzle.

I could see that this was a lady who was resistant to stress (because there is *regularity* in the *middle zone*, and also because the *currency* or smoothness and fluency of her writing is superb). I knew that she could keep a cool head under pressure (because although the writing is *compact* and there is *very close line spacing*, there is virtually no *interlinear tangling*. Also, the handwriting *pressure* is *medium*, which means Jessica could find a realistic balance in her work – there would be no under or over exertion). She enjoyed life's hustle and bustle (I have given the usual meaning for restless – seen in the *fluctuating lower zone* – a much more positive spin here, given the quality of her writing) and had the tenacity to succeed where others might give up (*angles, rising baselines, impatience ticks* and *hooks*).

Jessica paradoxically hated missing out on anything. She loved being caught up in the action and drama of a buzzing fast-paced environment, and yet was keen to find her own niche and work independently (*compact script, mixed slant, wide spacing around the personal pronoun I's*).

She was a lady whose headline theme was dealing in sensible practicalities slap-bang in the moment and had a firm finger on the pulse of what makes people's hearts sing (*dominant full* and *rounded MZ, garlands, stable baselines*).

This was an astonishingly articulate, animated and spontaneous lady, permeated with superb powers of expression and blessed with a keynote knack for timing (*clean* and *closed ovals, legible, fast speed, part connected, good clear letter spacing, aesthetic layout, sharp t-bars*). I sensed timing was a virtue worth coming back to.

Jessica was a versatile lady who exuded aesthetic sense, creativity and flair. She needed an audience to show off her abundant inner resources (seen in the fullness of the *middle zone* ego letters) and wow with her molten vivacity and sharp wit. The *large signature* aligned with a *small, stylish script* uncovered her secret desire to thrive on the oxygen of publicity. Jessica's presence could hold a crowd, and she wanted to be someone. (Not forgetting that I didn't know who she was at this stage – she could have been anyone.) It seemed that 'J Martin' was not so much an autograph as a pseudonym, and Jessica was locked into her persona. What scope of work could a woman like this entertain? To my mind, Jessica saw her world as bound up in the confines of the stage, although her inner qualities were less limiting. A thick vein of unexplored creativity was emerging and clearly worth tapping into.

I bookmarked that and dug deeper.

Next, I considered my client's motivation. The overall *small size* of her writing dictates that incentive must come from within. It recognises her ability to channel expression in a more precise and specialised way. It also reveals that she was motivated purely by precision – a sense of personal satisfaction would be derived from concentrating, remaining focused and tackling things thoroughly to get the job done well and to be spot on.

To find out more about someone's whole raison d'être, you would need to be looking at what is going on in the *zones*. Jessica's *middle zone* ego letters are prominent, and therefore hold the most influence in her life. In real terms, this corresponds with anything and everything affecting her ego, such as her self-image, her reputation and status. This meant she was only interested in recognition earned through dedication and the just-deserts of personal effort. Whatever Jessica does, she does it beautifully, and she needs well-deserved applause.

This was a lady whose true self was fused with her role in life. Her work and her image were closely meshed and related, both equally important to her. And with the benefit of self-control and self-discipline, she was able to achieve consistent results. It also mattered to Jessica that she should satisfy her esteem needs too. She wanted to do something different and was ready to go the extra mile to achieve that (*wide* and *widening left margin, angles, rising baselines*).

As we have seen, potential and motivation are closely associated and linked to the writer's strengths, rather than their weaknesses. However, there is always a complication or an obstacle or two, is there not? Things rarely run smoothly. In Jessica's case, something was holding her back, and this can be seen in plain sight in the *avoidance of the right-hand margin*.

It was not simply a matter of pinpointing a divergent career path. It was also clear that Jessica's private face was so wrapped up with her professional persona, that any criticism would affect her deeply. The huge *vanity loop* in the t in 'Martin' screamed out her sensitivity to professional criticism, and the *angular ticks* in her long y stems, together with some *angular points* in the *upper zone*, affirmed her own inner critique. Jessica feared public disapproval or rejection and was scared of failing. However, whilst she was at the front of the queue berating her own inadequacies, she was completely unable to step back and see the bigger picture from a wider perspective, because she had got so bogged down in the detail and could not see the wood for the trees. I knew this because her handwriting was so *small* and the layout was so *compact*. This tells you that all breathing and thinking space had been squeezed, sucked out and vacuum-packed. *Small* handwriting often means that the writer can get stuck in one segment of the problem and finds it hard to see things objectively. Jessica had lost perspective and needed guidance, direction and a trigger (hence my commission), but also subtle reassurance and encouragement to eliminate her little nagging insecurities. This would oil the key that would open the door to a whole new world of creativity for her.

Usually, when you are talking about someone being an actor, you would expect to see *large* handwriting (because they love the drama of being on stage at the centre of attention and projecting themselves in the public eye). However, just like their handwriting, people can be mixed bags, and sometimes the clues can be subtler. Here Jessica's writing was *small*, although the ego area was clearly a defining aspect of her character, as was her perfect timing. Jessica had the gift of being able to capitalise on ephemeral moments in time.

I had a hunch that Jessica was in the public eye and that she might be a stand-up comedian, actor or a one-woman TV or radio show. I imagined, if she were a comic, her timing would be perfect, and she would deliver dry pragmatic real life observational stories rather than the usual string of one-line chimeric jokes.

I suggested she could tap into her creativity and give expression a different route by diversifying into writing. This could be in the form of newspaper or magazine articles, or I had in my mind that she would have the self-discipline and dedication to go the whole hog and become an author – writing a book or an illustrated technical journal of some kind. I thought this might elevate personal feelings of self-satisfaction, and still earn her the kudos she desired.

My report was completed in 2010. Now I know that Jessica has gone from jazz singer to television impressionist to leading West End musical theatre actor, and more recently (because of my analysis) a comic creator and published graphic novelist.

'Thank you for the most insightful analysis I've ever had! I think even you'd have to agree that that was a pretty spooky, spot-on analysis given what you know about me now! I will be recommending you to all the curious people that show business is filled with!' (2010) 'Your work gave me tangible advice on how to explore my untapped creative potential. Look at me ... I'm like a machine now!' (2018)

Jessica Martin

'Mirror Mirror' – do we inherit character?
Exploring the handwriting of identical twins

We often inherit our looks, but do we also acquire character traits from our ancestors, handed down like well-worn trinkets? If so, would we expect identical twins to look exactly the same on the inside as they appear outwardly, as if they are clones of each other? Or would it be truer to say that whilst their phizogs might bear strong indistinguishable resemblance, that is where the similarities end? That gradually with the passage of time and separation, each twin will inevitably be confronted with a whole different set of circumstances as they navigate their way through life, and it is these events that will contribute to define their personal growth and mould their unique personalities and behaviour.

Tom and Theo (fabricated names, for the sake of anonymity) started off on a level playing field. They shared the same womb, attended the same schools and lived in the same family home, but what happened after that? They both chose to be right-handed, but that is not surprising because right-handedness is by far more common – about 90 per cent of the human population is right-hand dominant.

One aspect of their identity the twins are unable to share – where their differences are impossible to hide – is their handwriting. Their penmanship is visual proof that once you scratch beneath the surface there is a whole different foreign landscape to explore.

Let us look at their organic script and see if you can spot the disparity.

I am writing[4] this at my desk[5] as I recover from Covid ! Its been a journey, I am very fortunate to have had it mildly. But whilst the vaccine has clearly worked, my body is pretty[6] shattered, presumably having fought the virus[7] off, albeit successfully[8]. Thankyou, body! I am looking forward to being back to myself later this week, I hope. Gym, running and some socialising, post[9] quarantine – of course.

Theo, age 42, right-handed

Hi Tracey This is me doing
some handwriting samples for you.
Being honest I find that I seem
to have different-ish types of
writing depending on how I feel!
Sometimes I am quite rushed.
And that shows. Here I'm
just trying to write something for
you in the way I usually write
(a bit of a rush) but also I
am using my favorite pen a
on my favorite writing desk which
I find really helps me!
          Let me know if you need
anything else!

Tom, age 42, first-born, right-handed

Now. Imagine you are composing a portrait of someone. You have before you an artist's palette with all the primary colours. Mix some of the colours together and see how the various combinations produce entirely different shades. For example, take blue as your dominant colour and add a small amount of yellow. This will produce green. Add more yellow, and the green becomes lighter in appearance. Now a dash of red to the base blue as an alternative, and this will put an entirely different complexion on the resultant compound colour. Cooks conjure up recipes using the same principle. They combine ingredients in different quantities, and the resulting mixture will produce something different each time. Add spicy flavours in varying degrees to a sauce, and this will generate or create a different taste or flavour. If you have less of an artistic bent and are more scientifically minded, think of a mathematical equation or a formula. Again, the principle is the same. Depending on the chemicals involved, the composition and the proportions, you will have a concise way of expressing this information in a conclusion. In much the same way, graphologists can play with handwriting movements on their personality palette. The only difference is that graphologists do not choose the content – the writer has already provided this on the page.

Theo's portrait

Some of Theo's handwriting may be illegible and more akin to griffonage or scribbling when it is taken out of context (e.g. see 'desk' in line 1,[5] 'virus' in line 5[7]), but as an insight into character it is totally decipherable.

However, the *size* of his brother's writing is inclined to deceive. You are tricked into believing it is larger (than Theo's) because other factors encourage you to do so – Tom's thick strokes, the broad palette and expansive layout on the page compared with his younger brother's much finer, sharper, lighter pen strokes that seem to be squeezed, occupying less space. However, if you draw little horizontal lines along the tips of Theo's upper stems and again at the bottom of his lower extensions (the 'cradles' beneath the baseline) and measure the distance between the two poles (use words such as 'mildly' in line 3 or 'clearly' in line 4), you will discover that Theo's handwriting is not only big, it is bigger and consistently so (it averages 14mm, *medium size* is around 9mm). This means that Theo gives the appearance of being super-confident and will want everyone to notice him.

If you want to know what is really going on on the inside, you will need to examine the *size* of each *zone*, noting the proportions and how they interact. Theo's *middle zone* is disproportionately *small* and *weak* compared with the other sections of his handwriting, and this is your clearest indicator of a personality under strain, one that is determined to convert unconscious feelings of inferiority into pure driving ambition. This notion is supported by the *very large, tall stems*, which scream his orientation for achievement. The *upper zone* also represents our hopes, dreams, aspirations and spiritualism, so you could say that Theo's ambitions are centred around a desire for success and finding religion.

How much hard work is he going to dedicate to making his goals and dreams come true? To know the answer to this question you will need to look at the weight of the handwriting on the paper and see how much energy Theo chooses to invest. Theo's *pressure* is *light*, although it is *heavy* on the vertical. This immediately tells us that although status is vitally important to him (*heavy vertical pressure* is all about *'who I am'*), he applies more mental energy than physical to achieve his aims. So Theo works smart, rather than hard. This conclusion is backed up by the *sharp* pen strokes and underpinned by his enviable *high form standard (FS)*.

The *FS* (which comprises *speed, originality* and *layout*) reveals educational standard, hence the level of intelligence and creative power the writer is using. It also determines how positively movements should be interpreted. Theo's *FS* is *high*, mainly because the *speed* of his writing is fast and the degree of deviation from copybook model is substantial and noteworthy. Theo's agile mind enables him to think and grasp ideas quickly and easily and then express himself clearly and succinctly, without needing to work too hard at it. The *sharpness* of his handwriting enhances the theory that Theo's natural responses and powers of expression are enabled through his intellect. He certainly places more importance on mental processes than emotional feelings. Theo has left a wide space at the bottom of the page (so all his handwriting is concentrated at the top), highlighting his sense of idealism. The *leanness* (seen particularly in the *upper zone* – where there is a distinct lack of loops) reinforces this rationale by telling how Theo has good critical faculty and the ability to think and 'sift the wheat from the chaff'. He is the type who will be reluctant to share his feelings, and this meaning is boosted by some *left slanting LZ* (see the g in 'writing' in line 1 where the LZ pulls to the right[4]), which is an indication that he will not talk about how he feels deep down inside. This can make him appear cool and uncaring – not really the nurturing type. The *broadness* in his writing challenges this last interpretation, showing that there is more to Theo than meets the eye.

This is who Theo is.

Tom's portrait

Usually, with a piece of handwriting like this, I would start by talking about ideas and principles taking precedence over emotion. (This is because the sample is *aerated* – in other words, there is *wide word* and *line spacing* simultaneously.) Unusually, in this instance I also have to introduce the fact that Tom is endowed with emotional intelligence and explain that he cares deeply about his interpersonal interactions and relationships. (This is because the writing is warm, *pasty* and *broad*, with *heavy pressure*). He also has a lovely way about him and an ability to get on with all sorts of people, responding with lively interest once his attention has been caught (*horizontal emphasis, pasty, right slant varying*).

The *size* of Tom's handwriting is interesting because it is *medium* overall, but it zooms in and out (varying from *large* to *small*), highlighting his flexibility. The *zones*, too, are equally balanced but undulating greatly. It is also uncommon to see the perfectionists closely dotted i's in a script so large. This tells us that Tom can see the bigger picture and he is prepared to roll up his sleeves, dive in and tend to the finer details himself too. The *heavy pressure* confirms that he enjoys investing energy to satisfy his desires and 'own' his life.

In a nutshell, *zonal balance* uncovers a motivation to achieve and maintain balance in the writer's whole being, which means Tom tries to approach things sensibly by looking after every aspect of his world – material, spiritual and emotional. However, the yo-yo-ing within the *zones* makes us aware of what is really going on (at the time the sample was created). This desire for balance means that Tom is concerned equally with his headspace (fulfilling his dreams, adhering to principles and listening to his conscience whilst trying not to overthink things), his feelings (everything that is going on in his heart and affecting his moods) and practical considerations (security is also a headline motivator). However, the huge variation – where each *zone* oscillates to such a degree that the fluctuation exceeds the tipping point – shows that he is not able to manage all these needs at once, and this is causing him a problem. Tom is prepped and ready to respond to whatever may come (*broad, rising baselines, connected, right slant varying, complete LZ loops*), but this internal strife is not giving him an easy ride. In fact, it is all taking its toll and making him feel emotional and moody. Consequently, Tom is overthinking things, occasionally losing his temper (some *ovals* are filled in with pen or *flooded with ink* – see a in 'have' in line 4[10]) and generally feeling restless in every way. And this picture of psychological struggle is all reflected in his *avoidance of the right-hand side* of the page, which is always a tell-tale sign that the writer is worried about the future.

There is another significant strand to Tom's personality and that is his strong sense of aesthetics. He is the type of person whose visual order dominates his thought processes and therefore he insists on certain methods of presentation. This can be seen in the *stylish* handwriting and the combination of *pasty pen strokes* with *heavy pressure* and *close attention to diacritics*. If we also factor in the *fast speed*, it is abundantly clear that Tom is creative and spontaneous with lightening reflexes well suited to today's hectic world.

This is the essence of Tom's fighting spirit.

Let us swipe back, take another look at the evidence (on pages 41-42) and explore the resemblance (or kinship) and disparities in their handwriting. This will shed more light on their distinct personalities.

Similarities or dissimilarities?

First, the caveat here is that Theo's moods and emotions are understandably befuddled and haphazard at the moment because he is not well – Theo warned me in advance of his reading that he was suffering with minor Covid. We can see him struggling with this in the *meandering* and *tiled-up baselines* – short bursts of effort can be seen in 'pretty shattered' in line 4[6] (each word rises, but 'shattered' starts lower than the end of 'pretty') and also in the *greatly fluctuating middle zone*. This is fluid, malleable behaviour, no more than temporary and fleeting. These movements change constantly, like the ebb and flow of the tides, like our *slant* (the emotional barometer) or the fluctuation of the *size* of our letter parts (particularly in the *zonal sections* where we can see the areas we are most struggling to deal with inside – our heads, hearts and physical desires).

Notwithstanding, both have a congenital optimism and an inherited upbeat attitude on life (*rising baselines*), and both share a professional bent.

Both are highly intellectually driven, sharing top-drawer educational backgrounds, business acumen, curious natures, innovative strategies and a high-octane fast paced life (*high form standard* or *FS* and *quick speed*). They are problem solvers and go-getters, inspired by a challenge, yet they both feel a sense of prevailing discontentment (*pointed upper zonal loops*) and are driven by a shared concern of not doing well in life (*contracted writing, low t-bars* and in Theo's case a *disproportionately small* and *weak MZ, sharp writing, heavier downstroke pressure* and *stilted rhythm*).

The twins have finely honed social skills. They are well-versed and accomplished at getting on with people from all walks of life (*primary thread, broad*). They are stimulating company and fun to hang out with – both articulate and expressive, enthusiastic action-men keen to keep their options open and maintain an emotional high (*dynamic irregular writing, broad, connected, mixed slant, rising baselines*). Freedom is a powerful imperative for both (*horizontally expanded writing*).

Some of Tom's handwriting is big, but Theo's is bigger. This means that whilst they both come across confidently and enjoy a high profile (*large size, large signatures*), Theo displays ebullient confidence (*large–very large size, connected*) and is serious about his social desires and status (*lean* with *vertical emphasis* and *pressure*).

And this is where the similarities end and their paths diverge.

As we have seen, the twins use their energy in different ways. One sample has far *heavier pressure* than the other – one of the twins has a more intense grip of his pen pressing down on the surface, turning up the volume on his interpretations – and the sample with the *lighter pressure* (turning the dial down) also reveals *vertical pressure* (dialling up again on his stature). With his *heavy pressure*, this means that Tom's heart rules his head. He has deeper emotions and more intensity of feelings, so he will find that the pleasure and pain of experiences are prone to linger and his intelligence weighs more profoundly, deeply and poignantly on his soul. Theo's relationships and encounters tend to be more superficial, so he can bounce back quickly and he does not dwell on things so fiercely (*light pressure*, some *narrowness*).

Theo's head undoubtedly rules his heart and he is mentally resistant and resilient (*light pressure, sharp, double walling*), although in his quest to dare to be different he may become distracted and entertain moments of personal recklessness with a disregard for the consequences (*overly broad, meandering baselines, large*). He has a judicious sense of values and yet there is a part of him that challenges this headspace, these beliefs and principles. It is as if he needs jeopardy and introduces some conflict purposefully, for fear life might become too dull and boring otherwise.

Theo has a dry way of expressing his intelligence (because his pen strokes are *fine, sharp* and *light*), whereas Tom needs a mixture of intellectual awareness and creative energy to feed his versatility and satisfy his gourmet tastes and love of the arts (because his pen strokes are *heavy* and *pasty* and his writing is replete with *positive irregularities*).

They will both question and probe, but Tom will dig deep, wanting to explore the grey woolly areas in life, always imagining and worrying about what the world is going to do to him (*heavy pressure, horizontal emphasis, avoidance of right margin*).

At this point, their motivation paths converge once again. Theo slightly edges the race in his compulsive desire to achieve, whereas Tom is looking to find a work–life balance and musters a more realistic view on the world (*medium* and *smaller sized* handwriting compared with Theo's).

Could their similarities and dissimilarities stem from familial expectations and the way they were treated in childhood? Could they reveal contrasting parental influence? Perhaps one of them takes after their mother and the other has acquired paternal traits?

Parental or familial influence

The shortcut to revealing familial influence is by examining the *personal pronoun I*. Since the twins both use *simple stick* versions (which is an indication of maturity, independence and a confident self-concept), we must resort to other handwriting indicators. You would be looking at the *slant* of the handwriting to determine if the stronger influence comes directly from the mother or father, and then you would be examining other clusters of movements to tell you if this influence was a positive or a negative hang-up.

Where you have a *strong right slant*, there is inevitably a stronger father influence; conversely *a left slant* denotes a mother dominance. *Vertical* handwriting shows a fine balance between the two authorities. Here, both twins share a stronger masculine bias overall, but they both also clearly exhibit signs of a positive mother influence.

In Tom's script, the maternal influence is more developed and intense and can be seen in the way his *lower zone loops* sometimes cross their own *middle zone* (see the g in 'depending' in line 5[11]). This reveals how he can sometimes feel overwhelmed with emotion, but when he is in a positive frame of mind it also shows how he can think quickly and creatively, translating ideas into action. In other parts of the script, we can see enhanced thoughts of his mother by the way his *lower zone loops* are closed off below the *baseline* (see the y in 'way' in line 9[12]). This reveals how selective he is of his social contacts and intimates.

In Theo's sample, the beneficial mother impression delivers less clout but is still evident in the *cradle* style of his downstrokes (see the y in 'successfully' in line 6[8]). This means that the twins' mother exerted an influence on both her sons, albeit in an unconscious way (because in both cases the positivity stems from beneath the baseline). If the mother's influence had been negative, you would expect to see *angular ticks, triangles* or *distortions* in the *lower zone*, or *right tendencies* where *lower zone loops* shoot upwards or flick to the right (and we do see one example of this movement in the q of 'quarantine'[9] in the last line of Theo's sample, showing how awkward and argumentative he can be if someone presses the wrong buttons).

And in spite of the twins' strong desire to both emulate their father and take on the traditional masculine role in life, their frustration can be plainly seen in the *tall pointed upper zonal loops* in both their handwriting. This is an indication of dissatisfaction at an aspirational level and the key that drives them both on to achieve success in their lives.

Is our handwriting penned consciously or subconsciously?

Tom and Theo's handwriting is distinct in many ways, but could this be a conscious decision to be different in their search for individuality over uniform homogeneousness?

This leads us to consider again whether or not handwriting can be manipulated and changed. You would assume that handwriting is produced consciously, with complete awareness of our actions. After all, we are mindful of our faculties when we direct the pen across the page. Or so we think. The skill of handwriting, once learnt, is an automatic procedure and something we do instinctively without thinking about it, like riding a bike or driving a car.

Some aspects of handwriting are inadvertently subconscious. For instance, we may consider the holistic aesthetic layout on the page, particularly if we are creative types or concerned with spatial arrangement, but few writers contemplate the finer details – the subtle spacing and breadth of words and letters, or the gaps we leave between our sentences on the paper's canvas. When we prepare to write on a virgin piece of paper, we may fleetingly think about how wide we make our left margin as a starting point and even how we consciously intend to design and construct our pen strokes into specific shapes, but as our writing proceeds forwards, towards the right side of the page, far less thought is applied.

This is why it is more likely that conscious thought is foremost in our minds when we start out to make brand new marks on paper, and this is the reason why I always ask my clients to produce a handwritten sample composed of at least five sentences. The more someone writes, the more natural and less self-conscious their handwriting becomes and the more fluently it will flow across the page.

Movements which represent **conscious** and intentional thought in some way can be identified as follows:

☞ movements at the beginning of words, such as *upper case* or *capital letters* (because these represent the writer's outer image which they wish to project to the outside world) and *starting strokes* (because these show how the writer consciously prepares for and initiates action)

☞ movements at the beginning of lines, such as *left margin* formation

☞ *downstrokes* (because the *vertical axis* reveals how the writer intends to present themselves and discloses a definite purpose – the writer's conscious desire to make something part of their character)

☞ movements that appear on the left-hand side of the text generally

☞ our trademark *signature* (reflecting a designed and contrived pose)

☞ a *persona* or calligraphic style of writing.

Conversely, the following movements all represent **unconscious** thought patterns:

➣ movements towards the end of words, such as *end strokes*

➣ movements towards the end of lines, for the example the *right margin formation* (which you would normally expect to be higgledy-piggledy or *ragged*, because it has been given no conscious thought)

➣ *upstrokes* (brief moments or heartbeats when the writer is pausing to release tension and re-charge)

➣ *invisible pressure* (producing bent or arced downstrokes where you would expect straight lines. Meaning will depend on where this emanates – from the left or the right – and will show the writer's strong unconscious reaction to their home life or past)

➣ movements that appear on the right side of the text generally

➣ fluctuations in the *zones* (for example, unexplained emotions can be seen lucidly in the *middle zone section*)

➣ everything that happens beneath the *baseline*, which is the line of reality – i.e. in the *lower zone*, because this is where unconscious material resides

In fact, the most unconscious movements are ones that are not even there. That is the blank white space behind the handwriting – the *spatial arrangement* between lines, words and letters. *Large spaces between sentences* for example are produced subconsciously and tell how the writer often has difficulty recalling what they were thinking about.

It seems that nature and nurture have both contributed to the development of the twins' personalities. Character and behaviour are not just a product of pre-wiring, hence identical inherited genes, they are also acquired by exposure to life and different conscious and unconscious influences. So nature and the gene pool bestow their similarities, but in the broader scheme of things it is patently clear that nurture separates the twins. The family effect is also significant and should not be underestimated.

Beauty is not the only thing that is skin deep.

'That is incredible. You've captured exactly who I feel I am and everything that I grapple with in my mind about myself every day. I never thought I'd get this sort of analysis – you've uncovered bits of me that I've spent years trying to get a hold of! It's also incredibly helpful, as I contemplate my character and figure out how best to interact with the world, I can do so with confidence that I have a handle on my character and what makes me tick. Put another way, your analysis validates me and helps me connect with myself.'

Tom

CHAPTER 3

Compatibility

He Loves Me, He Loves Me Not
Can I trust him? Is he the marrying kind?

A young woman in her forties came to me with a personal quandary. She explained that she had just met a guy and thought she was falling for him. She said she had been hurt in the past and wanted some reassurance that she could trust him. She also wondered if he was the marrying type because she was keen to settle down again. The sample attachment provided a fascinating insight into his psyche and motivation in life.

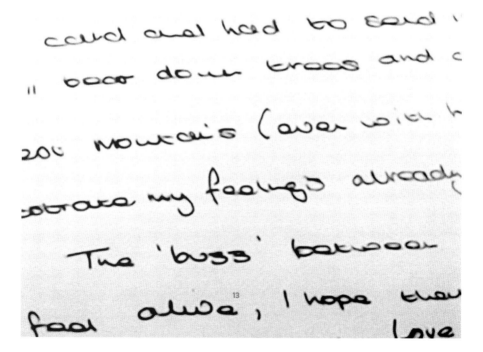

Male, age 51, right-handed

This was my response: I said he was a decent man – warm, straightforward, down-to-earth and thoughtful – someone who could be counted on. I could see this not only in the *regularity* and *legibility* of his handwriting, but also in his signature, which exactly matched the script (and has only been omitted for the sake of anonymity and out of respect for the delicate nature of the enquiry).

I considered the *simple* style of his writing, the *fairly slow measured speed*, the *rounded* shape of his *ovals* and the *unadorned* stick personal pronoun I's.

The style of writing represents the maturity of the writer and how natural they are. A *simple* style gives a child-like appearance, because copybook shapes have been reduced down to their simplest, most elementary form, but without any of the clever shortcuts you would expect to see in *simplified* writing (as illustrated by Lord Denning, later in the book on pages 191-192). It has no mannerisms, superfluous strokes or ornamentation, and the overall *form standard* is likely to be lower than you would see in a *simplified* hand, as it lacks the same intelligence and mental agility. Nevertheless, a *simple* style belongs to someone who is sincere, modest and unassuming. In its negative sense, it is penned by someone who is fairly mediocre, unimpressive and conforming, but here it is indicative of a mature man who is not interested in messing around or getting involved with anyone who is manipulative or prone to game-playing or throwing great dramatics.

The way his words hugged the *straight, stable baselines* further revealed that his feet were firmly on the ground, and he had a common-sense approach to life. I could tell my client, without any qualms, that there was good news. In my opinion, the handwriting sample indicated that he would make a loyal, steadfast, kind and dependable partner. He was a realist, eternally practical, emotionally stable and keen to put things on familiar and firm foundations.

The strong *left tends* on the *end strokes* of some of the letters (see the v in 'alive' on line 6 [13]) left me in no doubt this chap had probably also been hurt in the past and was keen to reflect on things that had happened, so that he could learn by his mistakes. People who exhibit strong *left tendencies* in the *middle zone* often find it difficult to give up and forget people who have meant a lot to them. However, without sight of an original sample (which would disclose the *pressure* applied), I could not be certain if that particular interpretation was relevant here.

I could, however, see that he needed bedrock security in his world, so I suspected he might already be thinking of wedding bells and keen to get married too, just as soon as he found the right lady. I ended my snapshot analysis on a jolly note, asking if I could come to the wedding?

My client was blown away and two weeks later sent me another email. This time she announced that he had proposed and they were getting married on his farm the following summer. I was invited to the wedding!

'Mr Right'

How is your sex life? What is really going on beneath the sheets?

An email popped into my inbox one evening last year, just as I was shutting down my computer. Andrea (not her real name), a middle-aged lady I had never met, explained how she had been in a long-term relationship with a gentleman who was keen to move in with her. The problem was, Andrea lamented, she was not convinced he was The One, so she was not sure she could commit to him for the rest of her life. Also, she made no bones about the fact there was another gentleman lurking in the wings. The whole situation was turning her mind upside down and inside out, to the point where she could not think straight. In the absence of objectivity, she needed some remote help and advice. At the back of her mind a minuscule cog was also concerned that she might be incapable of committing to anyone. Andrea wondered what I could see in her handwriting, and she was curious to know what I thought she should do next.

I could not help but note Andrea's *overly rising baselines*, which immediately spoke volumes. They revealed her courageous heart, unbending optimism and determined spirit, but equally exposed her unhappiness. Put simply, she was trying too hard. Andrea had bravely pasted on a happy smile in the face of adversity, advertising – for anyone who cared to notice – the opposite of how she was really feeling inside. No one would have guessed; anyone looking in would have seen the cheerful mask, without knowing what was really going on behind the façade. I was already beginning to suspect that Andrea did not feel comfortable with her current situation and would rather withdraw than push things forwards. It would be a delicate situation to navigate.

The next impression, which hit me almost simultaneously, was her *strong avoidance of the right margin*. This meant she was more than a little concerned and afraid about what the future held in store for her, and this was naturally making her reluctant to go all the way. Plus, when someone's tall stems (in the *upper zone*) seesaw to such a degree, you know that whilst their thinking processes are flexible (in a positive sense), they are invariably floored by indecision. This oscillation in the 'thinking room' also leaves the writer wide open to influence from other more persuasive individuals. It opens the door, giving free rein for all manner of other things to come flooding in, such as an opportunity for the writer to be manipulated. The intermittent *overly broad width* of some of the small letters n, h, and m's only served to reinforce this idea.

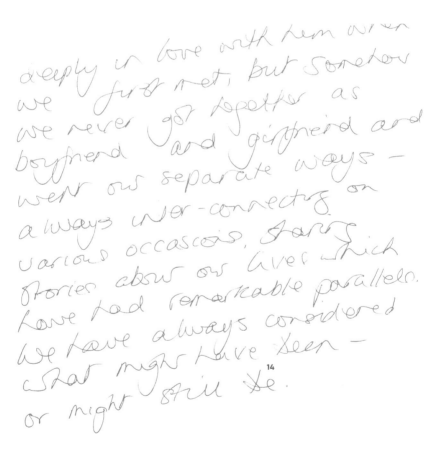

Andrea, age 60, right-handed
Medium–large size with dominant lower zone, greatly fluctuating upper zone and full middle zone. Light pressure. Marked right slant varying. Fluid rhythm. Connected. Overly rising baselines. Broad-overly broad. Compact layout with tangling baselines and close word spacing. Wide right-hand margin. Pseudo arcades. Disjointed letters and x-ing. Ovals with inner loops.

Andrea's *ovals* with *inner loops* exposed her own self-deception. She was trying to kid herself that everything was going to work out beautifully, but the tiny *pseudo arcades* (where there are clockwise loops within the middle stems of the letter m – sometimes these can only be viewed under magnification – gave away her worry. There was nowhere her writing could hide from the truth.

Further, if any more evidence was needed, she had *light pressure*. The trouble with *light pressure* writers is that the lack of force of the pen on paper generally means they hate any type of unpleasant confrontation. So, they go out of their way to avoid it. In this instance it meant that Andrea had become too accommodating and pliable – frankly a bit of a soft touch. She just wanted to proceed without friction, regardless of the outcome.

It seemed to me that Andrea was reacting to other people's wishes and going with the flow (see the *trizonal dynamics*: the way the writing dovetails between the *zones* – for example, in the word 'might' in the last sentence) rather than listening to her gut instincts and satisfying her own intrinsic needs. She had allowed herself to be swept romantically off her feet but now I imagined she felt stuck in a tight corner from which she could not extricate herself. The *x-ing* seen in some letters (notably the letter b in the last word 'be'[14]) only lent weight to this idea, showing her penchant to adopt a fatalistic attitude. She was hoping that things would magically work themselves out and excuse her from having to be proactive. Instead of taking control of her own life, Andrea was giving in to Mr Right. The occasional *disjointed letters* (letters formed in separate strokes rather than in one continuous fluid movement) meant that she found it hard to learn from her mistakes. My client was being manipulated by guilt.

The *medium-large size* of her writing (with the *dominant lower zone, fullness of middle zone*), together with the *marked right slant*, *compact layout* and *cursive style of rhythmic writing*, all contributed to reveal a warm and effusive character. Andrea was brimming with empathy and her emotional quotient was high. She loved life, enjoyed living in the moment and was stimulating company, building relationships with consummate ease. Often with *light pressure* writers, you have all the makings of a social butterfly – someone who enjoys keeping their options open and maintaining an emotional high. The thing was here you could not ignore Andrea's *close word* and *line spacing* and the overall *compact* layout. This highlighted a much more serious need for company. Andrea really did not want to be on her own and was scared she might crumble if she was abandoned. So the idea of someone moving in full-time was appealing in principle – but was he Mr Right?

A woman who could usually keep her head under pressure discovered that she suddenly could not see clearly – her judgment was impaired and she was in danger of losing perspective. You only had to look at the *close line spacing* with occasional *tangling* – where some of the letters bump into each other – to know that Andrea had become blinded by emotion and was unable to exercise reason or apply good old-fashioned common sense. In her head, she could not think straight. I think in her heart Andrea knew she did not want to be pinned down by this man. She knew in her gut that he was not the answer. However, she was well versed at instantaneously reacting to other people's needs (*marked right slant* and *garlands*), and she was too obliging. And of course, Mr Right, or at least this particular man, was taking advantage of this weakness in her character.

A lack of permission prohibits me from illustrating his handwriting. Understandably Mr Right wishes to maintain his privacy and confidentiality, but I can tell you, having personally had sight of a couple of his handwritten cards, this man was definitely *not* Andrea's Mr Right – not by a long chalk. His handwriting bore all the hallmarks of an unpleasant and difficult individual with a filthy temper. He could throw foul temper tantrums when he did not get his own way. Oh, superficially he was good at being romantic and schmoozing his way into her life – which was naturally hard for Andrea to resist – but much of this behaviour was a means to a selfish end. Beneath the fun and laughs, the charm, disingenuous generosity and gallantry, he concealed an awkward inferiority complex. This made him moody, tense and insecure, which was blatantly manifested in erratic and unpleasant behaviour. Mr Right was primed to fly off the handle at any moment. The only way he could live comfortably within his own skin and side by side with his own inadequacies was by effectively controlling Andrea, and I could see that he would make her life hell. Few people are all bad, but when the negatives outweigh the positives, it is time to move on.

Suffice to say, the message to my client was unequivocally strong. I implored her not to let him into her life permanently and predicted that their relationship would only end in disaster. I could see all this in the poor-quality *low form standard* of his handwriting; the *small* and *weak middle zone* which fluctuated dramatically to the extent where he obviously had an issue controlling and managing his mood swings; the rich *pasty* flow of the writing and inevitable *flooding* of *oval letters* (where they were unwittingly contaminated and filled in, smeary with ink), exposing and underlining his atrocious temper. The writing was littered with *irregularities* and the *rhythm* was badly affected and wayward, showing how uncomfortable he felt inside. The whole *layout* was invasive and intrusive, showing no boundaries, and pretty much reflecting the way he carried on in his life. If this was not all damning enough evidence, there were also *blunt endings* to letters (particularly his *horizontal t-bar crossings*, where you would expect to see the pen continue forwards freely in release), and random unprescribed *resting dots* (which are subconscious formations revealing some form of strained thinking and anxiety. They often uncover a writer who is having some difficulty in moving forwards in their lives and therefore has a propensity to leap into things without assessing the situation properly.

I was firm in my conviction that Mr Right was unable to come to terms with his demons. He could not relieve the extreme anxiety, and unacceptable levels of stress, tension and instability he was feeling. I also wondered how this might impact on his physical health at some point in the future. It seemed to me that Mr Right was potentially a candidate for some sort of physical illness, and I did not want this to become my client's burden too.

Andrea confirmed that everything I said about her was true and very close to the knuckle. I was right about Mr Right too. However, she revealed at this point, it was already too late – she had let him move in. Fast forwards six months, she has mentally gone downhill rapidly. So what happened? Mr Right had invaded her privacy, tapped into her vulnerabilities, eroding the sensitive fabric of her mind, manipulatively twisting everything for his own benefit. He had taken control.

Andrea's final remark was how funny it seemed that we had never met, but that I knew more about her and her life than a lot of her closest friends. Now we are back in touch and I am hoping she will find the strength to evict him from her house, so she can get her life back. The other gentleman, who was hovering in the wings, is still waiting patiently. I have analysed his handwriting now. Andrea has so much to look forward to.

Life is a masquerade
Compatibility assessment in the workplace

Rosalind Wyatt is a London-based textile, collage and calligraphy artist. One of her areas of specialism is writing with a needle. I first met Rosalind in 2018, when she invited me to her London studio and asked me to analyse the handwriting of a 20-year-old female contemporary, adding that Molly Martin was her Artist Assistant and she valued my feedback as to their compatibility. (Molly was complicit in this arrangement and just as intrigued to hear my comments, so no samples changed hands without permission.) Naturally, it was critical for me to have recent handwriting samples from both parties, so that I could compare their similarities and differences and find out if they had the potential to have an affinity and work well together, or if there was likely to be any jarring discord between them.

Rosalind submitted a sample of her natural handwritten notes for me to assess alongside Molly's, describing the random pencilled piece she extracted from her sketchbook as 'proper authenticate scribbly-mess'. This is her handwriting:

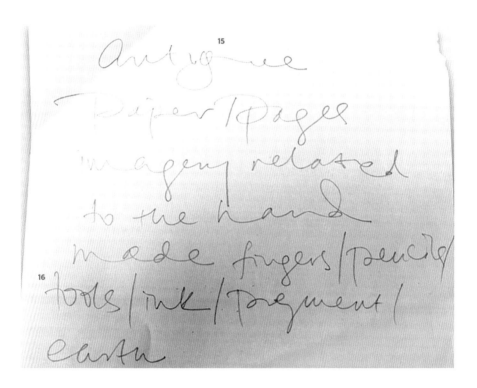

Rosalind Wyatt, 40s, right-handed

Rosalind's *large-sized*, flamboyant, loopy style of script mirrors her confident, larger-than-life personality. The expansive *broad width* (of the letters n and m) and the *horizontal emphasis* throughout tells how she is a forthright, potent, empathetic character who thrives on interaction with other people. This interpretation is supported by the joined-up writing with *garland* or saucer-shaped *connecting strokes* and *wide letter spacing*. The wider apart the letters, the greater the urge to interact with others and the more well-developed the writer's social ease.

Rosalind's work is her identity, and although she comes across as cool, chilled and composed (*upright slant*), she is super-proud, caring and respectful of what she does (*horizontal emphasis*). Her attention to detail is first-rate (illustrated by the closely dotted i's), although she sees the bigger picture and is equally adept at delegating (because her script is *large*).

Rosalind is a storyteller with a sense of the dramatic, and she enjoys a platform (*vertical/slight mixed slant* with *large size*). She thinks quickly and creatively, readily translating ideas into action (see the way the *lower zone loop* in the g of the first word crosses the *downstroke* well above the *baseline*[15]– cutting straight through the *middle zone*) and demonstrates immense flair and integrity for her industry (arched *arcade* shapes with *fullness*, together with *vanity loops* on the d's and *diligence loops* on the p's).

Rosalind is strong, and those little *hooks* (see the tip of the t stem in 'tools'[16]) tell us she will not be beaten if she wants something. She spots opportunities and holds on to her ideas tenaciously, occasionally allowing emotion to seep in and cloud her judgement, so a second pair of canny, sincere eyes is just what she needs.

Rosalind's *spacing* is generally *broad* and *wide*, which means she will not want anyone clingy or needy. She needs someone who is on the same wavelength – someone who is happy to beaver away independently in the background without supervision and who will deliver competently.

I carry your heart with me,
I carry it in my heart.
I am never without it, where
you go, I go, my dear.
I fear no fate, for you are
my fate, my true.
and you are whatever a moon
has always meant, is you.

molly martin.

Molly Martin, age 20, right-handed

Molly is a little treasure. Her *tiny* handwriting is a much more modest affair. She is disinclined to blow her own trumpet, although she gives a slightly bolder account of herself than she really feels (because she kicks off with a *larger sized stick style of personal pronoun I*). However, a little bit of bravado never hurt anyone, and she is very mature for her age. The point is, Molly has zero ego, so she is happy to be in the backroom, out of the limelight, assisting beautifully.

However, Molly should not be underrated because she is also very astute with the gift of the gab. We know she loves to talk and is brilliant at expressing herself orally, because all her *ovals* are *wide open* and most letters are *joined-up*. Both women talk openly and easily in a work setting, receptive to what each other has to say, but equally they need time out for reflection and would not want to be living in each other's pockets (teamwork simply is not their bag). They both also shy away from discussing any personal feelings, although this would not necessarily be appropriate in a work environment. The way Molly completes her *lower zone y loops*, and pertinently the fact that these *loops* are *crossed low* and *atrophied*, means that she pretty much offers exclusivity on partnerships and friendships for the select few. Nevertheless, I was sure she would enjoy a dialogue with Rosalind, thrashing out ideas and excelling at coming up with original ideas, often quite abstract ones.

Molly tends to be a dispassionate observer on life (because the *word* and *line spacing* is *wide* and *aerated* and the *pressure* is *light*) and highly proactive in the workplace (*right slanting* handwriting replete with lots of *angular shapes, joined-up letters* and *rising baselines*). She is happy to be left alone and can be trusted to get on with things (because the *spacing* is so generous). The *fast speed* of her pen strokes, without any loss of *legibility* also ensures that she works quickly, effectively and competently.

Molly is nearly always cheerful, enthusiastic and upbeat – she puts a positive spin on things – and she has an independent freshness and unique quality about her character. She is also a generous open-minded non-judgmental spirit. Her sense of aesthetic appreciation is finely honed, and this is another particularly important aspect in their line of work. Molly loves art, seeking out information, sourcing new ideas. She is also logical, intellectually driven, well organised and a good all-rounder. (All these qualities can be seen in the *aesthetically pleasing layout* with *signature* placed on the far-right side of the paper, the *aerated spacing, rising baselines, broad width, right slant* and the high quality of her script generally – when considering and evaluating the *originality* and *speed* of her writing.)

Molly's *signature* also matches the text, so she likes to be perceived as a straightforward and reliable lady who does what it says on the tin. Further, the *capital letters* of her *signature* have both been penned in *lower case* and joined to the next letter, highlighting Molly's desire to come across as humble and approachable. Despite all this niceness and affability, there is strength at her core, so she would never let anyone take liberties with her. We can see all this in the *sharp angular* tips of Molly's letters and the tiny dot or *full-stop after her signature*, which is an implicit barrier to stop people taking advantage of her. Dots following a *signature* are unconsciously formed and can also indicate effort, thoroughness and self-driving. All of these meanings are appropriate here. The same final full stop can also reveal the writer who likes to have the last word.

The verdict? Rosalind and Molly are a perfect blend and I said they should get along famously. I thought their work relationship was a seamless fit, like a hand in a glove. Rosalind commented that my appraisal was spot on. Molly and Rosalind are still working together today, although Molly now also works independently as a professional textile repairer and restorer, specialising in vintage and fragile fabrics. Molly's debut novel, *The Art of Repair*, was published in 2021.

CHAPTER 4

Children's handwriting

Does it matter if your child does not carry on writing the way they were taught?

Graphology can be helpful for different people of all ages, at different times in their lives. One of the reasons why personal human development is so important is that the adult personality has its roots in childhood. The ways in which we experienced events and the people we came into contact with during our youth largely determines who we are and what we do as adults. Learning to write is a critical step in this process, because it aligns with children learning to speak and expressing themselves eloquently. Handwriting analysis can also be invaluable for the successful development of children's personalities, particularly as it offers up some vital clues as to the child's feelings and thought processes at any phase of their growth. Sometimes it can be hard to express yourself clearly, no matter what age you are or what stage of development you have reached, so analysing children's handwriting can be the key that gives clarity to their parents and teachers.

Once children have mastered the correct pen hold and have advanced to learning how to write, they start by imitating the copybook model set by their teacher at school. In the UK there is currently no standard copy model – it tends to vary from school to school – and has changed enormously over the years.

Early efforts by very young children (between the ages of three and eight) are characterised by stumbles, awkwardness, insecurity and inexperience. This is shown in the handwriting as a lack of spontaneity, slow speed, cramped and unsteady movements, frequent hesitations and amendments. Children also often (but not always) write larger because they are still learning to form the letters (the smaller the writing, the more well developed and mature the child). The element of both the design and control over their pencil or writing implement is still of more concern to them than the thoughts they are trying to express. Their writing will not necessarily even be the correct way up – letters may be reversed or upside down – or stay in a horizontal line, and the baselines may be unsteady and meandering. All these things in a child's handwriting are perfectly normal, unless the signs are extreme, because they are going through a big learning curve. Some children may be still sorting out which hand to use in their writing – left or right – and some may be just learning how to hold a pen. Only gradually do they gain enough hand-eye coordination to trace the strokes properly and copy a template accurately.

Handwriting develops steadily during the primary school period. Once the basics have been memorised, practise improves the co-ordination. Children generally acquire sufficient skill to write with a firm and controlled hand and at a pace that suits their ability and temperament. Most children are taught school copybooks that have *disconnected print* scripts, which are made up of detached letters built by means of chopped strokes. Because this confines children to a sequence of short, abrupt movements, they cannot drive their pencils or pens at full speed across the paper. There are frequent interruptions, stops and starts, all of which waste time and energy. Print script may be useful as a learning tool, but once a child gains some skill with writing, most (but not all) children are taught to advance away from print to a cursive or joined-up script, so that they can write in one continuous movement. Naturally this provides them with the opportunity to start to increase their speed and fluency. At the same time, children are usually encouraged to write with a pen rather than a pencil, to encourage free movement. Graphologically, this is important too, since *connected* handwriting is an indicator of sociability and dedication.

This case study is about a little girl called Lily. She is fifteen now, but at the time of producing the samples below, she was only five and a half years old.

Lily's picture, age 5½, right-handed

Here (opposite page) Lily can coordinate vertical and horizontal movements. Note that the hairbrush in the first picture is not visually realistic, but she draws what she knows rather than what she sees, and she is a clever girl so she gives clarification by writing what the object represents underneath the illustration.

Next, her parents asked her to do some handwriting for me to analyse, and this is what she produced:

Lily, age 5½, right-handed (sample 1)

The interesting thing here is that both these samples were written on exactly the same day, and one after the other. Lily wrote the first sample completely on her own and without any supervision or hindrance, whilst the second sample was written under the instructions of her parents. They were a little cross with her, because she had not produced a piece of writing that followed the way she had been taught to

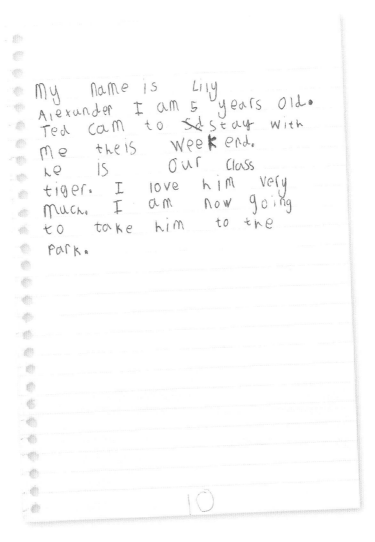

Lily, age 5½, right-handed (sample 2)

write at school. So, for the second sample they stood and watched over her shoulder as she wrote it, inhibiting her natural flow, spontaneity and expression, and thus preventing Lily's true personality from being uncovered.

This highlights the importance of a graphologist working with samples produced under natural, relaxed and unregulated conditions.

Note the *narrow* and *straight left-hand margin* in the second sample, compared with the spontaneity of the unsupervised version, where Lily beautifully (and unconsciously) demonstrates her emerging character even at this very tender age. The 'true' sample has a greatly *widening left margin, very wide* but *regular word spacing, small size*, a propensity to complete her *lower zone loops* (so the tails of her downstrokes come back up to the baseline, making a loop), tee-pee shaped d's and a simple stick *personal pronoun I* (as opposed to the *pedestal style* of *personal pronoun I*) in the subsequent more inhibited (consciously penned) sample.

This combination of movements reveals that Lily is mature and independent for her age. She is thoughtful and competent – a clever girl who relishes a project or a challenge. She can be quite motivated and enjoys having things to do and getting things done. She does not need other children for company all the time – she is quite good at playing on her own, and happy to do so. And she can be a stubborn little lady too, when she chooses!

So much of Lily's personality development is lost in the sample where her parents have persuaded her to try and emulate the copybook style she was taught by her teacher at school. We can even see her anxiety at being told off and being instructed to do what she is told – i.e. where the *wide word spacing* loses its natural *regularity* and becomes much more *irregular* and uncomfortable, becoming excessively wide in places – revealing stress as the interpretation rather than a natural propensity to enjoy her own company. It is an interesting aspect in graphology, where excess is the source of negatives, and where it steps in and alters the meaning.

Without the first natural sample, I would not have been able to evaluate Lily's developing personality in quite the same way. Neither would I have been able to give her parents the reassurance that her progress was coming along nicely and, like a butterfly emerging from a chrysalis, she was turning into a character with lots of positive skills and attributes. The second sample merely reflected how she had been taught to write in school; although it did reveal the stress and anxiety she felt under pressure to perform.

What are little boys made of?

Jimmy's parents sent me a sample of his handwriting when he was eleven years old. They wanted to know what I could glean about his character and development from his young writing, so they could have a better mutual understanding, with a view to considering the most suitable type of school for their son going forwards.

This is Jimmy's handwriting (Jimmy is not his real name) and the portrait that evolved through assessing the various components.

Jimmy, age 11, right-handed

Jimmy's letters are formed in a variety of different ways including *angle, arcade* and *garland shapes*. A mixture of different shapes of letter structures (purely looking at the n's and the m's) is a sign of maturity and the key to excellent interpersonal skills. It shows that the writer's body language is finely honed (at any age), so they are good at mixing with people and adopting different ways of behaving to fit in with all types of personalities. The clear spaces between the letters back up this interpretation. Few of the letters are glued together, which indicates less dependence on his peers and family. So we know that Jimmy is an independent, mature boy of eleven, who is turning out to be a people's person, savvy at getting on with all sorts of people he meets in life. The *close word spacing* also tells us that he enjoys company and having fun playing with his friends, although the way the y tails loop low down on the stem and finish well beneath the baseline (see, for example, the y of 'day' in line 1[17]) indicates that he prefers the company of an exclusive handful of friends; so Jimmy is quite fussy who he hangs out with. The distance between the *word spacing* varies too, so his appetite for company is a little fickle.

The writing veers from left to right (but mostly left) revealing that Jimmy's behaviour has become unpredictable and hard to read. This would no doubt be causing his parents some anxiety, and Jimmy would be catching his parent's vibes, soaking it all up, and this would affect him too. It is a bit of a domino effect, and a vicious circle. However, it would not be unusual to see an *irregular slant* in the handwriting of a child of this age. This movement simply reflects the exaggerated emotional responses Jimmy would have been feeling at this time of his life, entirely due to inner insecurities and uncertainties. It highlights the hidden worries that are affecting his outward behaviour and suggests that Jimmy is living in an immature state of shifting dissatisfaction. So this, and the *meandering baselines* and the weak ego area in the *middle zone* are all conspiring to make him feel unusually irrational and moody, prone to letting off some steam, generally blowing hot and cold and giving off mixed messages, and it is all because his purpose is fuzzy at the moment and he is inwardly sensitive and impressionable. The good news is that all this anxiety is temporary, but at the time it is all encompassing for a young boy of eleven, and may be distressing for the parents to witness.

The force of *pressure* Jimmy has applied on the page is *light*, which means he is keener on implementing mental rather than physical energy. Working smart rather than hard could be Jimmy's mantra, and being creative by playing a musical instrument or writing a story would be preferable to running around a football pitch or rolling up his sleeves and getting involved in a fight. That is not his style. He is likely to give up quickly under pressure, and certainly is not keen on confronting issues that cause him discomfort. Plus, he is likely to input the minimum amount of effort, unless he is particularly inspired by something. Otherwise this can lead to lethargy or laziness. Jimmy does not really like being made to do things he does not want to do, so he will not really like being told to knuckle down; he values learning by experimenting and finding out for himself – often the hard way. If you are going to tell him off and discipline him, take care, because Jimmy is a sensitive boy, so he will need gentle persuasion and intellectual influence and justification rather than a few badly chosen harsh words.

Another feature is the *medium-large size*, where the *upper zone* is dominant, the *middle zone* is smallest and slightly weak, and all the *zones* are fluctuating quite a lot. The *zones* allow an appraisal of the young inner character, and you would be looking for equilibrium and balance here to know that the writer focuses equal attention on all areas of his life. However, Jimmy's *upper zone* is the largest here, which means that he is excited and focused on projects that capture his mind. He lives inside his head. His dreams matter to him, and he thinks a lot about developing his ideas and philosophies, which are more important to him than having security or material possessions. However, the lack of *regularity* in this *zone* (as in all Jimmy's *zones*) tells us that he is struggling to cope with satisfying these needs, so there is a sense of dissatisfaction creeping in. The *large* and *dominant upper zone* also tells us that Jimmy places priority on principles and morals, which means he always considers other people's feelings and he cares and worries about letting people down. It will be important to him to have respect for his teachers, and the fundamental core values that underpin the school also matter hugely. The fluctuating *lower zone* is not dominant, which means it is not his priority, but nevertheless it offers some clues and tells us that Jimmy gets bored and restless and needs plenty of variety in his timetable to fully appreciate an all-round skills palette. The *small*, *weak* and *fluctuating middle zone* tells us that Jimmy's inner-contentment varies, he is finding it quite hard to control his emotions, and this can all make him feel despondent fairly quickly.

If Jimmy is not constantly stimulated, inspired and motivated, he will succumb to his bête noire – laziness – the easiest option for him. He does have expectations but needs interesting tasks to stop him getting bored and disheartened. He will appreciate a creative spin on lessons, which he will find more effective than dry lectures.

The letters are mostly *joined-up* and *legible*, showing his competence and desire to work single-mindedly on projects he finds challenging and fulfilling. This means that Jimmy would have particularly enjoyed writing the stories dreamed up in his imagination. Jimmy has a logical approach and likes doing things one thing at a time, finishing what he has started. He would be disrupted by too many changes to his routine. However, the *mixed slant* shows his valiant attempts to multi-task and adapt to changing situations. With encouragement, Jimmy works logically, diligently and methodically to a productive conclusion.

Age eleven, and Jimmy is developing nicely. You would not expect him to be fully mature at this age, but he is a well-rounded, bright boy with lots of potential, who sees life as an adventure. We have touched on Jimmy's individuality, and he will certainly need the freedom to explore this going forwards, so it will be crucial that his new school affords him the opportunity to explore extra-curricular activities. One of the most critical aspects of his selected school in the future will be the certainty that he is able to gain inspiration from his surroundings and facilities. A more contemporary form of teaching would work well for Jimmy, provided there is some discipline in a safe environment. Too much discipline would feel oppressive and unfamiliar, stifling his creativity and triggering his sensitivity, but not enough would encourage laziness to breed. It is all a question of degree, balance and moderation, but I suggested his parents might need to be prepared to dish out some tough love too.

Relationships are key in Jimmy's world, so he will need the gentle bubble of a small environment (as opposed to a large school, which may be too daunting for him to deal with), and he will respond better on a one-to-one personal basis where classroom sizes are small. I recommended a single-sex school, finances permitting, although Jimmy's teachers disagreed and felt that a mixed school and the 'gentler influencer of girls' might be beneficial. Jimmy's personality has nuances of a bohemian spirit, which is manifested in his creativity. So although he has all the makings of wanting to be a high achiever once he has found his niche, I suspected that his passion may not be going down a purely traditional academic route. I subsequently learnt that Jimmy was a violinist and had been offered a music scholarship at a private school.

What is going on inside my daughter's head?

It has been said of personality that in some ways we are like all other people, in some ways we are like some other people, and in some ways like no other person. Each of us, in many respects, is a little package of uniqueness. Little girls and little boys, in particular, can be quite different. This is the handwriting of an eleven-year-old girl called Belinda, and as you can see there are marked differences between her writing and Jimmy's; the only thing they share in common is the same age.

Belinda's handwriting speaks clearly and plainly about a walk in the woods with her dog Ruby, but graphologically there is a whole subtext going on to which Belinda's parents are blissfully oblivious. Are they aware, for example, that while on the outside she is so sensible, practical and well-grounded, on the inside she is dealing with all sorts of thoughts swirling around inside her headspace? Do they know that their young daughter is completely wrapped up in her self-image, her social life and friendships which currently define her? Do they appreciate the intensity of feeling she invests in sustaining these friendships, or how much energy she puts into everything with which she gets involved, and that she puts so much pressure on herself?

We know all this because the headline feature in Belinda's writing is the *middle zone* letters sitting on the baseline. Belinda's are large, full, some rotund and some square-shaped, bold, compact and all-consuming. And they have been formed with some considerable *pressure* on the page. What this all means is that Belinda cares, and her agenda revolves around focusing on her image, her family, socialising and everything that impinges on every minute of her waking day. Belinda unreservedly needs to belong; it is critical for her that she gels with her friends and she craves respect from her peers – recognition and positive feedback is the oxygen she breathes.

It is worth making special mention here to the advent of the *large* and *full middle zone* writings, which are so common these days, especially with young girls and adolescents, and now some older women too. It has a childlike appearance and shows that the writer has developed a sort of 'Smarties' hard shell that is used as a defence again the outside world that has often been challenging for them in their early years. It makes them feel tough, appear confident, but quite often the wobble in the height of the *middle zone* letters shows that, despite appearances, this is where they are most vulnerable. Positively, without too much of the wobble (or fluctuating size), it is indicative of someone who is bang on trend, image conscious, strongly in tune with the here and now, and living in the moment. These people's worlds revolve around their social life, and they are adept at personalising whatever they do, so that people remember them. They tend to enjoy standing out in a crowd and making an impression, and frequently desire acceptance, appreciation and respect to boost their self-esteem. Popularity is very important to them, so life is rarely dull around these people.

Belinda's writing does have a wobble and this vulnerability is reflected in the undertones – her *small personal pronoun I* in particular, which shows that she is a little unsure of herself at the moment and her self-esteem varies, so she will need plenty of encouragement, reassurance and hugs whilst she gains confidence with time and maturity.

Belinda, age 11, right-handed

Part Two

The mental health landscape

CHAPTER 5

The effects of the pandemic on mental health

Diana, Princess of Wales is perceptively quoted as saying in 1995, two years before she died: *'There's no better way to dismantle a personality than to isolate it.'*

At the end of December 2019, the BBC reported that the country was facing the biggest mental health crisis since the Second World War. No one could ever have foreseen the pandemic in the spring of 2020, in spite of all the warning tales coming out of Wuhan in China at the close of the previous year. Nor how wave after wave of enforced lockdowns and sustained isolation would make such a dramatic impact, chipping away relentlessly, creating uncertainty and fear, and ultimately affecting our psyches and causing a decline in our mental health – the very essence of our hearts, minds and souls. Particularly as we had no idea what the future held in store, nor any inkling of how long we would continue to be 'locked-down' or effectively 'imprisoned' in our own homes. However, one of the invaluable take-aways of this difficult period in time is that the whole mental health landscape can be clearly seen in handwriting.

Portrait of a quarantined mind

This is a vignette of a thirty-something male called James from northern England, taken at the end of the summer of 2020. James's mental health issues had been exacerbated by the lockdown, so his family commissioned me to study his handwriting because they needed help with pinpointing what was going on in his head. Reader, this handwriting may not look anything like yours, and there is nothing particularly striking or out of the ordinary about this script – no glaring horrors, no frills nor huge exaggerations or distortions – it could have been the boy-next-door's missive. However, I have chosen this sample as a template, simply because it comprehensively illustrates and showcases the effects of the pandemic on all our mental health, in one way or another. So you can cherry-pick the parts that relate to you.

It has to be said that in order to help someone effectively, you first have to get a handle on what the issues are you are dealing with, remembering that as a starting point the page symbolically represents the writer's environment and world, and writing patterns reflect ways of thinking and behaving in it. Sometimes it can help just by facing up to the truth – and knowing. So let us explore the graphic clues and take a peek inside his mind. This is James's handwriting:

Have you ever been close to tradgedy or close to folks who have? have you ever felt the pain so powerful so heavy you collapse? I've never had to knock on wood, all because of you and my mam. Thank Her for me. [18] I'd just like to take this moment to tell you how important you both are to me, [18] I'd be lost without you both. I guess this is my chance to apologise properly, [19] I didn't mean to do what I did, I'm not going to use drink or drugs as an excuse, I was out of control no matter what state I was in. Even Stone Cold Sober I couldn't be trusted. I just want to say thank you to you and my mam, I'm still suicidal but I would never do anything like that because I love you and my mam and I can't do that to you
S. Ford

James, age 37,
right-handed

James's script is clearly legible and easy to read, but again try to resist the temptation of reading the content. Do not allow yourself to be influenced by any spelling or grammatical errors, and try not to be impressed or prejudiced by your personal judgment of what you think looks perfect in handwriting, because none of these perceptions will give you true insight into the writer's psyche. You should be able to see other features emerging – anything that sticks out like a sore thumb. Only now can you begin to see what this living form of enduring expression is telling you about James's current mental health and his ability to deal with the pandemic, just by translating the pen stroke movements on the page.

These are the warning lights on the dashboard:

1. Depression

His baselines rise. You would not expect that from someone who is struggling with their mental health and feeling depressed. However, if you look at the second paragraph, halfway down the page, you will see that they begin to fall.

Falling baselines are a sign of tiredness or depression (or a more prosaic sign that the writer is left-handed), so it is important to distinguish between the two. Where a sentence falls away at the end of a line, this is happening subconsciously, so it is more likely to indicate depression. Let us piece the whole story together: James starts out boldly, wishing for normality and trying to put a brave face on things, but eventually he is overcome with sadness and exhaustion, and he cannot keep up the pretence any longer. Depression can take on many forms and guises in handwriting but *falling baselines* would have to headline this list.

Wavering or sinuous and *meandering baselines* is another indication of emotion creeping in, shining a spotlight on stress and anxiety. When we have lots of nervous energy and feel like we are on rocky ground, this is often replicated in *undulating baselines*. Alternatively, if you have *very straight baselines*, as if you have written on a ruler or insisted on writing on lined paper, this shows how far you will go to try to control things. You need stability and simply cannot cope with change in your life.

2. Loneliness

The whole piece of handwriting looks crowded (there is more black ink than white background on the page) – the lines and most words are close and compacted together. You would not expect that either. If someone was feeling lonely and isolated, you would expect to be able to drive a truck through the gaps between their sentences. Historically, wide empty spaces between words are symbolic evidence of a writer's desire for solitude and privacy, tagged with space to breathe. For many people lockdown means never *ever* being alone, because they are housebound with others in a confined space. However, when does a longing recalibrate into a loathing of too much time spent alone? The answer it seems is in 2020–21, during the multiple lockdowns, when a flip-side emerged (they say 'be careful what you wish for') and the *wide word* and *line spacing* had both begun to reflect uncomfortable feelings of isolation and detachment from the rest of the world.

So what does it mean if someone, like James, has *close or super-closely spaced baselines*? It tells us that he loves being involved with everything that is going on, even if nothing is going on – the desire remains. It also means that he struggles to get a perspective on what is occurring and would not be able to think straight, because he cannot see things objectively. So, you would assume that he would wrestle with the stark circumstances and social distancing. And the only clue to this admission is the *wide word spacing* around James's *personal pronoun I's (PPI's)* and also the individual words 'me' (seen in lines 6 and 9[18]). This is where he was feeling most lonely.

3. Mood

What about mood? How does James feel inside, and how do his emotions affect his behaviour? The writing is not too big and not too small – it is an average or *medium size* overall, which is prescribed by copybook model, and therefore nothing out of the ordinary. That is how James comes across outwardly – not too confidently (because his writing is not big), nor a shrinking violet (because it is not small either). To get a true handle on what is actually going on *inside*, you would need to drill down deeper and take a look at the size of all the middle bits of his letters sitting on the baseline (exclude the tall stems and any long downstrokes for the time being; we will come to them later). The technical term for this area is called the *middle zone (MZ)*.

We would expect to see some *variation in size* here, just because we are human beings with a need for social sensitivity and an inbuilt capacity for adapting to the needs of the moment. Also, very few people's moods stay on an even keel consistently throughout the day, every day. The problem arises when there is too much fluctuation in the size of these letter parts (a's, c, e, i, m, n, o, r, s, u, v, w, x's) and the undulation exceeds the tipping point. Here, James's *MZ* is fluctuating quite a lot

– too much (believe me, I have measured it) – which reveals the chinks in his armour, telling us that he is unable to cope with his emotions, and they are getting out of control. He is feeling emotionally off-kilter and anxious, with zig-zagging emotional mood swings – a whole corona coaster of emotion. It may not look like it from the outside, but inside life is causing James one big problem.

How is this manifested in his behaviour? If you knew this man in real life, what would you expect to see? (I have absolutely no idea what James's physical form, shape or face looks like, because I have never met him). However, I do know there will be mood swings, and that is where the *slant* or angle of the handwriting comes into play. A piece of handwriting may slope forwards, tilt backwards or possibly even seesaw one way and then another, and that is all you need to know. It is like the emotional barometer displaying the outward expression of behaviour. If someone is friendly, sympathetic, cooperative and responsive, in varying degrees, it will be *right slanting*. A *left slant* fits someone who is self-absorbed, withdrawn or aloof, non-conformist and potentially belligerent and difficult to deal with. The scale of the gradient will reveal if there is a balance to the writer's mood swings, or alternatively any excess flip-flopping backwards and forwards will have a negative impact on your reading.

Here, the initial *left slant* gives way to a swinging *mixed slant*, which means that James starts off on the defensive, and then blows hot and cold, lurching unpredictably from one state to another, exhibiting behaviour which is irrational and chaotic, making him very difficult to second-guess. I have to say that if the writing veered less dramatically from the right to the left or vice-versa, you would be able to tone down this interpretation and say that he was an adaptable and versatile sort of chap with a certain amount of 'give' to his make-up. However, excess is never a good thing. It is generally the source of all negatives.

Another way of recognising that someone is not feeling happy inside – and not at peace within themselves – is by looking at the *rhythm* of their writing. This will be a subjective evaluation (one of the few graphological movements that cannot be measured empirically), but no less authentic and insightful if you know what you are looking for. The trick is to liken handwritten words with musical notes, and then imagine the pulse on the page. This will instantly give you a feel for how smoothly or chaotically the writing either dances or trots unprepossessingly across the paper. Rhythm should not be mechanical and exact, like the ticking of a clock; it needs some natural vibration. Any jerks, jarring movements, flaws or stumbling blocks in the free flow of the writing will alert you to how self-confident someone is feeling, and how well they are adapting to their current circumstances and coping with their innermost feelings. Are they likely to be the type of people who panic in a crisis, or will they deal with problems in a calm manner when they arise?

Imagine that James was a novice on *Strictly Come Dancing*. He would be doing the movements (going through the motions), but not feeling them or doing them without thinking. It is easy to find a beat and manufacture the steps, far less easy to naturally vibrate to them unconsciously. James's handwritten 'dance' reminds me of the tango. There is a repetitive staccato rhythm that moves tentatively yet purposefully and proudly across the page, and then suddenly pulls up, in hold, before moving off again in another direction. There is plenty of passionate attitude, but not enough *speed*, too much control and some discordant activity. His unjoined letters set the (slow) pace, and then the changes in the *MZ height* and *varied width* of his letters interfere with the pulse. However, mostly any natural movements are hindered by the change in the direction of his *slant* and his preference to *disconnect* his handwriting. Any potential harmony is also impaired by the *irregularity* of his *word spacing*. James is not comfortable in his own skin. He has more than enough emotion and resources at his disposal, but this is just further evidence that he has absolutely no idea what to do with them or how to direct them.

4. Overthinking

Let us consider the tall stems (the top segments of the letters b, d, f, h, k, l, and t) in the *upper zone (UZ)*, because this is where you will discover if someone is overthinking or dwelling on things. Where you have a mixture of tall and shorter stems, as we have in this particular sample, you have before you a person with many thoughts – too many thoughts – that will all be rattling around in their mind, and they will be struggling to calibrate them. James plays his worries on a loop, rewinding them over and over, until they become negative thought sequences and stagnant behavioural patterns, and he is unable to make up his mind and be decisive or deal with anything logically or realistically.

The top section of the letters is also the home of our moral compass, defining and delineating our ethics and boundaries. The *size* and *regularity* in this *zone* will reveal if we are able to finely tune our beliefs or whether we lack a social conscience. James's *UZ* is *disproportionately small* and *weak* (compared with the other *zones*), putting a question mark over his willingness to behave in accordance with societies rules. Given the wrong set of circumstances, it is quite possible that his moral compass could spin out of control.

5. Restlessness

To complete the hat-trick, James is not getting enough physical exercise, and this makes him feel incredibly fidgety and agitated. He may also be feeling worried about money issues and practicalities at the time of writing, and unable to sleep at night. We can see all this in the *lower zone (LZ)* area, and specifically the long yo-yo-ing downstrokes, which again are so irregular to be malfunctioning. (Here, they all measure different sizes, and the variation between the smallest and largest size is huge.) If you have been furloughed or made redundant, or simply feeling cooped up with not enough scope to work-out, you will see exactly the same thing happening in your handwriting.

6. Fears for the future

As the penny dropped with the whole situation that we were only just beginning to find ourselves in and comprehend, there was a gradual realisation that this was the way things were now – strange, unsettling and scary – making it impossible to plan ahead. We can see that James became apprehensive and fearful of what may come next by his *avoidance of the right-hand margin* (it is quite wide in his sample).

7. Apathy

How can you tell if someone is feeling apathetic from their handwriting? We can see James's 'What's the point?!' attitude in his *t-bars*, which are crossed so low down the stem and occasionally *concave* or saucer-shaped, uncovering his fear of failure and propensity to self-sabotage. Life must have seemed like a steep climb that was overwhelming and insurmountable.

Drooping saucer-shaped connections between letters (sagging beneath the baseline) also pinpoint a passive, emotionally dependent and potentially masochistic nature that is inclined to let other people take advantage of them. This can derive either from a sense of guilt, depression or defeatism. Any of these movements seen individually or in clusters would be a living testimony to a general slowing down, and eventual giving up.

However, there is an even better indication of apathy. As someone's mental health declines, you would expect to see a drop in energy levels, unexplained exhaustion and general feelings of lifelessness. This lack of elan can be translated into weak or very lightly penned sentences. That is not all. Apathy can also be seen in a general sense of sluggishness or stagnancy that pervades the whole global look of the handwriting, as words are delivered monotonously on the page.

In this particular illustration, we have *light pressure* as opposed to overly light or weak weight being applied to the paper, which means that James is feeling stressed and cannot take on anything too taxing at the moment. It also tells that he is super-sensitive and needs careful handling, although he is not yet at the point of throwing in the towel. (Without handling the original sample, you could not possibly know that there is *light pressure* deprived of any imprints or ridges on the reverse side of the paper.)

And just look at his signature! You would not think it belonged to the same writer. It looks completely different from his 'normal' handwriting. It is quite common for people to adopt a style of signature that is quite unlike their longhand, and the diversity can be revealing. James's signature is *illegible* (it is not what you think it is), unlike the rest of his handwriting which is plain and easy to read, even when words are taken out of context. This shows that he is hiding something. He has even drawn an extra loop in his oval, cutting it in half. He is trying to be evasive and is playing his cards close to his chest, because he does not want people to know what he is really like, or that he is a kind, gentle pussycat inside, underneath the mask. However, the *tangling in the MZ* (where letters overlap) uncovers complicated emotions, along with a dependence on other people to understand him and be there for him, without James having to explain. The missing downstroke in the letter u of 'Pout' reveals that he was beginning to unravel, like a piece of knitting coming apart at the seams. Most of all, the *signature* has significantly *lighter pressure* compared with the main script. James is trying to give the impression that he does not care, but he cares more than he lets on. And he really cares about his social life because an *angle* makes an unexpected appearance in the oval part of the upper case letter P. The letter P represents his attitude towards his social life, and it is quite aggressive and ambitious. The cool apathy he projects covers a multitude of sins.

8. Stress and anxiety

Our brains operate on a need-to-know basis and most of the time we do not need to know. This is the reason why human beings sometimes unconsciously trigger the *repression* button, when things simply become too much and overwhelming.

Not many people would admit to anxiety at any time, never mind in times of national turmoil, such as during the Covid-19 pandemic. People cope with stress in an endless variety of ways, and the tactics they use help determine whether the stress has positive or negative effects on them. In fact, our mental health depends on our ability to cope effectively with stress. What is your go-to strategy for hiding anxiety? Do you bottle it up or push it deep down, or aggressively strike out at others or just give up? You may even resort to blaming yourself for things that go wrong. These are the most common coping strategies, but perhaps you might be the sort of person who uses a type of defence mechanism to protect your ego?

Sigmund Freud brilliantly explains how the process of *repression* (the 'don't-remember it' syndrome) functions by banishing unpleasant, unpalatable or undesirable feelings into our subconscious, protecting us from any memories or thoughts or traumas that might induce anxiety. In fact, Freud postulated that we have a whole range or system of unconscious *defence mechanisms* that help us to cope, by protecting our ego.

So how do we know that the writer chooses to forget things just by looking at their handwriting? One of the best indicators of *repression* is a *tense, rigid script*, with a *strong accent on the vertical*, revealing how hard someone is trying to control their energies. These people excel at keeping their true feelings under wraps.

People who attribute their failures to personal shortcomings are highly self-critical and tend to have pessimistic thoughts. Self-blame is seen in the *leftward ticks* or *angular upstrokes* of the ends of y and g stems.

Wide gaps between letters are another clue that some sort of mental strain, caused by excessive stress and anxiety, is going on, sometimes to the point where the writer may be close to a breakdown. *Erratic* and *extremely wide spacing between words* offers more proof that the writer is feeling completely out of their comfort zone. Stress can become chronic over a period of time, resulting in some sort of physical illness if the writer is not aware and able to manage it better.

The *currency* of the writing may also be affected. *Currency* is the graphological term describing the *quality* of the writing and is associated with health. Good *currency* is shown by the smoothness and fluency of the pen stroke. If there is any deterioration in the clear-cut edges of pen strokes, the production of disintegrating pigment (sometimes only when examined under magnified conditions), the appearance of minute jerks and tremors, any breaks in letters, superfluous *resting dots*, *irregular pressure patterns* or abnormalities in the stroke generally – any shaky pen strokes at all (as opposed to unattractive and illegible handwriting) – this may be an indication of a health problem or proof of tension due to physical or psychological conditions. It will reveal the extent of any deterioration in physical health, usually seen in elderly people's handwriting, or where the onset of old age has been accelerated. (And I should add that no sign of decrepitude can be seen in James's sample.)

In an ideal world, handwriting will look smooth, elastic and unimpeded, flowing naturally with *positive regularities*. This is certainly what you would expect to see in the handwriting of someone who is not hampered by tensions or inhibitions and has good mental and physical health.

Currency is usually measured hand-in-hand with *pressure*, because they are both key graphological movements that determine the mental and physical health as well as dialling up (or down) the intensity of the writer. *Pressure* measures how much energy is available, whereas *currency* determines the quality of this energy, and how efficiently or not the energy can be channelled and maintained.

There are other ways you can spot anxiety in writing. *Hesitant* writing means that the writer has difficulty getting on with their life due to inner anxieties and uncertainties. If, for example, the writing looks *jerky*, you can deduce that the writer is suffering from stress and fatigue. It could also simply mean that the writer is elderly. *Distorted* pen strokes that look twisted and fragile can mean that the writer is physically ill or emotionally disturbed (the exact location of the deformity will give clues as to the type of frailty).

Broken handwriting is a sign that the writer is living under unacceptably high levels of stress, and the fragmented strokes show that it is beginning to affect their physical well-being. It should, however, be noted that children's pen strokes can be suddenly interrupted, producing *broken* handwriting, but this is perfectly normal and does not have any gloomy connotation or cause for concern. It is also important to appreciate that any *distorted* movements penned during adolescence is also perfectly natural and indicative of glandular changes associated with puberty (rather than its adult interpretation around physical or emotional health).

There are a few more clues for recognising *repression*, tension and bottling of feelings, so the writer manages to avoid unpleasant feelings of anxiety. Sometimes you may see the upward loop of a long downstroke where the return loop crosses the downstroke and is completed *beneath* the baseline and *running parallel to it*. This can be compared to putting a lid on things, so you do not have to face up to them. *Claws in the lower zone* area is another detector of subconscious anxiety. (*Claws* look like upside down or inside out LZ loops. When the downstroke reaches its nadir or lowest point, it suddenly goes off in an anti-clockwise direction, and the loop is never completed.)

There is more, and it is clear that stress and anxiety are the cuckoos that hijack many aspects of this illustration and our portrait of James.

Here, we have a voice that begs to be heard, but because James consistently closes his *ovals* and unjoins most of his letters, he struggles to express himself and articulate his feelings.

In an attempt to avoid anxiety (or take responsibility for himself), James also employs another of Freud's defence mechanisms – *regression* – by reverting back to an earlier behaviour or developmental stage that feels safe, comforting and pleasurable. However, this has the effect of preventing him from trying to solve his own problems. *Regression* is very common in younger children who are trying to gain more attention. In adulthood, eating or drinking too much, or losing your temper when things do not go your way, are all good examples. Some adults sometimes go into severe *regression* following a major trauma – some event which affected them and brought a halt to their cognitive development. In order to identify the writer as having regressed, you would need to see several pieces of handwriting dating back from various periods in their life. Otherwise, it could be that the writer had never reached beyond a particular stage of development. Here, *regression* is seen in James's tendency to reproduce school-taught tunnel-shaped arch formations (known as copybook model *arcade forms of connection*), revealing that he has retained the mentality and mindset of a child. He is not well adapted emotionally, which means he is immature and demanding with a childish naivety. His coping mechanisms and behavioural patterns continue to reflect those expected of a child – one that has not yet learnt how to connect ideas and thoughts logically (and this interpretation is also supported or backed-up by his unjoined-up handwriting).

Finally in this collection of issues triggered by the pandemic, we have anger.

9. Anger
Triangular shapes in handwriting often expose tension in the writer, and a smattering of *angles* here, including a few *misplaced angles* in *ovals*[19] (where straight lines replace smooth rounded letters forms in unexpected places), highlight

lurking aggressive tendencies. Some of the full stops are also heavily *ground-in* (so they can easily be felt on the back of the page, unlike the rest of James's handwriting), symbolically depicting anger teetering on the brink of erupting. Little *ticks* at the ends of strokes also reveal signs of frustration, and the more *ticks* you can see, the more irritated the writer will be feeling. On a positive note, this type of annoyance may be acute, but it is generally short term and fleeting, particularly in this case where the overall *pressure* is *light*.

By the way, if you spot any triangular shapes *beneath* the baseline, then this is repressed aggression exposing some kind of control-freakery going on behind closed doors.

Moving on. It is not all bad news. In a more general sense, it would also be true to say that quite a few positive behaviours have emerged from this pandemic. James's sample, as most samples invariably do, offers some pegs from which to hang affirmation of hope and positivity. There is hidden potential here that is not even very well hidden in places. So, let us re-dress the balance and consider some beneficial effects, both relating to James's portrait and universally.

1. Kindness, altruism, solidarity

People were beginning to help each other more during the lockdowns. They were developing a social conscience and becoming more community minded. It did not take long before people developed a sense of solidarity – a 'we're all in it together' attitude, which has not been seen hitherto since the Second World War. There we were, all standing on doorsteps every Thursday evening at 8.00pm, clapping our hands until they were sore, showing our appreciation for the NHS by applauding, whooping, whistling, banging on saucepans like drums with wooden spoons for drumsticks, letting off some steam. Some of us had tears in our eyes or pouring down our faces.

Children's rainbow drawings were also popping up and adorning house windows around the world, cutting across culture and language barriers. The innocent dialogue was a message of courage and a symbol of hope – powerful and empowering.

In handwriting, you would expect to see lots of *rounded* letters and *garland* or saucer-shaped constructions within the letters n, m and h, when there is some element of kindness to be found. The script may also fall forwards, even just a little.

The letters and words might be joined together, like one long piece of uncut elastic or thread. There would be a strong emphasis on the horizontal breadth of letters (as opposed to vertical slashing downstrokes), with some cradle-shaped loops appearing under the baselines. All these features point to a caring nature.

James's sample ticks three of these prerequisites. His writing has a *rounded* style, which means that he is a people's person with a real handle on what make other people tick. He is a kind, sentimental soul with a good heart, a social conscience and the potential to nurture others. His heart rules his head and he strongly values relationships and family. His *arcade* arch-shaped letters also reveal incredible loyalty to his family and the people who matter in his world. He identifies with the underdog and needs a life that is congruent with his values. His big, round, full (almost bloated) letters are all part of the picture of a strong *anima* (or feminine side), which means that James has an emotional streak that empathises with other people, particularly women and children. He can relate to them and cares about them. There are enough *broad* n and m letters (if you drew little boxes around some of them, you would make rectangular shapes) which enhances the meaning that he has not entirely retreated into himself and can be personable, when he chooses, and when he is not being defensive and/or playing his cards close to his chest (because James's handwriting mostly slopes backwards).

2. Appreciation

People learnt how to be in the moment and appreciate and savour what they had in the here and now. Here, James is clearly tuned into the present, because his *rounded letters in the MZ* (sitting on the baseline) are *large, full and dominant* (disproportionately so, since they are being compared with his other *zones*).

We have looked at how the different sections of our letters reveal our emotions, our moods, thinking patterns, physical and materialistic needs. And we have seen how the *zones* will also tell you where the writer's interests can be found and where the writer directs most of their time and energy, brilliantly pinpointing motivation. The *largest* or *dominant zone* is where the writer focuses most attention, desire and drive. Here, James's *large MZ* shows how much he emotionally invests in everything that is going on, day to day and minute to minute. Popularity will be one of his headline priorities, galvanising his behaviour. James will be strongly affected and influenced by peer group pressures. He needs love and support, plenty of reassurance, praise and affirmation, clear expectations and benchmarks, and some recognition and appreciation for his achievements. He needs a human spin. Only then will he be able to tap into his potential, step up to the plate and become devoted to meeting other people's needs, but first James has to stop denying his own. It is like flight attendants always say in an emergency: you have to put your own mask on first, before you help anyone else.

3. Self-esteem

The English language provides graphologists with a gift. It is the only language that uses a single letter to represent the whole of the writer. This letter alone can tell us so much about the writer's true personality. The *I* symbolises the writer's self-worth, self-esteem and self-image. It relates to self-importance, pride, self-confidence (or lack of all these things), how we see ourselves in relation to other people, and how we want to be regarded. It is an excellent way to glean the writer's feelings of inferiority or vanity. In short, the *personal pronoun I (PPI)* is the exteriorisation of the self.

Naturally, if the ego is weak or impaired, it may not be able to keep us healthy. A debilitating loss of self-esteem is associated with feelings of personal worthlessness. This may have been brought on by furlough, redundancy or simply a change from normal routines. There are also likely to be signs of diminished self-confidence, and a rise in self-criticism and self-deprecation. There is a surfeit of other indicators:

☛ A *tiny PPI*, the *MZ* (representing the ego) will be weak and diminished, the overall size may also be *very small*. James is endowed with perhaps a surprisingly *large PPI*, which is promising and tells us that his self-esteem is good (considering all the underlying turmoil), although he will still need some support and encouragement.

☛ If the *PPI* is *huge*, the writer will be completely locked into who they are, with no understanding of the world around them. A *very large personal pronoun I* is the sign of an over powerful ego.

☛ If the *PPI* is *elaborate* in any way, this is someone who over-compensates by projecting a strong self-image. These people will need plenty of reassurance.

Warning bells should sound if you see any of the following types of the letter I:

☞ *Small/tiny* and *insignificant* (particularly with *light pressure*), sometimes penned in a lower case i (the crushed ego – feeling inferior and insignificant, and having poor self-esteem and poor self-concept).

☞ *Retouched* or *amended* (anxiety, lacks confidence, neurotic tendencies).

☞ *Retraced* (a deliberate, conscious motion where a stroke is redrawn. This is done compulsively, to reduce anxiety. It exposes inhibition and repressed feelings.)

☞ *Distorted* (illness or having tainted thoughts about the self, needing attention).

☞ *Isolated* (feelings of loneliness and desolation, yet unable to ask for help).

☞ *Split* or *broken* (split personality, disturbed self-concept with a fractured identity, leaving the writer with a legacy of insecurity and self-doubt. These people can also be petty and have odd views when it comes to social liaisons. They are quite complicated characters.)

☞ *PPI crossed through* (by obliterating their *personal pronoun I*, the writer is effectively and symbolically eradicating their own personal identity. These are free-floating individuals, without an anchor.)

☞ *Mixed forms* (disclosing an identity issue – the writer's behaviour may be unpredictable).

4. What would become of the extrovert?

I did wonder how this unprecedented situation might impact on the extrovert. It is the thrill-seeking extrovert's horror of being cooped up and alone. They are energised by the outside world, craving contact and interaction with other people. How would they cope without this stimulation? According to Carl Jung, introversion and extroversion are neither fixed states nor mutually exclusive. Apparently, we all possess qualities of both the extrovert and the introvert, and we flow between the two, usually with a preference towards one, at any given time, depending on the (external and internal) circumstances at different periods of our lives. This is epitomised in James's handwriting, where he has an equal number of handwriting movements symbolising both attitudes and highlighting his feelings of ambivalence at the time. The movements representing his penchant for extroversion are portrayed in his *closely spaced words*, the *full large* and *rounded middle zone* letters, the *broad width* of many of these letters, the partially *rising baselines* and the marginal dominance of the *lower zone*. Conversely, introverted indicators are detected in the unjoined, *arcade-shaped* structures, the *left slant varying*, the *avoidance of the right margin*, the *partly falling baselines* and the *slow speed* of his writing.

We know that handwriting analysis is a snapshot of a moment in time. So if you wanted to see a symbolic switch in an individual's script, you would need to have sight of 'before' and 'after' samples, or at the very least more than one sample taken from different periods in the writer's life. This would enable you to track the changing landscape of their shifting behaviour.

The global pandemic was forcing more people to go *within* to seek energy and generate strength. People were becoming more introspective and introverted, and simultaneously more self-sufficient and able to stretch moments of action into periods of just 'being'. There was time to reflect and search for meaning and purpose. Many people were beginning to learn to enjoy a quieter external life, and to create ideas or seek solutions by trusting what came from exploring their own hearts and minds, rather than using others as sounding boards for drawing opinions or making decisions.

The pandemic was a catalyst that saw an explosion of new concepts and inventions, not just with individuals but with businesses too. Companies had time to think and be more strategic, rather than getting bogged down in well-established but outmoded or stale routines of functioning. With this renewed focus, some took the opportunity to pivot away from their core business and successfully re-invented themselves.

CHAPTER 6

Stress and anxiety

A mid-life crisis

Peter (this is a pseudonym) had just turned forty, when he emailed a little while ago. Peter approached me because he was concerned he 'might have done something he may come to regret' and asked if I was able to spot stress in handwriting, and if so, could I help him? He did not offer any more details, so I was not privy to the underlying reason of why he was feeling stressed. I explained that I should be able to pinpoint areas of concern, provided he supply me with a current sample of his handwriting, so I could see exactly what was going on at that moment in time. It was critical for me to have sight of an original piece of handwriting in this instance, so that I would be able to assess Peter's *pressure*. This evaluation would constitute a vital component of the analysis, particularly since the remit was to examine and evaluate intensity of feelings, stress levels and disposable energy – which are all interlinked and discovered through the weight or force and depth of the writing on the paper.

True to his word, my client followed up his initial enquiry with a signed handwritten sample delivered the very next day in the first-class post. He asked me not to hold back and to *'say it like it is'*, which was a relief when I realised that his penmanship was an exemplary case of stress, tension and anxiety, as well as showcasing a number of defensive coping mechanisms.

We shall see how stress triggered anxiety and evoked fear to such a degree that Peter had become paralysed to act and impotent to resolve his problem. My client would indeed need broad shoulders to read my report.

I am going to deconstruct my analysis here, so you can read the respective clues and see how when you tie all the loose strands together, a complete portrait emerges, uncovering the workings of a human mind at a time of distress.

*things are getting better and there is up.
I am enjoying work and thought only a
few months ago that it was work calling
me to feel so low and wanted to sell
the business. I do not think I could
cope without it at the moment.
Well when I started the letter. I had just
finished the a hard gym session and was
very hungry. Just eaten my food now so
not as hungry. wonder if you see a change
owing to that.*

*I ~~do have to get~~ Need to go shopping
for work so cutting this off now.
I will speak soon.*

Peter, age 42, right-handed

Messy layout with some illegibility. Light pressure. Arrhythmic. Large–very large size with dominant UZ, disproportionately small and weak MZ, all zones fluctuating greatly. Left slant/mixed (particularly in the LZ). Non-existent left margin with some avoidance of right. Overly rising baselines. Connected. Irregularities including wide and irregular word spacing. Deep garlands and angles. Contraction. Covering strokes in MZ and LZ. Pointed UZ loops. Ovals with inner spirals and double walling. Tall d's with vanity loops.

The overall shape, contour and structure of Peter's handwriting reveals a picture of *irregularity* and *arrhythm*, echoing a man in distress. Writing tends to become more and more irregular in response to stress. Here it is very messy, careless and disordered. Peter was on the edge of coping. His behaviour had become increasingly inconsistent and unreliable, and his behavioural responses had become emotionally charged. He had already lost control of objectivity and was clearly feeling emotional and unhappy. The inner tension and mental stress was acute and he was worried about what was happening in his life at that time. The trouble was, he was also feeling overwhelmed and could not tolerate any more stress, but neither could he deal with it effectively. Nor could he cope with a mundane routine going forwards. It simply was not in his nature, and so it seemed like he was trapped in an impossible situation. Peter could not seem to progress forwards and he did not want to go backwards.

When baselines are *rising* dramatically, you always know there is a problem. It is like overkill, revealing that the writer is trying to put a brave face on things during difficult and challenging times. 'He doth protest too much, methinks!' is the Shakespearian line that recognises overcompensation, and the likelihood is that the opposite will be true.

The *slant* of the writing veers mainly to the left, although there is some *mixed slant*, which meant he was blowing hot and cold and behaving unpredictably, but he had also become accomplished at bottling things up and hiding his true feelings. It seemed Peter's way of coping was by sticking a plaster over the truth and hoping things would get better by itself, or better still, miraculously disappear.

The *large–very large size* of his writing and signature gave away his desire to be in the limelight. Here it was more a case of staying ahead and beating the Jones's than keeping up with them. Peter was an effervescent showman at heart – a sociable, outgoing, fun-loving, action-orientated, upbeat risk taker who loved life, relished a project and an adventure, and enjoyed interacting with people. However, the layer of fun was wearing dangerously thin and his confidence was fast evaporating. Another interpretation for *very large* handwriting is independence, and this man wanted to be his own person calling the shots. Furthermore, he did not necessarily want to be in his marriage.

A closer inspection of what was going on in the *zones* gave a deeper insight into how he was feeling inside. The biggest *dominant zone* was found in the upper section, where the tall letters spiralled high and measured more than the long downstrokes beneath the baseline and more than the rounded letters to be found sitting on the *middle zone* imaginary baseline (where the ego resides). Peter's chief area of motivation could be found here. The *upper zone* tells you how, and how much, a person thinks. If it is *large in size*, then thinking processes, a conscientious attitude and ambitious desires will form an integral part of the writer's make-up. If it is *small*, this does not automatically mean that the writer does not think, or that they have no conscience or even that they lack aspirations, but it is likely they are more inclined to size things up quickly – they are the practical types, the sort of people who get stuck in and do things, rather than overthink everything.

Peter could see the big picture and was driven to get out into the world and achieve great things to satisfy his burning ambitious desires. However, he was also affected by his principles. Peter was shot through with a noble code that dictated he must do the right thing. And it was this moral compass that was the barrier conspiring to stop him in his tracks and hold him back. Peter's conscience was playing havoc with him.

We see this visually in the way the tall stems fluctuate, like a desperate heart rhythm, interfering and influencing decisions, pulling him first one way and then another, responsible for ricocheting ideas around in his head. If, for example, the size of the tall stems had been more regulated and similarly sized, this would have meant that he would almost certainly be less impressionable or easily influenced (particularly if there was a degree of restraint and a few *narrow* letters made an appearance in the script). He would have been much less likely to be tempted to go against his principles, and he would not have been feeling so confused and dreadful. Plus, he would not have kept changing his mind every second. Peter was frightened of making the wrong decision, so he was overthinking everything and could not think straight. He also had a bee in his bonnet (see the little *hooks* on the very tips of some of the *upper zone* stems) and would not let go of all these different, conflicting thoughts.

The long tails in the *lower zone* also varied considerably, so they were all at different lengths. This added a large dose of restlessness into an already uncomfortable equation. And as for the small *middle zone* letters on the baseline? Well, they were indeed disproportionately small, inferior and weak in size compared to the other *zones*, and also undulating massively. Ergo, Peter's ego was diminished and fragile, and he was having the devil's own job trying to control all these wild impulses and desires. This only served to enhance his confusion and inability to make firm decisions. Peter was unable to cope rationally with anything that was going on in his life.

Discovering that Peter's *pressure* was *light* exposed his sensitivity and further uncovered a propensity to dodge any issues and take the path of least resistance. He was lacking any willpower or stamina to face his problems and was much more inclined to avoid than confront. He would walk away from his commitments, turn his back on his family and the people closest to him without trying to sort things out properly. The way some of his letters unravel confirmed to me that he was lacking backbone and struggling to deal with his problems at the time. I do not believe it was what he really wanted (I am not sure he knew what he wanted – that was part of the dilemma), but it was probably his only way of coping, because he was literally unravelling, just like his handwriting.

Some of the ovals had *inner spirals* and loops cutting the letters in half. Whenever you see this, it is a sign of self-deception. Here was further evidence that Peter was dodging issues instead of facing up to them. He was trying to convince himself that his problems were more palatable than they really were, so he did not have to deal with them anymore. Not only was Peter kidding himself, but he had become accomplished at fooling other people too.

The *left margins* were non-existent, but more importantly, the *right margins* were *wide* – very wide. My client was struggling to plan for the future. He was afraid of committing himself to moving forwards and potentially making the biggest mistake of his life. Something was stopping him from going all the way. He was paralysed with indecision, like a rabbit caught in the headlights. Peter was in the throes of a midlife crisis.

The trouble was that Peter had been living the life he felt he ought to live, rather than the life he wished he could. Something or someone had flicked a switch inside, triggering all these emotional responses. He was desperate to follow his dreams, but they did not fit in with his current situation and his family's needs and expectations. There was clearly an inner conflict between sentiment and reason and between ideals and practical considerations, and he was finding it increasingly difficult integrating the two. The whole scenario was causing him to feel stressed, anxious, restless, moody and confused, not to mention resentful and discontented.

The core issue had to be resolved, which meant a decision had to be made and he could not dodge the matter any longer. However, it could not be *my* decision – it was my client's decision to make. I could only reveal what I could see in the handwriting and advise accordingly. I suspected Peter was embroiled in an affair. It seemed none of this high principle counted for much when circumstances presented him with an appealing alternative adventure. Peter was being tempted by a chance to re-write his own narrative. I warned that he should beware of behaving recklessly and acting impulsively without considering the consequences of his actions, and explained that he was giving out so many mixed messages and behaving so irrationally that it would have been difficult for his family to know where they stood or what was going on in his head.

Peter was relieved that someone understood how he was feeling, although he thought I must have had some insider knowledge on him. He admitted it was a midlife crisis, and he also owned up to the affair. He could not resist the other woman or the prospect of a new adventure and a sense of jeopardy in his life. So they ran off together and fulfilled their dreams. The relationship is still going on.

CHAPTER 7

Negative parental influence

L ike all good fairy tales and since time immemorial, nothing is ever what it seems. Someone may appear to have everything going for them. They may be highly intelligent and give the outward impression of being well-balanced and enjoying their world. However, what if they have a difficult and possessive mother to contend with? How might that play out on the mental health of her son, and what could possibly be the repercussions in his later life? Having the gift of academic intelligence may open some doors, but it is not the same as being tough and streetwise. None of us can legislate for the family we inherit and the circumstances in which we may find ourselves. Some events can define us for the rest of our lives, if we let them. This story traverses time, revealing the intriguing compatibility between a mother and her University of Oxford student son, and we shall see how their relationship ultimately affected his future.

A story of mother and son

I have been transported back to November 1961, to visit the original handwriting of an undergraduate at Pembroke College, Oxford. My remit was to provide a graphological portrait of a young man whose character was deemed to be a 'work in progress'. It was fascinating for my client to read what her husband's handwriting said about him then – a time before she knew him, before they had even met, when he was in love with another woman. Graphology is not just about who we are now.

Time passes gradually. The younger years seem to go on for ever and the summer months are always long, warm and sunny, but then with a final whoosh of the last dregs of sand grains slipping through the thin neck of an egg timer, you can suddenly find yourself staring back at the past, clutching at snapshot memories in your mind, wondering where your life went and how it all evaporated so quickly. Ken Kerman was no exception.

Ken's charmed life began so innocently and beautifully. He was an only son with loving parents who lavished him with all the trimmings and privileges that life could offer. However, where did it end? What happened? Ken is eighty now. Who did he become in those intervening years?

Ken, age 20, right-handed

That old cliched question, nature or nurture?, still rings true, and they both play their roles in shaping a human's life. Graphology can make short shrift of the *nature* part of the equation, and can also deal with the *nurture* aspect too, provided sufficient evidence is available (i.e. a piece of handwriting penned by the person responsible for the child's upbringing – in this case, Ken's mother.)

However, that is not all. There is one more key powerful ingredient that frequently makes its Shakespearian appearance on stage, time and again, completing the picture of our personal trajectories through life. The joker of the pack is circumstance. Events *can* be planned, but often deliver the greatest impact on our lives when they arrive suddenly and unexpectedly out of the blue. John Lennon knew what he was talking about when he said that 'Life is what happens when you're busy making other plans.' We all know that circumstances can be dealt with positively, or allowed to influence and define us adversely, depending on our core nature and amassed nurture at the time.

As I say, it all began so well. However, who was Ken really, and how did he deal with the circumstances in his past and the people who crossed his path and made up his world? We shall see how a man who had everything on paper lost his true love and how this loss coloured the rest of his life. We will start by taking a look at the components of Ken's life – his nature and the person most responsible for his nurture, and then I will reveal the actual events, so you can see how closely his personality aligned with the reality, right up until the present day. We will explore how far graphology can predict the propensity for a person to behave in a certain way, given a particular state of affairs.

The son

By the age of twenty, the headed notepaper tells us that Ken had become an undergraduate student at Pembroke College, Oxford. His handwriting back then (see the sample opposite) confirms that he was academically talented and endowed with some life skills. In fact his handwriting, like Ken, seems to have everything going for it. The easy flow, the rhythmical grace and gentle charm, sweep you off your feet. On first impressions it would be easy to be blinded by the quality of his script too, and the maturity of his enviable intellect. However, if you roll back the beautiful layers, there is a destabilising element underneath that would eventually let him down and come back to bite him.

How do you know if someone has a quality script (known technically as *high form standard*) and what does this mean? The calibre of a person's handwriting is measured (early on in an assessment) by the *speed, layout* and *originality* of the pen strokes. Fast speed combined with novel and resourceful ways of deviating from the way you were taught to write in school is conducive to producing a high-quality script. The better or higher the standard, the more positive a spin you can apply to your interpretation. Ken's *very high form standard (FS)* meant that his intellectual abilities were strong and he was operating and expressing himself from a place of creativity.

Let us unpick some more handwriting movements. Ken used a fountain pen, and his writing looks quite faded, so the *light pressure* patterns appear unevenly distributed in places. This could be attributed to the natural patina of an old letter, but I quickly ruled out this possibility, knowing that it had been carefully stored in a plastic covering inside a closed box all these years. It was more likely that this *irregularity* (in the finish) pointed towards Ken's pent-up feelings, revealing hidden sensitivity and vulnerability. It was already becoming apparent that the brilliance of the mind does not always compensate for the fragility of the emotions and the heart.

As we have seen in previous chapters, *light pressure* is produced by sensitive, empathetic people, often with little will-power. Here we can also see, with the benefit of the *high FS* thrown into the mix, that it portrays good mental energy. However, that does not negate another interpretation for *light pressure*, namely Ken's dislike of confrontation and the likelihood that faced with an awkward situation he will always take the path of least resistance – anything for an easy life in Ken's book.

Overall, there is a *dry* quality to Ken's handwriting – where the pen strokes are distinct and the upstrokes are thinner than the downstrokes – uncovering his intellectual approach to life. There also appear to be pockets of *pasty* pen strokes, where the writing looks softer, warm and well-nourished, but also thicker – the up and down strokes are of equal thickness – almost as if the writing was painted or a thick nib was used. Sometimes, by using a magnifying glass or under a microscope, you will be able to see that the edges of the pen strokes appear to be *bleeding* or frayed. This can result from the relaxed grip of the pen, which allows for more ink to flow freely. What you get is a stroke that may look heavy but is in fact light.

Pasty writers can be highly cultured, sentimental, tolerant, sensual and tactile human beings, with a strong need to indulge their libidinal appetites and make the best of everything. However, the other side of the picture paints a shallow side that is inclined towards laziness and vulnerability, particularly when presented with the wrong set of circumstances (and/or a *lower form standard*). If this were a more negative appraisal, where the *pastiness* was excessive (and loops and ovals were flooded with ink), you could expect repressed anxiety and suppressed sexuality. These would be clues to the writer escaping through daydreaming or by consuming alcohol, or even resorting to drug abuse. Here, Ken's *pasty* strokes are subtler and not overdone and his ovals are mostly clear and uncontaminated, so we can park the more flawed aspects of this movement. Instead, the *pasty* hallmark reflects a man with artistic flair, creativity, a rich imagination and a good perception of colour.

Now we have explored the foundations of his handwriting, let me introduce you properly to the young Ken, again through the prism of his handwriting. As a twenty-year-old student he already had a lovely way about him. He was a kind man of exceptional warmth and benevolence, coupled with a dry sense of humour and a witty disposition. He was low key, humble, modest and unassuming. He generously accepted people for what they were and had an ability to see others' points of view. There was no ego about him, so he was not one for being in the spotlight and was perfectly happy trundling along in the background. You can imagine that he was the sort of person who everyone would want to befriend. He was erudite and operated from a very high level of intellect and creativity, with a supremely active, versatile and innovative mind, which empowered him to think and grasp new ideas quickly and fluently. He could certainly improvise and spin a yarn. (Reader, I know all this because of a combination of the s*mall, quickly written joined-up handwriting*, together with the *pastiness, broad and horizontally stretched letters, slight mixed slant, good mixture of letter formations* and the *significantly high form standard*).

Ken adopted a relaxed attitude and ran on mental energy (*light pressure*), which was partly why he had such a brilliant mind. He had a congenital optimism and a sense that everything would turn out well in the end (*rising baselines*). So there was a tendency to be swept along by life, as he took the easy options. Ken was happy to appreciate the journey, absorbed by his experiences, rather than looking ahead to The End. He revelled in the finer things and satisfied his sensual appetites. Self-indulgence suited him perfectly. He was not ready to make any commitments or settle down exclusively to one person at that time. Life was easy, and he was happy with the status quo. Ken seemed to have it all going on. This is who he was.

However, this only tells half the story.

It would be so easy and convenient to forget that people are complex, multi-layered creatures with good and bad traits, and just because they may be good and clever or super-kind on the whole, it does not mean that they do not have their bad points or weak spots too. Just because you are applying a positive slant to the overall interpretation, it does not mean you can brush over the flaws and ignore the less palatable aspects of character. As we have seen, each and every handwriting movement has more than one meaning. Some are positive and some can be quite negative or pessimistic – but no less valid. One good trait may compensate for a bad characteristic, but it does not eliminate it. It is still there, lingering in the background, waiting for the wrong situation to present itself, triggering that destruct button on the dashboard.

So it would be easy to overlook the fact that Ken's nonchalance hid emotional instability and anxiety. Or that his kindness protected his own sensitive heart and self-doubts. Or that his gentleness prevented him from standing up for himself and instead made him dependent on others, porously open to abuse from the wrong source. Or that his dislike of confrontation meant that he would wriggle out of uncomfortable situations by telling untruths if necessary. Or that his talent for being open-minded ultimately meant that he had so much rattling around in his head that he struggled to make his own personal decisions, and invariably needed other people to make them for him. Or that his desire for space and freedom meant that he felt isolated at times. (I know all this from his *greatly fluctuating MZ and UZ*, the *light* and *variable pressure*, the *mixed slant, missing downstrokes, overly stretched broad width, wide word spacing*, some *light* and *low t-bars, UZ loops* and *thready letters*, and last but not least the *embryo style of personal pronoun I* which curls in on itself uncovering his need to be mothered.)

Ken was not entirely a soft touch. There were glimpses of a man with ambitious desires for achievement (*widening left margin, connected letters*), hints at independence and autonomy (*strongly left slanting personal pronoun I's*), and small traces of defiance (seen in the *oversized letter K* in 'Thanks' in line 1[20]).

So let us investigate his mother's make up and defining features and find out what she was like.

The mother

Ken's mother's handwriting is intriguing, because it is apt to deceive, and the truth creeps up on you slowly, quietly and furtively. On the surface, at face value, she portrays the happy, soft little woman indoors. A bit of a do-gooder who comes across all nicey-nicey. The forward slope of her script talks about sociability, friendliness, cooperation and compassion. The *broad* letters are a nod to a big heart and a generous spirit. The *rising baselines* vibrate to a cheerful, upbeat tune. And the *small, rounded* letters complete her appearance of being a warm, unassuming and kind woman, just like her son. So much so, this piece nearly fooled me, and it took a little while for the truth to sink in.

The weight exerted by Ken's mother's hand on the page is *heavy*. If you look closely (see the sample on page 108) you can see the grooves or deep indentations coming through on the back of the paper. (You may see this best in the heavy downstrokes of the letters p[23]). Not only is it firm, but there is strong *horizontal emphasis* as well as *pressure*. Can you see the long, extended *t-bars*, some with blunt endings, towards the end of the script? Bludgeoning *t-bars* uncover a bossy person with a particularly strong will. These people can be quite cruel – it is all part of their power complex. The overall layout is also compact and crowded, with an undiscerning lack of margins all round, as if the writer is sucking up all the oxygen. The *MZ* section of the letters is dominant, so she would have been a social climber. If you factor in these stand out features, this instantly puts an entirely different complexion on things.

Sunday

Dear Ken,

Received your letter, glad to hear you received parcel safely & that you are well, although you do not mention whether your cold has completely cleared. Do hope so. Glad you are finding the sweater useful. How is it for size, would like to know, in case I should make you another & what about the neck, do you prefer this to the high type, which I suppose would be even warmer, although personally I don't think they look so nice. Let me know.

Well, you seem to be more cheerful. Yes, time has gone very quickly & it hardly seems 5 weeks since you left, although I suppose the next 3 will drag. By the way, as you start vac late, does this mean you will have over 5 weeks this time.

Nothing very exciting happening here, in fact things are pretty dull. I still have no char, & although I've advertised for weeks I haven't had one application, so it seems I shall have to carry on myself,

Ken's mother, age 54, right-handed

Pressure is the kingpin of an analysis because it will either intensify or tone down your interpretations. *Heavy pressure* is a prime indicator of intense deep wells of feelings that run deep and everlasting. These writers apply 100 per cent commitment to everything they do and whatever passion they choose to follow (and here we can see that it is strong attachment and devotion to her son). The *small size* (of Ken's mother's handwriting) tells us that she does not want to draw attention to herself, but – make no mistake – her heavy pressured pen strokes means that she will be the one ruling the roost. She will be wilful, tenacious and controlling in the way she goes about imposing her 'big heart' desires. And topped up with the heavy *horizontal pressure* and the *broad* letters, neither is she easily diverted from her objectives. Put simply, Ken's mother was pushy, overbearing and domineering.

What is more, her *pasty* pen stroke character has the appearance of being muddy or doughy here, taking on a much more negative meaning, revealing a superficial face. That, combined with many blunt *end strokes*, scream insensitivity and a desire to hurt. She was determined to get exactly what she wanted and would have been very awkward and nasty if challenged. Ken's mother just could not help herself.

So you do not have to scratch the surface too hard to be able to observe some of the finer details and see the undercurrent whispering. It is not long before a whole raft of mixed messages and complications rock up, and before you know it a can of revealing worms is opened. It seems that Ken's mother was not as understated or unassuming and endearing as first impressions may have conveyed.

Let us lay out the evidence and examine the smaller clues – the *miscellaneous movements*. Jealousy is seen in the inflated and bloated *ovals*, which also uncover a predilection for being a bit of a drama queen behind closed doors and making a mountain out of a molehill, so that everyone else ends up feeling guilty.

There are tell-tale little *potlids* (which is where the tips of the p stems rear their heads, shooting up and extending above the oval part of the letter[22]) uncovering a simmering argumentative streak. Ken's mother would poke her nose into everyone's business because she needed to know everything that was going on. She could not abide being wrong about anything. Her upper case H's have a concave shaped initial downstroke[21] revealing incredible obstinacy plastered on the face of someone who is quite different to the person they portray. Some of her *ovals* are also drawn in a clockwise direction, which depicts someone who likes to do things their way.

There is a caveat here. There are various handwriting movements which are accepted as normal for a left-handed writer. These include blunt endings on t-bars, reversed *ovals* penned in a clockwise direction, and falling baselines. *Falling baselines* sometimes occur when a 'leftie' is trying to avoid smudging ink. So it is important to recognise which hand the writer uses before jumping to any incorrect conclusions or making any sweeping accusations. It may be that their only crime is simply a preference for sinistrality – i.e. writing with their left hand.

Mixed messages crop up when you have two strongly featured handwriting movements whose interpretations seem to contradict rather than complement each other. At first sight, they appear to coexist as a conundrum, because they do not blend well. You may even be tempted to think that one automatically cancels out the other, but that would only leave valuable insight lying on the cutting room floor. So if you can get a handle on how to amalgamate the two opposing meanings without being clumsy, you would effectively be pinpointing the paradoxes of someone's personality, and for that reason enormous understanding and perspicacity can be gleaned. Here, the mixed messages can be found in Ken's mother's social behaviour and her way of dealing with people. This can be visualised graphically by the formation and structure of the letters n, m and h. The powerful combination of sharp *angles* mixed with loose *thready* letters is an insider way of dissimulating emotional manipulation. These people can be slippery operators, which means you cannot trust them. Ken's mother also mashes her *angles* with *garland* or saucer shapes and this alludes to her iron fist in velvet glove approach. The non-existent *left margin* and some extended *end strokes* (seen more clearly in other pages of this letter) show her double standards: she kept people at arm's length so they could not encroach on her territory, although she did not afford other people the same courtesy and was quite disrespectful of their privacy.

Ken's mother made herself indispensable by devoting herself to her son's every need, self-righteously believing herself to be the source of all his happiness and welfare. She did not think twice about interfering in his life, always believing that she knew best. However, her love was not nurturing; it was stifling, laced with selfishness and envy. She was jealous of any woman who threatened her position by trying to steal her son's heart and affections. She was over-protective and only too ready to 'swallow up' Ken and sabotage his world in the name of love. And the trouble was, Ken was only too prepared to let her. He was too accommodating and weak.

It was fascinating to see how a brilliant man could unravel, despite all his access to wealth and academia, at the hands of his own mother. And it begs the chilling question: How well do you truly know those closest to you?

You may wonder *why* she behaved this way towards her only son. I did. Few people are all bad, and I liked to think her intentions were consciously well meaning. There is generally a prosaic reason behind people's behaviour. It is just a case of finding the clues that triggered her actions. They were there, clear as day. Not just one clue, but a smattering of handwriting movements that held the answers. Part of the trouble was her low boredom threshold. (This is seen in the *huge variation* in the *size* of her *long stems* beneath the *baseline*). Another revolved around the fact that for whatever reason she was unable to do the things she wanted to do. (This is apparent where the upstrokes, which would normally become loops of y's and g's connecting to the next letter, instead retrace the stems so that straight lines replace loops). The technical term for these movements is known as *greatly fluctuating lower zone (LZ)* and *covering strokes in the (LZ)*.

Also, the levels of dissatisfaction she was experiencing inside and the frustration she felt at an aspirational level (seen in the hugely *fluctuating MZ* letters and the appearance of angular tips of some of her *tall, pointed loops*) could only lead me to believe that she was unhappy with her lot in life and had taken to living vicariously through her son. Her tall loopy stems uncover a touch of Walter Mitty, and also an adventurous streak that craved excitement (see the letter t when it's followed by an h – the h is always penned much taller in comparison).

It is a curious relationship between *heavy* and *light pressure* writers. They do not understand each other, and one always thinks the other does not care enough. It can be quite a miserable, troubled and frustrating mix. Initially, a *heavy pressure* writer (Ken's mother) may admire the *light pressure* writer (Ken's) breezy approach to life, but it does not last long. The *heavy pressure* writer always feels that their counterpart is not pulling their weight and will invariably be frustrated by the lack of commitment and refusal to confront or face up to issues. And the *light pressure* writer is always overwhelmed by the intensity of their opposite. Ken's mother was never going to be satisfied, because nothing was ever good enough, and these feelings were pumped up by the belief that her son's talents were wasted on him. She may have secretly resented his easy manner and charmed lifestyle – she was always envious of other people who she assumed were having a better time than her – and this could have been the fuse that detonated her intense controlling behaviour towards him. It was a sad story that did not end there. The consequences continued to unspool.

Everything I have given you so far has been seen purely through the framework of the script.

The big reveal

Since graphology is unable to see circumstance or the precise details of what is going on in someone's life, Ken's wife, Catherine, kindly joined-up the dots for me. She filled me in on the gaps about the fabric of their lives and the chronological events, but only after my commission had been wrapped up and delivered back to her. I could do no more.

It turns out that Ken got a first-class degree in Philosophy, Politics and Economics. He developed a love of the theatre at Oxford and became the stage manager, working behind the scenes. He did not just excel academically. Ken's school reports also praised his social skills and ability to connect and integrate easily with people from all walks of life. He was known for being personable and popular.

Then Ken met Melanie – not her real name – early on at his time at Pembroke College. She was a local girl and they met in a bar one evening in Oxford. It was an attraction of opposites. She was no great beauty and possessed no intellect, but she loved Ken for what he was, warts and all. She appreciated his sharp mind and great sense of humour and she really understood his character. She was perfect for him. They courted for six years, even after he graduated and went back home to Golders Green in northwest London, where he was welcomed warmly back into the familial nest.

Ken and Melanie were extraordinarily in tune, really complementing each other, with one major exception: Ken had no backbone and Melanie was very brave. She propped up the relationship as best she could and tried to make them strong. When Ken returned to the bosom of his home, they carried on their long-distance romance by writing to each other, although Ken lied profusely and creatively to his mother, denying that such correspondence ever existed.

Ken's mother was very mumsy, even as a young woman. She was plain and overweight with flat feet and thick ankles. The roly-poly appearance generally associated with kindness can be very deceptive. When she was out socialising with her husband, she would play the meek, sweet, subservient, adoring wife, but as soon as they were back home those trousers came out of the closet and she was wearing them.

She was fiercely ambitious for her son, but he was never good enough. She was not only a homemaker, she was also very capable with money and investments and buying shares. Ken inherited the meekness and anxiety from his father. What ambition he had came from his mother.

When Ken took a summer holiday job, he used to leave home early so he could speak to Melanie or clandestinely visit her. The mother must have caught on, because she used to call his employer to check what time he started work and then she would call Melanie's parents to find out if they were together. She made Ken feel very guilty for consorting with an unsuitable woman (who she said was beneath her son), always maintaining that he was ungrateful and selfish. Ken's mother went to enormous lengths to 'protect' her son and to get her own way. She even used to read his personal letters from Melanie, when she eventually found his secret stash in a shoebox on top of his wardrobe. And when Ken's mother strongly suggested he should not marry Melanie, he did not.

By the time Ken stood up to his mother and decided to go ahead with his marriage to Melanie without his mother's blessing, it was too late. His mother was already one step ahead. She had intercepted, read and hidden all his girlfriend's recent letters, so Ken did not even know that Melanie had finally given up waiting and had left the country, heartbroken. She flew into the arms of another man, marrying on the rebound within months. By the time Ken found out, it was too late. Melanie had gone.

His mother's deception devastated him, and when he realised he had lost Melanie for good, he was a broken man. He started smoking, drinking and eating excessively. His mental health deteriorated and he eventually ended up in therapy. As we know, Ken disliked confrontation and was good at wriggling out of any uncomfortable situations. Still, he could not bring himself to tell the truth and reveal his soul. He engaged a psychoanalyst and paid £150 a week for the privilege for ten years, only to lie constantly.

Ken could not have his love, so he set his cap at a string of unsuitable, strong and domineering women who were just like his mother, but all with their own unique set of issues and invariably never with his best interests at heart. Eventually he met and married his convent-educated current wife, Catherine Jamet Kerman, in 2003 at the

French Consulate, and then ten years later he was cruelly diagnosed with Posterior Cortical Atrophy (PCA).

This disease is otherwise known as Benson's syndrome. It is a rare form of dementia that affects your perception of space and vision. To this day, Catherine poignantly believes herself to be 'collateral damage at the end of the chain'. She says that when she discovered Ken's nature was weak, it was too late for her, but finding out he had no backbone at all was a severe blow. She feels she married an Oxford first and ended up with someone who was first outsmarted by his mother and then by an incurable disease. Nowadays Ken has full-time care. He can no longer recognise his own face, and he does not think his limbs belong to him. Sometimes he has the sensation that he is walking on the ceiling.

Mother Kerman passed away in 1993.

Melanie got divorced and is currently living a solitary existence in Ireland. She is a social worker and continues to keep in regular touch with Catherine.

CHAPTER 8

Dementia

Unpicking the mind of a lady with dementia

Just over a decade ago I was approached by a sixteen-year-old schoolgirl called Caitlin, who was studying for her AS levels and preparing an Extended Project Qualification (EPQ – introduced in 2006 by Sir Mike Tomlinson) for a practical diploma in Society, Health and Development. Caitlin contacted me initially via the post. She explained that a handwritten letter addressed to her parents had turned up out of the blue. The letter had been penned by an eighty-year-old lady called Bernice, who was suffering from dementia. (Dementia develops as a disease in the brain rather than as an illness, so it is part of our mental well-being. Syndromes like dementia are caused by the mis-folding of proteins in the body into an alternative shape. This can result in toxins building up in the brain cells, aggregating into clumps and causing the disease. As the population ages and people live for longer, it has become one of the most important health and care issues facing the world. Dementia is an incurable condition which causes a gradual loss of mental ability, including problems with memory, understanding, judgment and thinking.)

Bernice used to know Caitlin's Grandma Laurel. Caitlin said that the letter did not appear to make any sense at all. She described the handwriting as topsy-turvy and 'all over the place!' Caitlin asked me to analyse the handwriting, because she thought it might be an original and insightful way to 'unpick her mind' purely from a graphological perspective. Caitlin said she was 'fascinated by graphology and thought it would be a far more interesting route to take than getting a psychologist to look at it'. So this is all about Bernice's handwriting and her story, gleaned from frozen snapshots in time.

The evidence immediately and overwhelmingly suggested to me that 'unpicking her mind' and revealing Bernice's character was going to be difficult, given that she was already clearly a shadow of her former self. It was also hard for me to know how much of her character could be attributed directly to her condition, since the symptoms of dementia were causing her to behave in extreme ways, and how much was inherent. However, what was clear was that this condition did not sit comfortably with the writer and was at the very least exacerbating traits of her personality that may never have come to light under different or 'normal' circumstances.

Usually you would be looking for clusters of handwriting movements, but occasionally the dominance of one solitary handwriting movement is so extreme that it cannot be ignored. As we have seen, excess in handwriting is always a source of negativity. Here this particular excessive movement relates to the overall layout of the writing on the page.

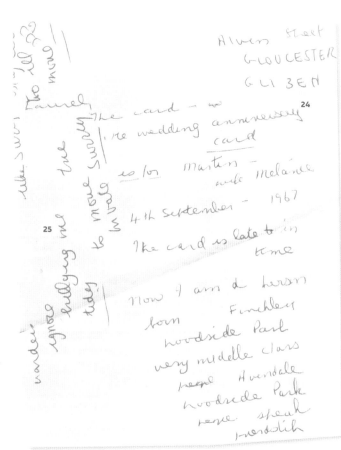

Bernice, age 80, unknown hand (original letter, page 1)
Note the chimney funnel effect produced by extremely wide and widening left margin together with avoidance of right margin. Note also the consciously formed straight right margin, which you would normally expect to be ragged.

The first and most significant feature of the writing that hits you is the unusual layout of words on the pages. There is a *strong avoidance of the left margin* – Bernice's *left margins* are all wide, and progressively widening – and the *right margins* are also mostly wide, and in some places less naturally *ragged* and more consciously 'straight'. The striking cumulative effect produced is one of a *chimney funnel*. This is a common theme that repeats itself on every page of the letter.

The significance of this layout is a claustrophobic feeling of entrapment. Bernice is trapped in a time bubble, caught up in the present, and appearing to be moving further and further away from her past, yet unable to move forwards into the future. Whether that was because she did not want to go back to the past, because of something that happened to her or because she could not go back because her memory was failing, we can only speculate. It is as if she is living in a cage and locked into a world she could no longer understand or of which she could not make any sense.

I do not believe it was a self-imposed situation, but it does reflect her confusion and her fears, her frustration, anxiety and restricted mobility within her mind through the time frames. Occasionally Bernice feels the urge to fill some space within the *left-hand margin* with what appear to be random words. This can be attributed to her lack of organisation and her ingrained thrift.

The *extreme wide left margin* is a clue to Bernice's distress and feelings of disconnection with her memories from the past. The avoidance of the right-hand margin also reveals her inability to see a way forwards, her fears for the future and a social anxiety in a broad sense.

Where the right-hand margin is dead straight, this shows a conscious effort and restraint on the writer's part to try to control what is happening in her life going forwards. It shows that she is struggling to adapt and is much more comfortable with a structured lifestyle. Appearances still mattered to Bernice, and it is highly likely she was worried and concerned about what other people were thinking.

Bernice cannot go back, and she is afraid to venture forwards, so the *chimney funnel* effect has her firmly trapped within the present. It is interesting also that the *left margin* is *progressively widening*, because this reveals her desire to keep busy. Regardless of everything that is happening in Bernice's world, she is still the type of lady who is keen to be productive. It tells us that she is independent, possesses self-respect and feels impatience. This movement can also mean that she has become less trusting of others and may be keen to escape from certain individuals.

A further interpretation is that she possesses a sense of propriety and courtesy. There is a lot of dignity in Bernice's make-up, yet it is all being compromised by her medical state. What is vital is that all these interpretations can be backed-up and therefore justified by other elements of her handwriting, as we shall see.

Within the left margin on page 1 of the letter there are a few words infilling the space. Two of these words read, 'bullying me'. There is a *shark's tooth* within the letter 'm' of 'me' (on the second arch or arcade[25]). *Shark's teeth* are very unusual handwriting movements in graphology, fortunately rarely seen, and they never have a positive interpretation. It is a strong indication of someone taking advantage, either financially or emotionally. It tells of a courteous exterior hiding cunning

Bernice, age 80,
unknown hand
(original letter, page 2)

manipulative behaviour, and often implies a sadistic element. These people can be nasty when pushed, although this may only happen under duress. I am not suggesting that Bernice is an exploitable party here, but given that this movement is only seen once in the entire script, and found on the word 'me', it begs the question: does it refer to how flagrant Bernice's behaviour could be, when faced with a difficult situation and the inevitable progression of her state of dementia?

The impact of handwriting *pressure* is always an informative evaluation because it can completely transform an interpretation. This third dimension (of pressing downwards, rather than simply directing the pen from one side of the page to the other) modifies everything. So, with *heavy pressure*, the depth accentuates and intensifies the overall meaning, and where the force of the writing on the page is *variable*, which it is here, we can see how Bernice unconsciously directed her emotions, and her emerging behavioural problems. The *irregular pressure* means that she struggled to regulate her mental state and was quick to lose her temper, creating a bad atmosphere. So she was easily roused, anxious, sensitive and nervous, and lacked the self-discipline and willpower to control her reactions and frustrations.

The global *light–medium pressure* patterns suggests that Bernice's anger would take on the form of sudden indignation, sporadic irritability, tense emotional outbursts and unpredictable over-excitability. This happened because she was no longer able to use her energy in a systemic way, and this would probably have been entirely due to her illness. One minute her conduct was agreeable, tolerant and receptive, and the next she became antagonistic, barely containing her anger, or even completely unresponsive. This assorted emotional volatility was due to inner feelings of dissatisfaction and tension. It was also indicative of the dementia and her inability to accept her new reality and see things for what they really were. For a woman who had been used to communicating her thoughts and principles at an intellectual level (we know this because the *upper zone* is *large* and endowed with *full loops*), it must have been very frustrating and disheartening indeed. For everyone else, she must have been a difficult person to be around, and her behaviour must have been bewildering, particularly for people who knew her well in the past. I suspect Bernice had become quite a handful.

The *very wide (*and *intermittent) word spacing* reveals memory loss, anxiety and forgetfulness. The occasional *resting dot* backs up this meaning. A *resting dot* can be compared to a walking stick that leaves a mark whenever it pauses for a moment, causing interference with the brain's motor action. Often it is a sign of obsessional behaviour, which originates in anxiety, and this may have been reflected in Bernice's behaviour, although we will never know if this was true in her case. It is, however, likely that Bernice was racked with anxiety and insecurities, and suffering generally from mental stress. *Resting dots* are formed unconsciously and mean that something is causing the writer to feel tense, worried and uncertain. It may be due to something that happened in the past that they are subconsciously ashamed of and want to try and block. Whatever the reason, it was causing Bernice to reflect on things anxiously. *Resting dots* are also thought to show some form of oppression or strained thinking, and this would also fit in with Bernice's condition.

Wide word spacing is generally seen where the writer enjoys their own company, space, freedom and room to breathe. Yet here it conveys Bernice's feelings of isolation and convinces us that she felt trapped by her condition. The *fullness* in the *rounded middle zone* continues to reflect how much her social life still mattered. So we have a reversion to impulsive, emotional, childish behaviour, all punctuated with subjective judgments and unreal perceptions. We see how Bernice was holding people at arm's length, perhaps because she knew something was wrong, and she knew she was not behaving like her old self. It was her way of maintaining a 'proper' distance from others – sparing people from her difficult disposition, deteriorating moods and resentment.

While the total or *absolute size* of Bernice's writing is *small*, all three *zones* are *large* and *fluctuating greatly* to such an extent that there is a serious problem in every area of her life. You would describe this outcome as an unhealthy degree, where the writer's inner control is relinquished. This means that every part of Bernice's being, including her principles, were being compromised and affected by an inability to regulate or control her emotions, feelings, thoughts, actions and reactions, all leaving her with a legacy of immense dissatisfaction.

In plain speaking, Bernice was very restless and cranky, and she was losing her memory. Her mental and physical faculties were failing her, she was emotionally in turmoil, so her behaviour was becoming increasingly erratic. All her experiences in life were coloured by unfamiliar mood swings, feelings of uncertainty, anxiety, weakness and helplessness. It is clear she was not in a good place and in the grips of paranoia. She is powerlessness to do anything about her situation.

It is interesting to note that in spite of all these changes, her spirit battled on. This optimism is witnessed in her *rising baselines*.

Bernice, age 80,
unknown hand
(original letter, page 3)
*Note the very wide
word spacing and the
resting dots. The
pressure is variable,
and all three zones are
fluctuating greatly, to
an unhealthy degree.*

The *small size* is evidence that she was trying hard to concentrate, to remember things. Sight of an older piece of her handwriting taken from a time pre-dementia would reveal if her writing had become smaller (directly in line with her desire to recall memories) or if her writing had always been small, indicating modesty and a desire to maintain a low profile. If this were the case, she certainly would not have wanted to make any fuss, or be a nuisance.

Still looking at the size of writing, it is evident that in places Bernice's *middle zone* letters *progressively increase in size*. This is key to the analysis because it is equivalent to shouting on paper. Bernice was trying to find her voice. It seems, perhaps in her desperation, she found that voice clumsy, and she simply could not help herself from blurting things out, probably at inappropriate or unexpected moments, Tourette-style.

Bernice's writing is *mainly connected* or joined-up. Cursive handwriting reveals a desire for routine, a high need for involvement with other people, a good mind for trivia, single-minded thought processes, tenacity, focus and a desire to finish what she has started without interruption. This was a woman whose mind and actions were in perpetual motion, and this is seen in a combination of the *connected* writing, the *rising baselines* and progressively *widening left-hand margin*.

As I say, Bernice's *rising baselines* disclose how desperately she was trying to keep her spirits up and put on a brave face – she did not want to be beaten. In fact,

Bernice, age 80, unknown hand (original letter, page 4)
Note the rising baselines.

her bright disposition lends itself to the theory that she may not even have been aware of being ill, just frustrated by her loss of memory, inability to follow her usual logical thoughts and, perhaps, a change to her usual routine and domestic situation. There was a desperate battle going on for some comprehension of her dilemma. She was torn between wanting to understand and communicate her feelings, and not realising that she was simultaneously in the grips of denial. So she found herself trapped, going round and round in circles. It was a vicious loop that was winning the battle and exacerbating her stress and insecurity. Bernice may have been afraid, but she was trying. The oppression and negativity she felt, the anxiety and strained thinking were all debilitating for her and prevented her from moving forwards. The letters show that she was reflecting, trying to get some perspective, trying to adjust emotionally to her shifting circumstances and trying to come to terms with her unfamiliar situation. However, she needed plenty of reassurance, understanding and gentle nurturing.

The *slant* of Bernice's writing *varies* mostly on the *right* side of the emotional barometer, although there is some vertically *upright*, and some *mixed slant*, in all the *zones*, particularly in the *middle zone*. The further the writing slants to the right, the more the individual is influenced by emotion, and the more subjectivity will prevail affecting the writer's thoughts and actions – these people emotionally invest in whatever they do, finding it hard to remain impartial and objective.

Bernice's personal *slant* pattern reveals the importance of communication to her, combined with a desire (at the time of writing) to keep a stiff upper lip, but also the inability to control her emotions, and this is exposed in her behaviour by wide mood swings, and a variety of emotional reactions to people and situations. At any other time (without the imbalance in the *middle zone*) perhaps in the past, Bernice might have exhibited a talent for people skills and the ability to respond to others appropriately.

The construction of Bernice's n's and m's mostly consists of *copybook arcades* with a smattering of *angles*, and all the letters are joined together by *garland cursive strokes*. This smacks of the old-fashioned traditionalist for whom appearances and self-control matters. This means that Bernice would have been very conscious of how things looked. Again, we see a sense of propriety, a propensity towards conventional behaviour and a dislike of change. Bernice would have enjoyed a certain amount of routine in her life. There is also a sense of duty, so she preferred keeping busy and being productive, and she also made a loyal friend. However, the *angles* pop up to remind us that she could also be intolerant and aggressive, depending on the situation. By and large Bernice was good at dealing with people – she undoubtedly had a knack for friendship – but if she could not get what she wanted, she would take the quick and easy way out by adopting a more belligerent and tough approach. Perhaps the *shark's tooth* I uncovered (in 'bullying me' in Bernice's letter, page 1) reflects a manipulative streak and propensity to say one thing and do another?

There is *broadness*. So the width of Bernice's arched *middle zone* letters are mostly rectangular, hence broad. This translates into an inherently confident, optimistic, expressive soul who enjoyed social contact and understood how to connect with people. She was a woman naturally inclined to behave and react spontaneously to people's requests and the things that were occurring; and also just as likely to show a lack of restraint when things were not going well. And perhaps most tellingly, she was also open to influence from other perhaps less scrupulous people (again, see the *shark's tooth* on page 1 of her letter). At a time pre-dementia, it is likely Bernice would have been able to use subjective gut-reactions to guide her seamlessly through life. However, now she found she was unable to employ her acquired life skills, and this left her in a very vulnerable place.

In addition to the stand out *dominant* features of Bernice's handwriting, there is a host of other *miscellaneous movements* that lend themselves beautifully for the purpose of backing up and validating every trait that has been outlined above, adding weight to the meanings. These are, in no particular order, as follows:

1. **Potlids** (see letter, page 2, 'speak', on page 118[26]): these highlight an argumentative, contentious streak of someone who does not like to be wrong. This tells us that Bernice was locked into her own viewpoint and was not afraid to speak her mind. In normal circumstances, there is often a desire to get at all the facts through questions and answers.

2. **Short d stems** (see letter, page 3, 'difficult', on page 121[27]): she can be quite a tough cookie, but whilst she is direct and blunt, she is also sensitive to people's reactions. The loops within the d's reveal hyper-sensitivity, and a need for approval and acceptance on a personal level – so we know that Bernice wants to be liked.

3. *Loops*: emotional expression and sensitivity. A need to interact with other people and have social stimulation. Someone who knows her own mind.

4. *Vanity Loops*: sensitivity. Reveals a need for reassurance and approval.

5. *Good clear letter spacing*: good interpersonal skills and independence.

6. *Occasional tangling* (where *middle zone* letters overlap): moments of dependence and neediness. Where you have regular interlinear *tangling* (between the lines), this can reveal a much more negative progression revealing where the writer is not only blinded by emotion, but also rapidly losing all sense of perspective and objectivity. The writer will not be able to think straight anymore.

7. *Open ovals*: a desire to communicate. A chatterbox. A need for attention. Indiscretion.

8. *Misplaced angles*: resentment. Where there is an *angular oval* on the baseline, you can expect the writer to have a sharp, aggressive and often unpleasant tongue.

9. *Abrupt end strokes* (some tucked under and *left tending*): bluntness, inner aggression or self-protection. Mistrusting of others.

10. *Pseudo garlands* (unprescribed anti-clockwise connecting loops in the *middle zone*): the writer is not above embellishing the content of what they say in order to make themselves heard. It is superficial charm.

11. *Closely dotted i's and carefully numbered pages*: the writer has an ingrained sense of organisation and an eye for detail. It is an attempt to maintain some perspective and understanding of what is going on in her life.

12. *Letter y lower zone forms with a left tending angular tick* (see letter, page 1, 'anniversary', on page 116[24]) revealing that Bernice is self-critical, so she probably blames her condition or ineffectual behaviour on herself. It is all about repressed regression, and this may be symptomtic of the dementia. The *short, sharp straight lower zone* strokes in y's show impatience and determination. The straight

downstrokes reveal that all attempts at discretion dissipate instantly. *Covering strokes* in the *lower zone* (see letter, page 3, 'Blessings', on page 121 [28]) show how much responsiveness Bernice has blocked out of her life – she does not want people meddling in her private affairs and she is shying away from physical contact. The impulse may be to give, but caution and uncertainty rules against it. It is another indication of guilt, as if she is somehow to blame. It also tells us that Bernice is not doing what she wants anymore.

13. *Legibility* is apparent, although the content is mainly gobbledegook. Bernice's clarity of communication has therefore been impaired dramatically by dementia.

Now we have stripped back the writing and captured the essence of Bernice's character, we can certainly see how mental health issues have had an impact on her world, affecting both her behaviour and lifestyle. How far she has moved away from her natural default personality setting is harder to assess without witnesses who knew her before she had dementia, and/or without sight of previous handwriting samples. So it is difficult to gauge how much or to what extent dementia was affecting Bernice's personality, or exactly where her true character begins and ends. However, what is clear, from a graphological perspective on a frozen snapshot in time, is that this was a lady trying to find a voice. Bernice wanted to talk, but most of all she wanted to be heard. It certainly appears that she had lost contact with life as she knew it, and was living in a sort of abstract, self-protective, unrealistic world that was causing her mental pain and anguish. It must have been very difficult to communicate with her, not just because her mind was constantly distracted, but because her exclusion of people probably meant she had begun to respond inappropriately too. Bernice was patently afraid and emotional, but how much paranoia mirrored her condition, and how much was for real, no one will ever know. What we have witnessed is a tragic situation evidenced through the writer's handwriting.

'A fascinating, thought-provoking and very readable article that pushes the boundaries about our understanding of what goes on inside the mind of the mentally ill. I never fail to be impressed by your insights and observations, which are always so powerful.'
Mary Black BSc M.BIG(dip), former tutor at the British Institute of Graphologists

CHAPTER 9

Chronic mental health

L et us extend the mental health landscape and explore some more chronic and significant repercussions of mental health issues.

Waterloo Bridge – a story of hope
Getting inside the head of a man suffering with a schizoaffective disorder

This is the story of Jonny Benjamin and his herculean journey through mental illness. It is the unvarnished version, witnessed entirely through the prism of graphology, but ultimately one of hope and about a life saved through the goodness and humanity of a passer-by. On 14 January 2008, Jonny discharged himself from hospital, and as he stood on Waterloo Bridge in London on the verge of committing suicide, a stranger took the time to stop and talked to him. The stranger suggested, *'We could go for a coffee ... talk it over? Whatever it is, it isn't worth your life.'* The stranger saved Jonny's life that day. Jonny did not even know his name at the time, but subsequently called him 'Mike', and six years after the event a campaign was launched on TV and social media to try and reunite them. The *#findmike* campaign went viral and six years later, in 2014, the two men eventually met on the bridge again.

Rewind to a few weeks before the first meeting in 2008, when Jonny was still in hospital, waiting to be diagnosed with a schizoaffective disorder – a combination of schizophrenia (a mood disorder defined by abnormal social behaviour and failure to understand reality) and bipolar (characterised by swings in a person's mood from high to low – euphoric to depressed). At his lowest ebb, out of a difficulty in communicating his personal thoughts and inner turmoil, Jonny began writing notes and poetry (a book entitled *Pill After Pill: Poems From A Schizophrenic Mind* was subsequently published in 2012 – see page 128). Writing gave Jonny a brief release from his often violent thoughts. Who knows if it was the outpouring of the sentiments on the page or the actual physical process of directing a pen that helped release something positive inside his brain? Perhaps we shall never know. However, the clues

Pill After Pill: Poems from a Schizophrenic Mind
An extract from the original, tatty Sainsbury's notebook.

Inject Some Happiness

Inject some happiness into my blood,
So it can swim to my brain and flood
Its cavities. Let it fill every cell
With its pure red joy, and cast a spell
To morph these tear-stained lips into a smile.
This content is the summer shower, to last a while;
It will cool and replenish the barren leaves,
But like my ecstasy it soon will leave,
And I am back in the afternoon heat.
I gasp for cool air, I burn in the sun,
I am back where I started, with the
Sadness in which I began.

to the workings of his mind were all there on the page, recorded for perpetuity.

Many of Jonny's original poems were handwritten in a pre-lined Sainsbury's notebook. Jonny not only emptied his mind of his deepest thoughts during the darkest moments of his life, but he is now bravely allowing permission for a graphological exploration of his inner psyche through his handwritten words on paper. This is an illustrated audit of Jonny's original handwritten poem entitled 'Suicide' (see page 130), penned on a piece of plain, unlined paper, when he was aged twenty and in hospital, in those final days leading up to the Waterloo Bridge incident. The analysis of his handwritten words in hindsight gives enormous value into other people's mindsets – those who may be going through similar thoughts and feelings of depression, and suffering from frightening moments of confusion and inner turmoil.

I first met Jonny anonymously, on paper, when Rosalind Wyatt (see pages 59-64) asked me what I thought about the handwriting she had in her possession. (I later learnt that Rosalind was inspired to stitch the story for the project *The stitch lives of London*. She met Jonny and Neil Laybourn, who was the 'stranger', to understand their story. Jonny subsequently donated the white t-shirt he was wearing on the bridge that day, along with his handwritten diary. This became the artwork *life restored*.) The tatty Sainsbury's notebook was opened at random; I cannot even remember which poem I was shown, or even whether it was just an extract of a poem, but I do know I was not wearing my reading glasses at the time (so was unable to read the content). I was instantly blown away and stunned; the writing literally made me gasp. It took my breath away. The only details I had been given was that the author was male. I was asked to give a quickie on-the-spot snapshot analysis. We had just met, so I think Rosalind was trying to test out my skills.

I said something along the lines of: 'This is a very intelligent guy who has lots of different ideas pinballing around in his mind, but he's afraid he will never be able to pull any of them off – to make any of them happen. It's as if he feels he's invisible, like he's not really here in this world, and he's desperately trying to put the past behind him... He's very angry with himself... Why is he so angry?' I stopped to draw breath and racked my brains. At that point Rosalind jumped in, revealing the identity of the writer, and she gave me a little bit of his back story. I was so intrigued and excited by how much I could see in his handwriting with regards to pinpointing the mental health issues going on, that it inspired me to investigate further. Tucked inside one of the notebooks was this loose-leaf sheet of unlined A4 paper, and all the clues were right there, in plain sight on the page.

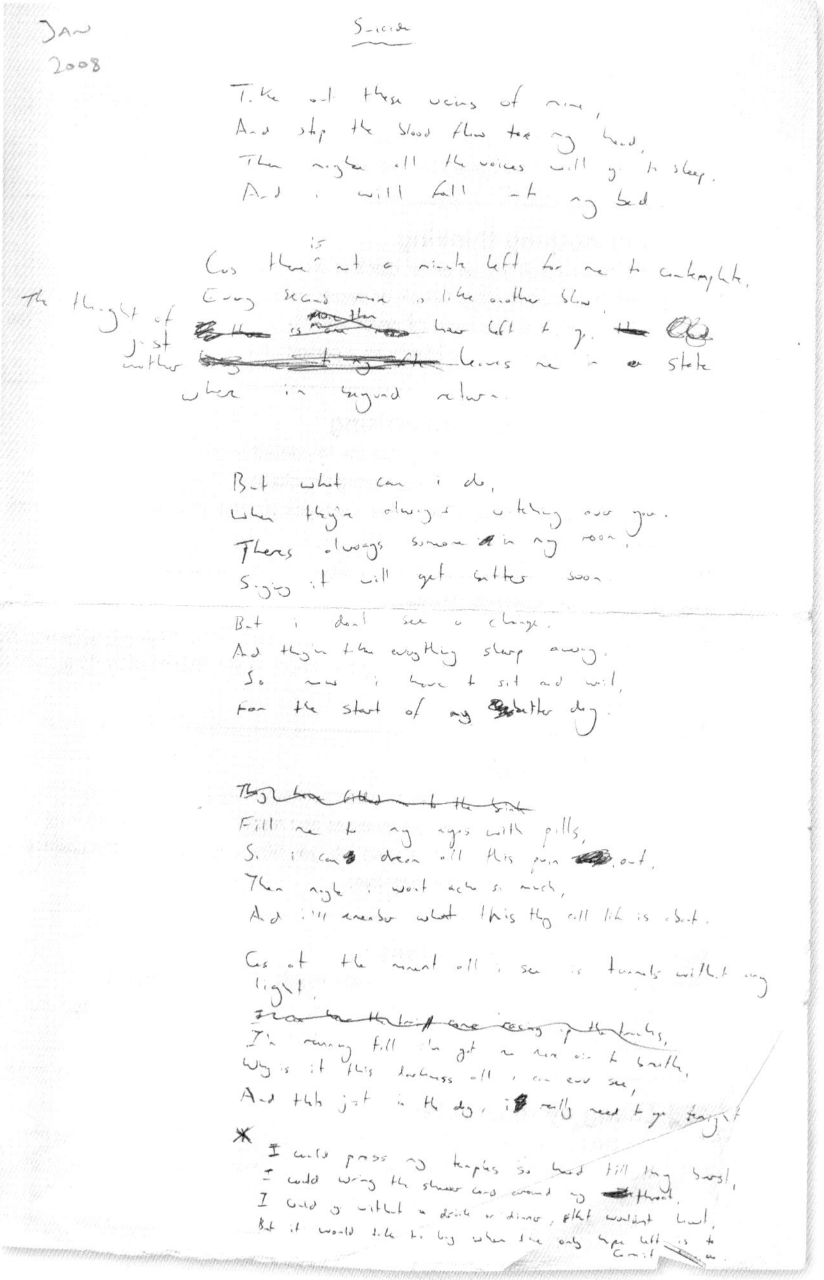

Jonny Benjamin, 20, right-handed

First appearances show fragility. Initially, Jonny's handwriting reminded me of the point of the story, *The Emperor's New Clothes*, because you could hardly see it. It was the most delicate of light fine touches, as if butterfly wings had gently brushed the page. His pen strokes reminded me of daddy longlegs, and this thought popped into my mind: 'Their legs are fine black pencil strokes that come apart, like some bad joke...' There was tremendous mental energy going on, but it was all inside his head, and any physical energy and vitality had forsaken him. The fine writing was whispering, as if the writer could not find his voice. The longer I looked, the more I noticed that all the other usual ingredients were beginning to crop up, so the warning signs were there as clear as daylight on the page. Jonny's brittle handwriting mirrored his fragile state of mind.

Let us take a closer look at the components.

1. The pressure behind the pen

Extremely *light pressure* is indicative of fatigue or ill health, extreme sensitivity, apathy, weakness of will and a general lack of self-esteem. So we instantly know that Jonny was likely to cave in under pressure, and was floating through life with nothing in the tank but his thoughts. He was almost totally devoid of any stamina or willpower, because physical energy resources were depleted. He was running on empty and had lost all sense of reality.

2. The tiny size

His handwriting is microscopically *small*. The tiny size reveals that Jonny was shrinking into himself. Like Alice in Wonderland, he had escaped into a private world of his own and had seemingly knocked back the entire contents of the bottle marked 'drink me' in an attempt to avoid reality. The introvert who prefers to put his energy into thinking rather than doing invariably produces *small size* writing. Judging by Jonny's *very light pressure* too, it would be a fair assumption to say that he might struggle to convert his thoughts into action after a period of concentration, and this would have been very frustrating for him.

3. The zonal scales

If we then zoom in on the *zonal rooms* (encapsulated within the *microscopic* writing) and measure the average size of each section – the upper tips of long stems, the lower tails hanging beneath the baseline and the small letters sitting on the baseline – it becomes clear that Jonny's *zones* are imbalanced and fluctuating greatly. We can also see that his areas of priority (the *largest zones*) were split equally between his unfettered intellect – his ideas, aspirations, principles and beliefs (all detected in the *large upper zone*) on the one hand, versus his most basic physiological and safety, security, stability needs (seen in the *large lower zone*) on the other. However, he was struggling to cope with any of these demands effectively, because he lacked self-confidence and had lost control. We know this because his ego or self (seen visually in the *middle zone* area) was disproportionately small, diminished and weak, compressed and stressed to the max. And also, because all of Jonny's *zones* were varying tremendously in size. So much so, there were unresolved issues in every area of his life, and a paranoia had been sparked. The inner turmoil meant that Jonny's psyche was compromised, and this translated outwardly into erratic, irrational and restless behaviour.

Of all the qualities we possess, self-image, self-awareness and self-esteem are very special, unique characteristics of humans, and have far-reaching consequences for human development. Self-image is the self you suppose yourself to be, and people are generally strongly motivated to maintain a consistent view of themselves. Self-awareness is being aware or conscious of yourself as you actually are. Self-esteem is the evaluative component of self-image, and refers to the degree to which you value yourself. Low self-esteem occurs when self-awareness is less and therefore the self-image is unclear. And when there is a large discrepancy between the self-image ('myself as I think I am') and the ideal self ('myself as I would like to be') there is also likely to be anxiety and over-sensitivity in close attendance. There may be disconcerting swings from self-hatred to self-depreciation. These traits are all manifested in Jonny's personality.

The weak, diminished, stressed and greatly seesawing *middle zone* is relevant, because it tells us what was going on at Jonny's core and how his ego was functioning. A disproportionately small *middle zone* is commensurate with an exceptionally under-developed self-esteem. Here you have the classic inferiority complex, and where you have an inferiority complex, you have a personality under strain, believing they are less important and less deserving than others. People with *small middle zones* are usually not very in touch with their feelings. Jonny believed he was worthless and felt full of self-contempt, and this was the direct trigger for causing him to punish himself. This anger is lucidly seen in the *heavy crossings out* that litter this illustration.

People suffering from an inferiority complex can potentially behave in two very different ways: either they become overwhelmed and entrenched by inferiority, feeling they are not measuring up and are goaded to compensate negatively by acting forcefully and sometimes violently (towards the self or others). Or they are empowered and driven to compensate positively through self-success. Either way, the writer will be keen to follow their own path, so with the right assistance (depending on whether it can be seen in their own handwriting, or alternatively supplied through the help of someone else) energy can and will be channelled to a happy or bad and sad conclusion. There was nothing else in Jonny's handwriting to suggest he could be the master of his own destiny, so he was powerless to direct his inferiority complex down a positive route. This meant that until he sought outside assistance, he could only succumb to negativity.

The disproportionately *tiny size* is tantamount not only to reduced self-confidence and self-esteem, but also to feelings of helplessness and heightened sensitivity. And because Jonny's inner contentment was compromised, his behaviour became volatile and his reactions to situations manifested as temper tantrums. Jonny's nucleus was under strain, so it was vital that he received words of encouragement and help as well as affection at this time. Of course he did not know how to ask for it, and in the meantime he was busy being very grumpy and pushing everyone away. He was not helping himself.

4. Mixed personal pronoun 'I's

The *personal pronoun I* is an interesting letter because it cannot be abbreviated. Our I is the exteriorisation of ourselves, symbolising our sense of self-worth, self-esteem, self-image and self-confidence (or lack of all these things).

Jonny's mixed bag of different types and styles of *personal pronoun I's* are proof of the confusion he was feeling about himself and his diagnosed schizophrenia. He did not know who he was and the cause of his 'self' being seriously disturbed was likely due to worry, fear and anguish, all whilst coming across as perfectly 'normal'. We can see how his tiny little lower case i's juxtapose with the business-like upper case I's with tops and tail horizontal bars. The almost invisible, lower case i's reveals his crushed ego and impaired or weakened self-confidence, as well as modesty but to the point where he felt impotent to act. The *spacing* is also particularly *wide* around the little 'i's, exposing his strong feelings of isolation and loneliness whilst simultaneously attempting to hold people at arm's length. The more business style of *personal pronoun* with the broad lines, top and bottom, is a stab at independence, telling us that he was trying his hardest to project himself. There is also evidence of slightly *broken personal pronoun I* formations, although they are hard to see without a microscope. This can highlight someone with a split personality and shows how Jonny's identity had been fractured, leaving him with a legacy of insecurity and self-doubt.

5. Mixed messages on the emotional barometer

Let us talk about the direction the pen takes on the page and the *slant* of the writing. Jonny's is mixed, and different segments of his writing tilts in contrasting ways. His *upper zone* is sloping forwards and his *lower zone* (his unconscious private area) is reclining, or *left slanting*. What this tells us is that whilst he was happy to share his thoughts and ideas with anyone and everyone who would care to listen, there was a strong sense of dissatisfaction with his sexual and security situation, and he would not or could not disclose his deepest or darkest feelings. However, we do know that the extreme *left slant* in his *lower zone* area meant that change was threatening to him. Excessive *mixed slant* overall always exposes some confusion going on, and here we can see Jonny's unhappiness reproduced clearly on paper.

6. Wide word spacing

Jonny's *wide word spacing* is irregular and more than occasionally *very wide*, pinpointing where his propensity to be quickly stifled (hence his appetite for personal freedom – space and room to breathe) tilts to the other less healthy end of the scale, telling how much he had become unequivocally withdrawn and reclusive, living in his own fantasy world. Very *wide* and *irregular word spacing* is also a strong indicator of stress. We have seen Jonny's raging mass of insecurity and now we have evidence that he was shot through with anxiety, very nearly propelling him into oblivion.

7. Very wide margins

The *left margin* is *very wide*, excessively so. This discloses Jonny's desire to escape from his past. It also tells of an unprejudiced nature and a deliciously polite and courteous demeanour. The fact that many of his left margins are also *widening* uncovers his need for autonomy and independence, his ability to be creative and a willingness to take challenges on board. I would like to be able to say that in spite of everything, Jonny was raring to face his future. However, I would have to stop short of delivering this one positive glimpse of light on the horizon because many of his right-hand margins are also *very wide*, revealing social anxiety – a fear of social involvement – and critically also a fear of what the future holds in store for him. Jonny was dreading what was going to happen next. It was a bleak picture for him at this snapshot moment in time.

8. Disconnection

The majority of Jonny's letters are not joined-up; they are *disconnected*. In this context, given the overwhelming back-up movements, this means there was self-inflicted tension and loneliness going on. Letters are often *disconnected* by people who want to do things their own way, without becoming too involved with others to any great extent. Jonny was one of these people. He may have been reluctant to share his feelings, he may not always have come across as logical, he may have been easily distracted – flitting from one thing to another, his communication skills may have endured periods of being abysmal, he may not even have understood the dynamics of his behaviour and was lacking in self-awareness (all valid interpretations for unjoined or *disconnected* handwriting), but there was no denying he was equipped with a reflective, curious and inspired mind that was particularly honed at being abundantly intuitive, inventive and coming up with lots of original thoughts and ideas. There is inevitably more than one meaning for every handwriting movement, so (again, with appropriate supporting strokes) a broad palette of different interpretations can be applied.

9. Broad letters

The width of many of Jonny's n's and m's are not just *broad* and rectangular-shaped, they are *overly broad* and stretched out horizontally. This is another important strand that should be given credence and weaved into the analysis. If your writing is *broad*, this can mean that you are non-judgmental and unprejudiced, personable, generous and creative. However, when the *broadness* (of these *middle zone* letters) become *overly broad*, they tip the balance, taking on another more extreme meaning. Now the writer is fantasy-filled, lacking restraint and being highly impressionable, leaving themselves dangerously wide open to influence, both from oral substances and from more dominant personalities. It can also mean that they have a propensity to act carelessly, which can of course have dangerous consequences.

10. The baselines

Some of Jonny's sentences begin to fall towards the tail ends, and then they dip. The end of the theoretical or imaginary baseline conveys our unconscious feelings, highlighting someone with suicidal tendencies. This is what Jonny was battling against – his black or 'indigo' mood swings (as he called them). At that point, he was besieged and burdened by emotional heaviness. He found himself in a serious depressive state with a sense of foreboding and pessimistic anticipation that things would go wrong. He had become excessively self-concerned, and perhaps, most poignantly, he felt inadequate and impotent in his inability to realise his dreams. Jonny was lacking all hope, filled with despondency and feeling that his outlook was barren and grim.

Looking closer at the first few baselines, they are also partly *convex shaped*, which means he got exasperated, vexed and bored easily, and then gave up too quickly. Jonny may have made resolutions, but they only lasted a short while, and then he fell back into his old self and old habits again. There is *buoyancy* (in some of the *baselines*), so even in his darkest moments Jonny remained receptive, which is why 'Mike' was able to talk him down from the bridge. Johnny does attempt to rally, but his bravery is short-lived, and the baselines dip once again in the last paragraph.

Jonny's problems stemmed from putting so much pressure on himself to achieve and succeed, that much of his despair was because he was afraid he would not be able to pull off his dreams. He was scared he would fail. (I was reminded of a daddy longlegs once again, and thought of another extract from one of my poems, 'Daddy Longlegs': 'On fragile legs, they stagger round, drunken, skidding, on the ground. A frantic waltz on window panes, to try to get outside again. And when the morning comes around, they leave without a single sound. Never flying high at all, perhaps afraid that they might fall.') I think this is where we came in.

11. The loose ends on the cutting room floor

When all these strands come together, we can see that the overall portrait of a man in turmoil, suffering from neurosis, is irrefutable beyond doubt. There were just a few final loose ends to tie up. The pen stroke character of Jonny's writing was *lean* and *sharp*, which highlighted his strong idealistic principles, his intellectual approach to life and his reluctance to share his deepest feelings. The writing often appears *neglected*, because he seems to no longer care, and is unable or unwilling to communicate cogently. The initial *vertical downstrokes* on some letters are missing, which means the formation of individual letters is amorphous, and like a piece of thread it can just unravel. This is because there was something upsetting the balance of his personality, which meant he could not take on anything taxing, and if he had a problem with someone, he would simply avoid them at all costs. The little individual *tee-pee style of d's* reveals his stubbornness and provides further evidence that he did not allow people into his bubble, even when he so clearly needed support.

The handwriting *currency* or quality reveals some wobbles under the microscope; it seems there was an occasional impeded flow of an otherwise quick (*fast*) script, and tells us once more that Jonny was stressed and anxious at the time of writing these poems.

However, ultimately the *high form standard (FS)* convincingly rescues this global analysis and affirms Jonny's intelligence and potential. If he could just get his mojo back, he had what it took to express himself clearly and articulately, and he might turn his life around. This would enable him to act as a mouthpiece for other people going through similar experiences, and even dispel the stigma of mental health issues. Jonny had the ability to offer a clearer understanding across the main arteries of society, and inspire others in his quest for a better quality and healthier life for all.

Ten years later

An original note by Jonny, handwritten on unlined paper, came into my possession in March 2018 – ten years on. This time it was sent to me in the post, directly from Jonny himself. He was keen to know if I could see any changes or progress in his character. The new sample offered a very interesting update on the mind and development of a man who had once experienced suicidal thoughts and was diagnosed with a schizoaffective disorder, for which he is being treated to this day. Jonny still has relapses.

Comparing this sample with his 'Suicide' poem, it is clear Jonny has made tremendous headway, both personally and professionally since 2008, although his current handwriting suggests that he is still very much a 'work in progress'. In fact, if you read the content of the note, Jonny admits this himself, so it is hardly groundbreaking news. Nevertheless, the differences in his handwriting – hence personality – are interesting to observe. We can see how hard he is working to try and direct his inferiority complex through positive channels. We can see how much he cares about personal development, with a view to being productive and potent within the world, so that he can help other people too.

The positive take-aways

The main difference is that his handwritten *pressure* has increased from *extremely light to heavy*, with some *vertical pressure*. This is an extraordinary turnaround, and showcases tremendous progress, but also potentially uncovers a double-edged sword. Whilst Jonny is in much better physical health and has vitality metaphorically injected in his veins, so now he is investing effort, energy, commitment and passion into everything he does (there is a life force streaming like a heavy torrent and coursing through every corner of his being), he is also simultaneously experiencing more intensity in the realms of his own personal feelings. And whilst this makes him feel alive and 'real', it also creates a whole new set of problems for Jonny to deal with. Because he cares so much now, everything will hit him harder, with stronger emotion, affecting him more deeply and lasting for a longer period of time. So any difficult feelings will make a bigger and longer lasting impression. It seems Jonny has made a journey from a place of feeling insignificant – where he was tiptoeing through the world, believing he was invisible and everything around him was an illusion – into a deep bubbling cauldron of pain, pleasure, pathos, appreciation, sensitivity and perception, a place where everything is authentic and tangible and therefore has the potential to affect and wound him even more deeply. The *vertical pressure* (on the downstrokes) tells us that he also cares about his status and *who* he is, and means that he is trying to be more assertive and putting himself under pressure to achieve his goals. He may even give the impression that he is tougher and stronger than he really feels on the inside.

Action is winning the battle over reflection, but is Jonny prepared for a whole different set of possible consequences? Can he cope with this? I believe he can, so let us see why.

March '18

Things are very different now for me.
That's not to say i didt struggle-
i still do.
But i dont feel broken and unfixable
like i did before.
What i really struggle with is
paranoia and insecurity.
I used to absolutely loathe
myself - there are times this
still occurs but, again, not like
before.
In recent times I have actually
experienced moments of self-love!
And that, i now believe, is the
meaning of life- for myself at least-
to learn to be truly loving of
the skin you are in.
It is, and I am, a work in
progress!

Jonny Benjamin, age 31, right-handed

The baselines are all *rising* now, with a few that *step up*. This means that Jonny's spirit is consistently upbeat, trusting and optimistic, and any bad emotion creeping in is instantly zapped by willpower and strength. Jonny is making a continued effort to keep his feelings on an even keel, so no pessimistic tendencies or 'indigo moods' are allowed to filter through.

The size of his writing is now *medium*, so it is larger overall. Jonny is no longer disappearing on the page. He is more realistic and well adjusted. Looking at the *zones*, and what is taking place on the inside, there has been a dramatic change of focus here too – from the upper/lower balancing act to the *lower* only. In fact, the *lower zone* is now disproportionately large in this letter, which means Jonny's got his practical hat on in his search for security. His focus is now irrefutably fixed on the sensible practicalities in his life.

The *upper zone* continues to fluctuate wildly, which means he is still easily distracted with a propensity to change his mind a lot, and a plethora of ideas are still ricocheting around in his head, but the *large sized lower zone* is clearly the main focal point and motivating area, and this is a consistent fact (because it hardly oscillates at all). What this all means is that he is still open-minded about things, but there is stability in his life now. Restlessness has been replaced with a feeling of being more grounded. This in turn has generated maturity, and currently ensures practical considerations are taken care of. In a nutshell, Jonny is touching base with reality.

The general *irregularity* in his handwriting is toned down and no longer excessive, which lends a more productive interpretation, giving a positive spin to Jonny's portrait. It shows that he copes with change by improvising and thinking on his feet. And he derives pleasure from working in a stimulating environment with new challenges. He may still be susceptible to changing moods and hypersensitivity, but this is usually concealed by a stronger front. Jonny is morphing into a powerful character with an artistic bent.

Jonny loves keeping busy and achieving results, and his enthusiasm and spontaneity is growing by leaps and bounds as he gets more involved in new challenges. We know this because the *left margin* is *strongly widening*. He is still racing to leave the past behind, and now he is raring to carve out and embrace a rewarding future. However, this preference for extroversion continues to be challenged by a fear of what lies ahead in the future. Jonny still sees a fear of failure (owing to the strong avoidance of the *right margin*) like a brightly lit neon sign that sometimes seems to be mocking him. And this is why the brakes keep slamming on, stopping him in his tracks.

The glitches

The script continues to be punctuated by tiny isolated *personal pronoun i's*, which is the main evidence of continuing lack of self-esteem and paranoia at work. In fact, the *pressure* on the little downstroke i's is also *very light* (as opposed to *heavy*, as it now is in the balance of the note) which tells us that he still struggles with positive images of himself. And the *personal pronoun I's* continue to be mixed. The tiny little lower case i's still juxtapose with the business-like upper case I's, continuing to reveal his confusion about himself – who he really is – and also exposing pockets of the old Jonny, with his crushed ego and strong sense of personal isolation. So although we have seen definite improvement in the personal reconstruction of Jonny Benjamin, the fracture of his identity remains unhealed, and he still experiences moments of fear and doubt. Impotence has been stripped away, allowing Jonny to function productively (most of the time) in the real world and take baby steps towards gradually fulfilling his dreams. The split personality is being physically driven out; I suspect largely through his own determination, stubbornness and defiance. Jonny's desires are beginning to outweigh his fears.

Jonny's *middle zone* moody letters (in the ego area) are still squashed, and fluctuating greatly, telling us that he is still emotionally off key and more than a little awkward under wraps. How much these moods can be attributed to genuine feelings and the complexities of his character, and how much was due to the drugs he was taking at the time, we cannot know for sure. However, we do know that he was not too emotionally over-stressed, because his *left margin* is straight.

Most of Jonny's 'social letter' d's are *left slanting*, which means he still feels mistrusting and defensive, which would explain why he is so often reclusive and socially withdrawn. The majority of his *t-bar crosses* are *low* and set beneath the height of the top of the other *middle zone* letters – emphasising Jonny's fear of failure. This fear is self-defeating, restricting his progress. By underestimating his abilities, it is equivalent to self-sabotage. Jonny has so many ideas and dreams for personal success, such high standards and expectations, but simultaneously he continues to struggle with self-belief issues.

Yet, it is a dynamic evolution. The more success Jonny achieves, the more self-confidence he builds, and the greater his feelings of self-esteem and self-worth enhance his soul. The bar was being raised slowly, little by little, small victories gathering momentum.

It would have been so easy for Jonny to have become overly self-absorbed and retreat deeper into himself. Instead, he has turned his own personal devastating experiences of mental health into a brave exploration and positive support structure for other people to benefit from. In spite of (or perhaps because of) his imperfections, Jonny is converting his dreams into hard reality right before our eyes, revealing a magnanimous generosity, and under the circumstances that is no mean achievement. He is now an award-winning mental health campaigner with royal connections.

> 'Wow Tracey. This is incredible. I think my psychiatrist would have a field day with this insight! Thank you so much for producing what you have. I can't tell you how accurate it is! Staggeringly accurate, almost painfully so in places! This is so exciting! It could help so many people to gain deeper understanding and insight! This actually helps me to understand and gain further insight into my mental health! I think you have an indescribable gift to share with this world and I feel so touched that I can be a tiny part of this!'
> **Jonny Benjamin MBE (March 2018)**

CHAPTER 10

Suicide

Ernest Hemingway said, *'The world breaks everyone...'* but how do you know when someone is broken? How do you recognise the mental health indicators in their handwriting?

Can anything be gleaned from the writing of a man who is driven to committing the most extreme act of personal violence?

The story of Daniel

Why does someone commit suicide, and how does it affect the people left behind? There can be many reasons why, but the after-effects are invariably the same – heartbreak and devastation. Even when a suicide note is found, explaining the reasons, lingering questions remain. A note can offer an explanation as to why a person has taken their own life, but it does not always divulge what they were really feeling at the time. So graphology is a way of enabling the suicide writer's voice to be heard from beyond the grave. As a graphologist, there is a huge sense of responsibility to help families understand not only how their loved one was feeling on the day, but possibly in the weeks, months and even years leading up to their suicide. Can we unlock any secrets in their life? The handwriting holds the clues, and this is a true dialogue.

Later in 2017, I received a long-distance email from a woman who was in possession of her late husband's suicide note. She approached me while the incident was still raw. She explained that the inquest into his death was complete, so the point of the report was purely personal. All she wanted was to try and see inside his head. To try and make sense of his actions. To try to understand what he was feeling and what he may have been thinking on the day he took his own life. It was as simple as that. There was never any question that my analysis would help her or her family to 'move on'. How do you ever move on from something so drastic and final? It was all about grasping some comprehension and insight. She explained that she only had a photocopy, because the original note was still being held by the police, at the coroner's office.

Handwriting reveals many things, including the essence of personality, behavioural patterns, anxieties and stresses, and it is also a snapshot in time, so I assured my client that the note *would* reveal how he was feeling at the exact time of writing. I also explained that from a graphological perspective, content rarely matters, because I evaluate *how* people write, rather than *what* they write. I agreed to analyse the handwriting, on the basis that we wait until I could have sight of the original. This would be essential for such an investigation, because it would offer up the ability to assess the *pressure* of the handwriting, together with the true *currency* – the quality of the pen strokes.

Both *pressure* and *currency* are prime evaluators for revealing feelings and health. *Pressure* is the weight of the pen that the writer exerts on the page. It represents not only the individual's energy and vitality, but also *how* it is used and the intensity behind the drive. In other words, it reflects how strongly the individual feels things and, pertinently, how long experiences affect and stay with them. *Pressure* increases or decreases in response to stress, and stress can often be detected in writing long before the body produces a more obvious and serious response. So it was vital that I could find out the *pressure* of the writing, if I was ever going to be able to tell my client what her late husband was really feeling at the time.

What is more, the *currency* of the writing would give an appreciation of how he was likely to act or react, and quality is always clearer in an original version. The health of the writer is shown by the smoothness and fluency of the pen strokes. Any deterioration in the clear-cut edges of pen strokes, any production of disintegrating pigment, or minute jerks and tremors, or any abnormalities in the strokes at all would all have indicated an underlying problem with his health (and this would cover emotional disturbance, distress and anxiety, as well as physical illness). Sometimes these movements are so tiny, they can only be viewed under a microscope, and then they would undoubtedly be lost in translation once photocopied. Although the outcome (of suicide) was already known, it was part of my investigative process to understand if physical health had played any part of the reason behind his actions.

So I asked my client to wait until the original sample was retrieved from the police and sent on to me, which she did. I also asked her to provide another recent handwriting sample from her late husband, which would allow me to compare any discrepancies between his 'usual' handwriting and the writing in the suicide note, at a time of heightened emotions. I was keen also to see his signature and explore his public face or image. This would give me a handle on how he wanted the world to perceive him. All these things were duly provided, so I could begin work.

Naturally this was an extremely sensitive, personal and highly emotive case study, so for the sake of anonymity, the protagonist's name has been changed to 'Daniel' to protect the identity of his wife and family, who have had to rebuild their lives. Grateful thanks are extended to my client, 'Daniel's' wife, who generously and bravely gave permission for me to unlock and decipher her late husband's handwriting on a public platform, in the hope that it may help someone else who is struggling to come to terms with their own issues and shifting changes in difficult circumstances. I asked no questions and was furnished only with the barest of frameworks – the handwriting samples. My work was to confine myself to analysing the symbols on the page; so I ignored the content entirely. (The content includes considerable aggression towards his wife, which the reader should ignore as well.) Everything I had, I give to you now. This is what I found.

Daniel's suicide note, unknown hand
The prevalent handwriting features in the suicide note above are the very heavy pressure (there is a firm imprint on the reverse side of the note), the strong wavering baselines (mostly rising at the end of sentences, and one falling), the larger size (compared with his other 'normal' samples) and some increasing size writing. The note is penned in upper case letters throughout (classed as middle zone), the slant is variable and the header is repeatedly underscored (which is commonly done when the writer knows the end of their story and they want people to notice and remember them)

DO NOT RESUSCITATE

▄▄▄, I CANT GO ON ANYMORE LIVING WITH YOUR CONSTANT THREATS OF FALSE PROSECUTION OR LIVING IN FEAR OF BEING ATTACKED BY YOUR MATES / FAMILY. YOU HAVE TAKEN MY GIRLS FROM ME WHEN YOU ARE THE ABUSER! I HAVE NOTHING LEFT. YOU WIN.

WHOMEVER - MY ESCAPE FUND IS IN MY WALLET, WONT BE NEEDING IT ANYMORE. ANY MONEY OF MINE IS TO GO ONLY TO MY DAUGHTERS

PLEASE CHECK MY PHONE FOR EMAILS / MESSAGES , THEY WILL TELL YOU ALL YOU NEED TO KNOW.

PLEASE SAVE MY GIRLS FROM THAT MONSTER

GIRLS, I AM SORRY I COULDNT PROTECT YOU FROM YOUR MUM, I WILL ALWAYS LOVE YOU BOTH, NOW AND FOREVER. DAD.

First impressions revealed Daniel was a people's person. He was a warm, sentimental, easy-going and trusting man who had charming manners and formed deep attachments to the people he loved. His feelings were true, deep and strong, and undoubtedly contributed to his downfall. So how could such a seemingly gentle caring man go to such lengths and end his own life? What was in his mind at the time, and what was he feeling?

You cannot help but notice that Daniel's note is written entirely in upper case letters. My client did point out that as long as she had known her late husband, he had always only ever written in upper case letters throughout, so there was nothing unusual about this. In fact, it is quite a common occurrence for men to write this way. There are many reasons for this (just as there is a whole raft of different interpretations for all handwriting movements observed), but in this context I would say it tells us that Daniel wore his upper case letters like a suit of armour – to make him feel tough and strong.

Writing in upper case letters is a primitive defence mechanism or unconscious strategy for people who like hiding behind a fringe and do not want to disclose too much about themselves, particularly what they are feeling. This is why it is more commonly seen for men to write in this way, because they are more inclined to bury their heads in the sand rather than talk about their feelings. Matt Rudd reported in *The Sunday Times Magazine* at the end of 2020: 'According to NHS figures released before this pandemic year, one in five women suffers from anxiety or depression, compared with one in eight men. Yet men are three times more likely to take their own lives.' Writing in upper case letters is an attempt at wearing a mask to keep emotions under control, and to protect the writer from anxiety arising from thoughts or feelings with which they do not feel comfortable. These people want to give the impression that they are straightforward, but actually they are anything but underneath.

Beneath the mask they are much more complex. They may lack confidence, they may feel inferior, they may have something to hide, they may even be recovering from a recent trauma or illness. Whatever the truth, they do not want other people to know about it. So they deliberately project the opposite of what they are really like, either to convince themselves that they are okay, or to withhold the truth from others. This does make it slightly harder for a graphologist to peel away the layers and discover what is going on inside the writer's mind, but not impossible. What we do already know is that Daniel found it difficult to face up to himself as he really was, and this undoubtedly resulted in guilt and the very anxiety he was trying to avoid.

We also know, from the *rounded style* of the *small middle zone* letters, that Daniel was a personable, unassuming man with a nice way about him. The *rounded* letters tell us that he was not tough enough to confront issues openly and was likely to overcompensate for this with aggressive behaviour, which was driven inwardly (directed internally) with disastrous consequences. We know he was emotional and sensitive beneath the façade (because the *middle zone* upper case letters throughout fluctuate greatly in *size*, and also the *baselines* – the ground of reality that we walk on – meander dramatically, showing more and more emotion seeping in). Daniel was clearly someone who had his ups and downs, but did not want to wear his heart on his sleeve. He did not want the world to know that he could be soft and sentimental, and he certainly did not want people to know what he was really like behind the playful disguise. He came across modestly – someone who did not need to be the centre of attention – but in truth he needed more attention than anyone realised, and of course he did care very much about what people thought, and he wanted to make a good impression. These things all mattered to him.

Daniel was keen to project the 'right' social image. He was super-conscious of how things looked and what other people thought. (The rigidly *straight left margin* rubber-stamps this message.) He wanted to be seen as a great guy, perhaps a little bit different from the norm; a little less ordinary, and a little more special. He cared deeply, and wanted people to think well of him. I think Daniel struggled with facing up to the man he really was, and was disappointed in himself – perhaps he felt he was not good enough. Writing in upper case letters would have been his way of holding his real personality in check. However, the fact his *middle zone* letters were also dominant tells us that he would have wanted some recognition and appreciation – someone to acknowledge he had achieved something in life. Daniel was very hard on himself.

By running my fingers gently over the back of the note, I could easily feel deep indentations or grooves on the reverse of the paper. So I was able to record that the all-important *pressure* of Daniel's handwriting, as I had suspected, was *very heavy*. It was rather like reading braille. This immediately put a much stronger spin on all my interpretations, accentuating and magnifying every trait, dialling up the intensity. I also noted that there was a fair amount of *horizontal pressure* (for example, on the *t-bar* transmitters and the multiple *underlinings*), which tells us he was not going to be easily diverted from the course of action he had planned to take. Daniel put himself under unnecessary pressure, because he suspected opposition or attack from other people, but this paranoia may not have been warranted. Although he ascribed to the supposed hostility of others, the repressed aggression he felt stemmed from within himself. He may have maintained that it was in response to antagonism from other people, who he believed were deliberating persecuting him.

Daniel's *very heavy pressure* also tells us that he would have been inclined to see his problems in black and white, and was ready to address and resolve them in a way that was direct. He was dealing with a lot of pent-up or bottled anger at the time. And the tiny *impatience ticks* (see, for example, the second downstroke of the H in 'HAVE' [29]) reveals that he was frustrated and wanted to get things over with as soon as possible. He would have needed a quick-fix physical solution, so his pre-planned actions would have been wilful and determined. I do not think anyone could have talked him round, because he had made up his mind, and that was that.

The *wavering* yet *rising baselines* tell us that even in dire straits he tried hard to put a brave face on his unstable emotions. It would have been difficult for anyone to have known that anything was wrong, because Daniel always tried so hard to project a cheerful disposition. Clearly everything had got too much for him, however, and it was more than he could bear. There is only one *falling baseline*, much further down the page, and this touches briefly and poignantly on his depression and exhaustion at the time of writing the note.

The oval 'o' in in his signature (removed from the top of the page to preserve anonymity, and therefore unseen) is the only *oval* that is open in the entire piece. This is significant, because it informs us that Daniel was ready to spill the beans and speak his truth. The letters in his wife's name (also removed) are squeezed tight, as if they are glued together, and *narrow* in formation, which reveals how much more needy and dependent on his wife Daniel was, than perhaps either of them realised. He felt he could not go on without her, in spite of anything he says (in the contents of the note). And I think, for this reason, he had come to terms with what he was going to do.

Daniel's *mixed slant* reveals that his emotions were unstable and volatile, but the *very heavy pressure* dictates that these emotions would have been suppressed and bottled up, deep down. He was clearly struggling to cope and contain his feelings, but grappling equally hard to express them, and this would have shown in unpredictable behaviour. The trouble with *very heavy pressure* is that it represents writers with very heavy hearts. So we know that Daniel cared deeply, and the weight of emotions he concealed would have been intense. So much so, they must have been too severe and agonising for him to bear any longer. He knew well enough that he could not get over whatever was upsetting him, and he also knew that the hurt would stay with him and be long-lasting. Daniel was suffering from chronic stress and felt he was not strong enough to endure it any longer.

Daniel would have been totally committed to whatever he did in his life, and at the time I suspect he was struggling to deal with any changes that affected his lifestyle or his relationships with the people he cared about most in the world.

The *size* of the handwriting in the suicide note is larger than in the other samples provided. Some of the words in the note are *increasing* in size too. Also the overall layout on the page could be reasonably described as *compact* or crowded. This means that Daniel was trying to get attention and be heard – it is like he was shouting on paper, which would have been unusual for him. It is as if he felt he was unable to express himself any other way than by talking big and exaggerating – laying it on thick.

The *close word spacing* and crowded layout uncovers a man who loved being involved in everything that was going on. He really enjoyed and craved other people's company, and could not bear the thought of being alone and lonely. His sense of isolation at the time is clear in the *wider word spacing* specifically around his *personal pronoun I's*. Daniel was the kind of man who was dependent on a sustained relationship for emotional fulfilment, and was unlikely to get over emotional wounds easily, however sensible and practical he may have appeared on the surface.

There was a huge inner conflict going on – sentiment versus reason, feelings versus practical considerations. So, perhaps surprisingly, given the circumstances and intense emotionality at the time, there are also signs that Daniel had got it together in some respects. There is a sense he was well organised, considering what he was planning, and the inevitable appalling conclusion that lay ahead. This can be seen in the *straight left-hand margin*, the *regularly spaced baselines*, the matching business-like style of *personal pronoun I's*, the *normal higgledy-piggledy* or *'ragged' right margin*, and perhaps even more tellingly, in the lack of *disturbed currency*. There is an absence of any *hesitant* or *jerky pen strokes*, any *retouched* or *retraced writing*, any *resting* or *scatter dots* or *ink trails*. Sometimes we can learn more from what we cannot see. Even a lack of *start strokes* eliminates the possibility of procrastination. This evidence all leads me to believe that he had capitulated and come to terms with what he was going to do, and that his actions were premeditated.

Whatever the truth, Daniel was a versatile and adaptable man – good at thinking on his feet – and really good at pretending that all was well. I would say the underlying anxiety bubbled away gently and self-indulgently beneath the surface for quite a while, but given the right or wrong set of circumstances was prepped and ready to be triggered violently, in a way that might have seemed irrational and unbelievable in the immediate aftermath. Daniel's actions could be abrupt and seem out of character, and his reasoning skills were impaired at the time, all because he was overcome by emotion. I think we are all capable of doing most things in life, given the 'right' set of circumstances, and who knows what tipped him over the edge that day. If his actions were deliberate and intentional, perhaps the day itself held no particular significance.

His handwritten note represents a violent emotional outburst on paper. It was a huge venting of pent-up anger. He was supremely vexed and emotionally unstable at the time, and his behaviour was becoming increasingly unpredictable. Daniel realised he was unable to adjust or cope with the demands life was putting on him, and he was lion-proud and so wrapped up in his own misery, he simply could not see beyond the end of his nose. So although there is an impression of realism in Daniel's make-up, all common sense had been compromised, and he had reached breaking point emotionally. He was deeply affected, acutely weakened and ultimately ruined by his intense feelings and emotions, his expectations in life and his desire to keep up social appearances. And this was the lethal concoction that contributed to his subsequent violent actions and demise.

> *'Thank you for the report, I have to say it was one of the most insightful things I've ever read, and I can see a lot of truth in it. It definitely adds up. I found it helpful, as it is an insight into not only what he was thinking at the time, but in the weeks, months and years before. I find it oddly comforting, as if it is the only way to have an idea what was going on with him. I can't thank you enough!'*
> **Daniel's wife**

The story of Bernard and Gladys
Between the years 1927–9

It is not all about who we are now. We are often contemporary versions of older family members, usually our mothers or fathers. We inherit our looks, so we frequently share similar phizogs. However, we are also often bestowed with familial character traits, and these are replicated in our handwriting, as the brain connects with the fabric of our related psyches.

Unravelling genealogy, by shaking the branches of our family tree and getting a first-hand account of where we come from and what our ancestors were like is not only fascinating, it can also be extraordinarily revealing and helpful, giving posthumous insight when it comes to understanding people's characters, feelings and behaviours in different times. It is so curious, the marks we leave behind, the little traces of ourselves.

Turning back the clock and three generations, this is a portrait of two people – Gladys and Bernard (the protagonist's real names have been changed to protect their descendants' privacy) – who lived together as man and wife, and whose lives were cut violently short late one evening in 1929. This very human story is composed and told almost exclusively from a graphological perspective.

It was during the early hours of 22 March 1929, in a big detached house called 'Overlands' which stood in an acre of land in the heart of a little village called Bushey, located on the outskirts of northwest London, that Bernard shot Gladys dead and then committed suicide.

Fast forward to today, and Gladys's descendants decided they would like to find out more about her and the man who was purporting to be her husband, but who ended her life so tragically and violently.

There were many mysterious, unanswered questions. What were Gladys and Bernard really like? What sort of characters did they have? What reason could Bernard possibly have had to murder Gladys? And why had he subsequently taken his own life? What sort of person would do something like this? Had Gladys contributed in any way to her own premature death – had she driven Bernard to kill her? Was it cruelly planned, or did events spiral unexpectedly out of control that night?

When I analyse handwriting and prepare profile reports, I always try to see the best in people. I go out of my way to see two sides to a story and always try to present a positive spin. However, just occasionally there is no palatable way of describing someone or saying something, and by glossing over the clues (in the handwriting), I am allowing the truth to be left uncovered.

So for the sake of the family's feelings – Bernard and Gladys's descendants – I had hoped and tried to imagine a more palatable set of excuses and reasons for what happened that fateful night long ago, but handwriting does not lie, and the truth will out. Few people are all bad, but sometimes there are no redeeming features.

So what did I know at the outset? I was furnished with various original handwriting samples and informed that Bernard was aged forty-four when he passed away (I was not initially informed that he had taken his own life), and Gladys was only twenty-six when she died (again, I was not told that he wilfully took hers). Two of the letters provided were written by Bernard, and dated 4 April 1928 and 11 March 1929, respectively – the latter was written only ten days before the incident happened. There was also a typed letter (dated 1927) showcasing Bernard's signature only. A handful of postcards, and a letter composed by Gladys were written on 28 January 1929 – two months before she was murdered.

I went through the usual questions, including *Do you know if the writer was right or left-handed?'*, not expecting the client to know the answer, and certainly not expecting the answer I got: *'I'm afraid I don't know, but the gun was found in his right hand!'* The rest was left for me to fill in the gaps.

My client (on behalf of her wider family) commissioned me to do a historical handwriting analysis. They were interested to learn as much as possible about the couple, and were particularly intrigued to know more about Gladys's character (my client's great-great-aunt), because they knew so little about her. They were also keen to find out if I could see any significant changes in Bernard's personality in the lead up to the fateful night (by comparing two handwritten letters dated a year apart), and which might shed some light and insight into what may have happened.

Bernard's portrait
(Born in July 1885, aged forty-four, at the time of writing)

Bernard was essentially an imperious, haughty, cavalier, very private and sombre man with delusions of grandeur. He probably had a disciplinarian father who made him a perfectionist. So Bernard tried his very best in life and put himself under a lot of pressure in doing so. He took his responsibilities very seriously and felt like he had the weight of the world on his shoulders. Bernard was also a control freak who always had to have the last word, and ultimately we shall see that there was nothing redeemable about him at all.

Socially, Bernard epitomised extroversion in so much as he loved and needed other people around him and could not bear the thought of being alone, although people would not have known what he was really like underneath or what his motives were, because he kept his true feelings strictly under wraps. The face the world saw was one of an intelligent, cultured man, who came across as incredibly polite, correct and civilised – a gentleman of etiquette. However, he was not the nice guy he made himself out to be at all – far from it.

Bernard should have carried a government health warning, because underneath the façade he was very different indeed. Bernard was bi-sexual, who got his kicks from sadomasochism. His obsession was with pain. He enjoyed inflicting it on other people as well as on himself, and he had a predilection for domination. There was a very cruel streak hidden behind the civilised exterior, and he would have undoubtedly led a secret life. Furthermore, he was obsessed by death – he thought about it regularly.

Bernard's approach to life was selfish, inflexible and rigidly obsessional. It was extremely unlikely that he would have done anything on the spur of the moment (without extenuating circumstances) and he intensely disliked being in situations where he felt he was not in control. He had set ideas about things and felt very threatened by change. It is clear there was bottled anger without release, which made Bernard potentially quarrelsome, contentious and reactionary. However, he was immensely emotionally repressed – inhibited, tense and anxious. He was also intransigent and intolerant of other people's points of view, so he would have systematically and aggressively opposed them. He had an obstinate nature and never knew when to throw in the towel. Once a chain of events was in motion, Bernard struggled to press the stop button. He simply had to finish something he had started. Bernard also had a sensitive pride that made him very reactive to criticism, and under stress he could become easily aggravated and frustrated. He was not the sort of man to compromise and if he lost control he was apt to act rashly and with the speed of a knee-jerk reaction.

Bernard was a complicated man who had also been suffering from depression for years, so he may have used murder and suicide as a vehicle for sadomasochism. He loved company, but I suspect he was fearful that anyone who got too close –

close enough to see the real person beneath the stiff and starchy façade – might uncover his ugly truths and secrets, and discover who he really was.

Regrettably, all the 'real' components of his character were a recipe for disaster. Bernard did have an inkling of decency. He did have a conscience and was inclined to suffer from feelings of guilt. So it is quite possible (simply from a graphological perspective) that he held a secret from his past that was choking him. This, coupled with his potentially long-term depression and an innate dignity that refused to let him share his anxieties and worries with anyone else, may have all conspired to push him over the edge. As we have seen, graphologists are unable to see the peripheral situation at the time. We can only extract and pinpoint the innate character traits themselves, and it will depend on an outside trigger to reveal what happens next.

So let us examine the graphological timeline in the lead-up to the shootings.

The evidence

Timeline:
November 1927 (one year before the bloodshed)

We begin with Bernard's professional signature on a typed letter. It is much more formal in style compared to his 'normal' signature when he signs off his personal letters (a more informal style can be seen on page 159). The signature is a conscious projection of identity (so it does not necessarily tell us what is going on unconsciously behind closed doors). Bernard's signature transmits the persona of a civilised man. He wanted people to believe he was a level-headed, responsible, down to earth, admirable man who was very much in control. Bernard wanted to create a presence because appearances mattered. He also wanted to be perceived as a character who was always on the go – keeping busy, being productive.

The placement of the *signature* on the right-hand side of the page is evidence that at the time he still saw a future ahead.

Upper case *capital letters* represent your ideal self, and the face you show to the world. They relate to appearances, pride, social prestige, egoism and vanity. From Bernard's huge upper case letter 'C', it is clear that this was a man who had pipe dreams of nobility. He craved respect and believed he had a reputation to maintain,

Bernard's professional signature, 1927, unknown hand

Here we have a very large size stylised signature (with just the initials shown, for the sake of anonymity), right slant, stilted rhythm, huge upper case C for the surname with lower zone extension and strong horizontal underlining, two final full stops, clever linking with the long t-bar leading into the big C, large potlid extension on the letter p (unseen here), narrowness (particularly in his middle name), connected, angles with angular connecting strokes, diligence loop on the B, misplaced angle in the lower zone of the big C; the speed of the family name is written more carefully than his given Christian names.

Note also the open B on the baseline revealing Bernard's duplicitous nature, which may be hard to believe, as he seemed so respectable. It is never enough to accuse someone of being deceitful or dishonest based on one sign alone (and no list is ever finite), but given a cluster of other indictors of dishonesty (seen here in the stylised script, the excess of covering strokes in the upper and middle zones, extreme rigidity and narrowness, the fairly slow speed depicted in the mechanical regularity of the writing), it would be fair to say there is a lot of secrecy and withholding going on.

so he set himself impossibly high standards. He felt a strong need to dominate others and if he was not taken seriously, he would have been quite annoyed. Bernard would not have been able to live with himself, with the guilt and the knowledge of what other people might think and say, after what he did. His family and status in life would have been of utmost importance, but he also needed to feel that he was worthy of it.

Bernard's signature also tells us that he was a hardworking, diligent man who always put family first. He was a very private man who would have covered up any perceived weaknesses from the eyes of the outside world, and this could have given vent to irritability or unexpected outbursts from time to time. He was the sort of person who would rather argue than smooth things over. He was uptight, anxious and emotionally repressed, but he wanted to come across as someone who meant well; a man who did good deeds and provided for everyone – certainly not someone who intended to do anyone any harm. He was just a man who bore his responsibilities in life seriously.

Nevertheless, his obsessive-compulsive behaviour could already be seen in the extreme *rigidity* of his handwriting, and in the way he makes two symmetrical full stops at the end of the signature – one above the underlining of his surname, and the other below.

Essentially, Bernard was a man who had a preoccupation with 'want' – he wanted things (financial, material possessions). He wanted so much in life, to the extent that he could lose sight of reality. These desires piled more and more pressure on him, as he struggled to adapt and fulfil his dreams. All his personal concerns were buried, finding no outlet. He was also capable of bearing grudges and taking revenge if he felt it was warranted.

The clues are already there in plain sight in Bernard's formal *signature*. Here we have a man who was controlling and domineering – tough, self-assertive, dogmatic and argumentative. Someone who could hold a grudge. Someone with buried aggression in his subconscious. Someone with huge personal pride. Someone experiencing too many pressures and battling with repressed emotions, tension, anxiety and angst, all swilling around inside. And let us not forget one more thing – someone with an absolute desire to have the last word.

It was already potentially a recipe for disaster, given of course the right circumstances that could have exacerbated or pushed the wrong buttons at that fateful moment in time. It was a very sad story.

April 1928 (one year before the incident)

Moving on to the first handwritten letter, one of the stand out features here are the regularly *falling baselines*. We have no reason to suspect Bernard was left-handed (remember, the gun was found in his right hand), and the *baselines* are *falling* quite steeply, which points to him suffering from exhaustion and depression. We can also see that he found it hard to express himself, so all his emotions would have been pent up and contained, no doubt festering. The marginally dominant *upper zone* also tells us that he had a conscience, and this could have been a driving factor that won out in the end, but not necessarily in the way we might expect.

We see brief glimpses into Bernard's sensitivity, but overall the signs continue along the same vein of deep emotional repression, self-restraint (he was very hard on himself and put himself until constant pressure), anxiety and control, and last but certainly not least, almost debilitating depression (which I imagine he would have effectively covered up and hidden from the outside world). Bernard was like a pressure cooker, waiting to explode.

4 April 1928

My dear Jack

Bernard's letter, April 1928, unknown hand
Note the marked right slant, falling baselines, extreme rigidity, narrowness and contracted (or cramped) rhythm. Angles and angular connecting strokes. Small-medium size with large and marginally dominant UZ, large LZ and small, weak and fluctuating MZ. Close word spacing. Variable pressure patterns with smeariness. Covering strokes in all zones. Straight lean LZ downstrokes (occasional right tending). Arrogance arcade and short angular starting strokes. Defiant K's. One fat vanity loop on d. Compressed and mainly closed ovals with misplaced angles. Fast speed. Narrow margins. Left tends. Small high t-bars. Twisted tight forms.

Bernard was not able to express himself or communicate his feelings with Gladys, and this would have exacerbated things further, causing more inner tension and repressed emotion. He felt he was very much the man of the house, and in charge not only of his young wife but also his brother-in-law (known alternately as Jack and John – for some reason he was known by both names), who meant so much to him. However, Bernard was impatient and likely to fly off the handle in a blink. He would undoubtedly have been the type of man who would have been happier working with facts and things rather than with people and emotion. The *straight downstrokes into the lower zone* reveal that this was a man who with all his morals, rules and discipline did not always think about the consequences of his words and actions. It also meant that he was poor at communication and tended to talk at people, rather than with them, which may have been like a red bag to a bull in his relationship with Gladys.

There is an impression that he thought the world of his much younger 'wife'. The size of the upper case G for 'Gladys' in the letter dating back to April 1928 is larger than any of the other upper case letters, which tells us that he held her in high esteem. The *close word spacing* also uncovers that Bernard could not bear the thought of being without her. I imagine that for all the repression, rules, discipline, principles and hard words, Gladys would have been his world.

The eighteen-year age gap between Bernard and Gladys suggests that his brother-in-law was also much younger than him. I suspect, seeing Bernard's authoritarian and conscientious nature, he bore a strong sense of responsibility to look after the family, and this weighed heavily on him, causing more pressure and adding to his feelings of tiredness and depression.

The *stilted* quality of Bernard's writing, where the natural rhythmic flow of the writing is restrained and held back in check, demonstrates on paper the control, repression, immense pressure and self-discipline he put on himself. He needed structure and security in his life, and he could not cope with change. He had set ideas and did not like making mistakes or getting anything wrong. Perhaps also, given Bernard's proclivities, one is left wondering what feelings he may have had towards Glady's brother?

March 1929 (eleven days before the murder and suicide)

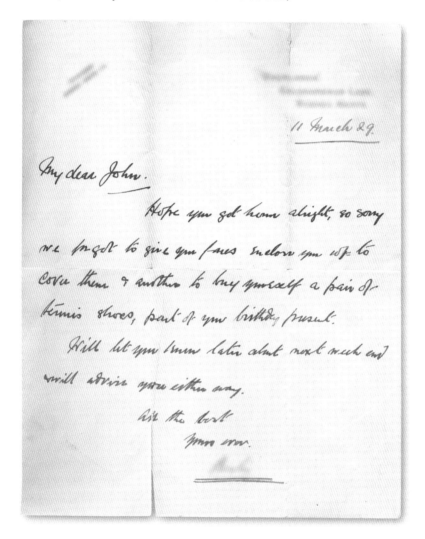

11 March 29.

My dear John.

Bernard's final letter, March 1929, unknown hand

Note the rigid tension, the strong marked right slant, the medium-large size with large and dominant UZ, a significantly smaller LZ, and a larger and greatly fluctuating MZ. The pressure patterns are still variable. The writing is sharp and lean, although some flooding of ink is noted. The baselines continue to fall, although less dramatically – but the word 'and' in line 6 falls away at the end of the line. There is also a notable preponderance of angles in ovals on the baseline.

One year on, and there is a significant difference in this piece of handwriting: The *zones* are weighted differently. The *upper zone* section is still dominant, but now it is not 'marginally' dominant – now it is disproportionately *very large* and dominant – and simultaneously the *lower zone* has diminished, which means that the writer's internal balance has been compromised, and all emphasis is now on the *upper zone*.

The *zones* are important because they tell you how someone is feeling on the inside. They tell us about the writer's inner character, and where their motivation lies. The *upper zone* comprises all the tall stems that are extensions of the small letters (seen in b, d, f, h, k, l, t) and are associated with the upper part of the body. This is the realm of hopes, dreams, aspirations, imagination, spiritualism and desire for achievement. It is the area of ambition, but also the spiritual area – a desire to be righteous, principled, moralistic and responsible. Taken to the extreme, and we see further evidence of Bernard's delusions of grandeur. He had become even more authoritarian and moralistic, with a sense of dissatisfaction with himself and also a tendency to overthink things – so there would have been a lot whirring around in his mind at the time. He would have been unable to accept that he had made mistakes, hence the delusional or unrealistic and deranged thinking patterns.

The *lower zone* (the long downstrokes that hang beneath the baseline – seen in the lower section of the letters f, g, j, p, q, y) represent the strictly private, secretive and subconscious area of practical considerations and sexual desires. So, the fact this zone had substantially decreased, also tells us that not only was he still emotionally cramped and challenged in this respect, but also that his physical needs were diminishing. This throws up the possibility that behind closed doors their private sexual lives had dwindled or even ceased, and perhaps Bernard was not fulfilling his young 'wife' in the bedroom (for whatever reason). The gross intensity of his emotions can be seen in the *variable pressure* patterns with some *smeary* handwriting.

In the meantime, the *middle zone* – the small letters sitting on the baseline – continue to fluctuate, but here the size is fluctuating emphatically, highlighting a problem area, meaning that Bernard had become prone to dark moods. We know that he also had a lot going on in his head and was struggling to deal with his gloomy thoughts too.

All the other changes in Bernard's handwriting are seen mainly in the small nuances. For example, the script becomes increasingly more *illegible* (if you compare the two samples), which tells us he has got something to hide and he is becoming ever more secretive. The *size* of the writing is *larger* in his last letter, but this could just be because he was writing on a larger sheet of paper with more space to fill. And the *ovals* are less *rounded* and have *more* and *sharper angles* on the *baseline* with some flooding of ink. This means he was just as inhibited emotionally, just as blunt and critical, but now he was more likely to be verbally destructive. Bernard was never able to take things at face value. He always had to check everything out, and he had a tendency to be suspicious of things – he was hopeless at reading between the lines. Maybe he could see the way things were going, and he did not like what he could see?

Here the *baselines* are not falling quite so steeply, although the last few sentences do fall. You may think that his depression had lessened and he was feeling a little better, and perhaps that makes it all the more poignant that the final emotional outburst happened. Perhaps something occurred out of the blue, or something was said – something that triggered him, sending him into a rage, and because Bernard had so much emotion bottled up, he simply could not control himself any longer? Also, the first few words, 'My dear John', are a little *wavy* along the *baseline*, which is another nod to emotion.

On the other hand, if he had had time to come to terms with his impending death, perhaps that knowledge was a relief, alleviating his feelings of burden. We have seen before when someone commits suicide and the *baselines* are rising rather than falling. Perhaps this is when the victim has become accustomed to their decision and accepted their fate as inevitable or a fait accompli? The *baselines* are also *wide* and *regularly well-spaced*, which is a prime indicator that Bernard's organisational skills were exceptional. So, what was he planning?

Finally, the *double underlining* of his signature is significant. People accentuate their name, because they are proud and want to draw attention to themselves. A double or multiple underscoring is quite unusual and would enhance this meaning. It is almost as if Bernard had a premonition and wanted to be remembered ... or perhaps, he already knew? As we have seen, multiple underlinings are common when someone is preparing for suicide.

Gladys's portrait

(Born in June 1903, aged twenty-six, at the time of writing)

January 1929 (three months before her murder)

Gladys was mature for her age, intelligent and like a breath of fresh air – the ubiquitous crowd pleaser. She was a real fun live wire who knew how to enjoy life to the full. She adored getting out and about and socialising. She was captivating and alluring and enjoyed any attention immensely. You would always know when she was in the room. She would have been the boisterous grand eloquent, making lots of noise, talking for England and generally busy being the life and soul of a gathering. She had a gift for being friendly and getting on with people. She probably loved nothing better than having a good chat and putting the world to rights. Gladys loved to talk but did not always listen. She could be described as a little OTT, although we can see from the *closed* and *occasionally squeezed ovals* that discretion was assured, so whatever went on behind closed doors, stayed there. Gladys would have kept a lid on it. She was not inclined to air her dirty laundry in public.

Gladys had all sorts of ideas and was keen to share her views and opinions with others. Her *positively rising baselines* tells us that she always looked on the bright side – she was definitely a glass half-full type of woman – and she would have been adept at putting a brave smile on her face, even when things were tough. You might describe her as a cool, sassy, street-wise, ambitious lady blended seamlessly with a carefree, fun-loving joie de vivre. She was charming and seductive, and may have given the appearance of being frivolous, but behind the smiling façade she was anything but. I suspect, given the very *wide* and *irregular word spacing* that she was not infallible and did suffer from inner anxieties that she kept to herself and never spoke about.

Gladys was also a grafter, who worked hard and played hard. She would undoubtedly have been an expert housewife, practical, magnanimous and capable of acts of great sacrifice. Although she loved socialising, it is clear that she enjoyed her privacy – quiet time alone – she was quickly drained by other people's needs and commitment. She was a restless independence seeker who relished personal freedom and travel, when the opportunity presented itself. New places, new faces – she loved them all.

Dear John

Am in the middle of cooking much Steak & Kidney Pie, so cannot stay long, but want you to know that we expect you this Friday as early as possible. Please ring up at Queens P/c.

4 o'clock. Dne hem tired ever since. However, hope you are feeling a little less law spirited. We are running out to Tring Saturday afternoon. I think you will like the run its a very pretty place. Chero' John love G

Gladys's letter, January 1929 (three months before her murder), unknown hand

Note the large size with weak MZ and all zones fluctuating considerably, revealing problem areas in UZ and MZ. Marked right slant. Rising baselines. Connected. Aerated. Word spacing wide and irregular. Letter spacing overly wide in places. Primary thread with angles, arcades and garlands. Angular garlands. Broad width with unexpected narrowness. Flourishes and small elaborations. Vanity loops on t's and d's. Pointed UZ and LZ loops (see, for example, the UZ J for 'John' and LZ f in 'of' in line 3). Starting strokes with full, flourished arcade m of 'middle' and an angular starting stroke followed by an arcade on m of 'much' and a garland starting stroke on w of 'want'. Big potlids. Strong t-bars. Some horizontal pressure. Covering strokes (see for example the LZ g of 'long' in line 5). Straight slashing downstrokes in LZ. Mostly closed ovals.

Underneath the smiles and light-hearted niceties, Gladys would have been quite a formidable lady in her own right. She was not backwards in coming forwards and she would not do anything she did not want to do. She was also perfectly happy getting on and doing her own thing. She was quickly stifled and actually thrived on her own breathing space in order to operate effectively. I could imagine that in another century – perhaps in this day and age – she would have carved an interesting lifestyle and workspace for herself. Gladys was self-sufficient and independent, imbued with the spirit of ambition and adventure.

The strong *horizontal pressure on the t-bars*, with sharp points and some placed high, transmitted that she was no one's quiet mouse and could stand up for herself. She was perfectly capable of taking charge, confidently speaking her mind as and when necessary. In truth, she could be quite bossy and contentious, and also had a sharp tongue that was prone to sarcasm. Some of the *t-bars* are *flyaway* on the right-hand side of the stems, revealing her impatience. Gladys could not always hold her tongue. The *angular connecting strokes* and *angular* letter forms, combined with the *marked right slant* (where the words are strongly inclining), the *large size, wide word*, *line* and *letter spacing*, and also the elongated *potlids* (where the downstroke part of the letter p rises high into the UZ), all collaborate to illustrate this interpretation.

All those *garland* or saucer-shaped formations linking the letters at the *baseline* tell us that Gladys had a bit of a battle going on in her head. Her mind told her to try to be conciliatory, good-natured and pleasant – to try to avoid confrontation – but her heart would not always follow suit. This meant there was a tendency to get carried away by her feelings and Gladys was inclined to jump to conclusions in a heartbeat. We can see this in the interference of the *marked right slant* on the emotional barometer, which often causes instant reactions.

Now that we have revealed Gladys's personality, we can see the pattern of their compatibility emerging, and once all the shapes are slotted together, we will have a deeper insight and understanding into how Gladys *may* have contributed to the events on that fateful night in 1929. Could it be that she was simply with the wrong man, in the wrong place, at the wrong time?

The compatibility

There are so many different perspectives you can take when looking at this union, as with any compatibility, and of course that is because people are complex creatures, particularly when it comes to the mechanism of the mind. It may be that Bernard was initially attracted by Gladys's youthful beauty. One of the things that graphology cannot do (apart from see current or future circumstances) is recognise physical appearance or the undefinable chemistry between two people.

Superficially Gladys and Bernard were probably a good match on a level playing field. They both would have enjoyed a flamboyant lifestyle with plenty of partying. I do not think either of them would have ever been happy in a conventional style of relationship. However, whilst I suspect that sombre Bernard may have found Gladys's company uplifting, there may have been other times when her light-hearted cheery, carefree attitude was annoying. He might also have got frustrated and irritated when she did not appear to take life as seriously as he did.

Bernard was committed to Gladys, but probably showed this by trying to control her – he was a control freak, so it was the only way he knew how to behave. Bernard would not have been an easy man to live with and he certainly was not someone you would have wanted to goad or tease. I suspect he had been suffering from depression for years, which would have been debilitating for a man who found it incredibly hard to express himself and communicate effectively. As we have seen, Gladys was an impressive lady in her own right – someone who would not have appreciated being dominated or controlled or bullied, despite the age difference between them. I suspect it infuriated Bernard when he could not control her, especially when she answered back! If Gladys was fed-up with Bernard, she would have told him so, and if she did not want any more sex with him, she would have made no bones about her wishes either. (Sometimes the very things that attract us to a person in the first instance can be the dividing and the defining factor further down the line, can they not?)

Gladys's strengths and abilities may have impressed and excited Bernard to begin with – pushing all the right buttons – but I suspect Gladys could take boldness a step too far, to another level. She was quite the rebel. Gladys could be antagonistic and stubborn, unlikely to let things go, and she could also be resentful, just like Bernard. This means that the two of them were potentially combustible material in a heated discussion. They were both capable of being contentious, unafraid to speak their mind or say hurtful words, loaded with venom and spite. Plus there were sexual tensions and frustrations, all stewing and playing their part. For Gladys, anger flared up out of the blue, but then dissipated and calmed just as quickly. For Bernard, his anger barometer exceeded acceptable limits, but it was all bottled up and festering deep down inside.

Gladys knew what she wanted in life and had high expectations. However, she was also impatient and short-tempered and Bernard may have found her sarcastic tongue disrespectful, especially coming from the mouth of a much younger woman. He undoubtedly would have taken anything she said very personally. Gladys was not really the nurturing type (there are few loops under the baseline and the majority of her y's and g's are all *straight sticks* or *slashing downstrokes*), so she may well have seemed uncaring and lacking empathy in her intimate relationships, and unwilling to pander to his sensitivities.

We know that Bernard set himself impossibly high standards, and Gladys may have inadvertently tapped into his low self-esteem, diminishing it further on occasions. Gladys may have misjudged her 'husband' too, perhaps unaware of how much anger and tension was being suppressed. It is unlikely she knew about his hidden secrets, personal stresses, anxiety and depression. Bernard was prone to dark moods and evil thoughts, so who knows what might have triggered the violence?

Gladys was a curious woman who did not listen to her instincts, and who dared to go intrepidly where angels feared to tread. Did the fun unravel quickly and the relationship between Bernard and Gladys combust catastrophically, in one last final heated exchange? Or was the nature of their union a red herring? Did the events unfold because that was exactly the way Bernard planned it, chillingly and cold-heartedly? We know that Bernard had an obsessive-compulsive disorder, so it is much more plausible that he planned the entire denouement meticulously in advance.

The final outcome

The evening of 22 March 1929

As an amateur sleuth armed purely with graphological evidence, I would say there were two distinct scenarios about what could have happened that night. First and foremost, control was key. Bernard was an obsessive control freak, with OCD and cruel destructive tendencies. He could easily have planned the violent climax with precise detail in advance and Gladys would have been oblivious of what was to come. So my first guess was to suggest that he calculatingly prepared for what was going to happen, and deliberately and wilfully took both their lives.

There was, however, another possibility that could not be discounted. This was my second theory: Bernard had been suffering from depression and was extremely emotionally restrained and suppressed. With so much emotion bottled up, it only took something small to happen unexpectedly, something silly that might have acted as the trigger, and he could have exploded violently with unforeseen consequences. We have seen that Bernard and Gladys's relationship was contentious and potentially volatile, so it is not impossible that an argument got out of hand, spiralled out of control, and it all happened very quickly in the end – a spontaneous outburst of violent emotion. And as soon as the deed was done, Bernard immediately regretted his actions and took his own life as a way of atonement. Perhaps the deaths were not premeditated. Perhaps Gladys was a contributing factor to the events that night.

The twists

Once my work was complete and I had delivered my report, I discovered that Bernard had in fact previously prepared and written no less than five suicide notes! My client told me she had found old records revealing that he was in huge debt and had evidently been planning his suicide for a while. In fact, he had never even owned 'Overlands', the house in which they lived. Neither had he 'owned' Gladys. They were living together as man and wife, although after their deaths the police could find no marriage certificate. Bernard had previously been married and did not appear to have been successful in securing a divorce.

Somehow Gladys and he had been living in a large, detached property they had never purchased. Bernard had even hired a gardener, a chauffeur and maid in the weeks leading up to the event. They had enjoyed a wonderful lifestyle, but it seems Bernard had been living beyond his means and could no longer keep a lid on all the secrets and lies. (In his final suicide note, Bernard stated that Gladys should not be blamed or made accountable in any way, because she knew nothing of his financial problems.) Bernard could no longer control events, and circumstances had spun out of his control. He shot Gladys dead in her sleep, before turning the gun on himself. How much she knew, if anything, remains a mystery, but judging by the contents of his suicide note I suspect Bernard had kept her completely in the dark. Why he had to kill her too, we will never know, but it was probably all part of his insatiable need for dominance and control. The gardener found them both in the bedroom in the morning. The maid had called upstairs and when no one answered, she asked the gardener to go up and check on them.

There was one more unexpected twist in the tale. After the deaths, 'Overlands' was demolished, and two detached houses were built on the plot (in Coldharbour Lane in Bushey Village), and then again in the 1960s these two houses which had been sitting empty and derelict for years were also demolished, and a row of four Georgian-style houses built in their place. My client was vaguely curious to know what had happened to any of the families who subsequently lived in these properties. She wondered if bad vibes had endured, permeating and affecting the people living there years later. My stepmother-in-law happened to be a leading local estate agent in Bushey Village at that time. So I thought she might know who bought the plot of land and built on it. I asked her the question and much to my surprise she said, without any hesitation at all, *'Well, yes, actually. We did.'*

The ripple effect often traverses time, but the coincidence that this story touched on my own family's background was entirely unforeseen and unexpected, creating a final shocking twist in the tale. According to my stepmother-in-law, it seems that anyone who ever lived in any of these properties either died prematurely or their marriages broke down irretrievably. Was that bad fortune or was the writing on the wall?

Even though Bernard had caused so much devastation within my client's family, they tell me that they do now feel they can offer him forgiveness. My client's initial reaction, when I delivered the character sketch was: *'Oh gosh Tracey, goose bumps here! This is amazing! You have confirmed so much of what we had suspected about B... from the inquest, but it's wonderful to have him 'fleshed out' so well. Wow! Thank you so much.'*

CHAPTER 11

Inside the mind of a serial killer

Dennis Nilsen – 'Killing for Company'

What sort of man would write like this?

This is the voice of a serial killer.

We have explored the good, delved into the bad and now we will scrutinise the ugly.

On 12 May 2018, at the age of seventy-two, Dennis Nilsen (who became known as the 'Muswell Hill Murderer') died in the high security HM Prison Full Sutton in East Yorkshire, having spent thirty-five years and half his life serving time for the murder of fifteen men – most of them homeless homosexuals – at his north London address. It is well documented that he lured his victims, murdered them by strangulation and then bathed and dressed the victims' bodies, which he sodomised and retained for extended periods of time, placing them around his home and sleeping at their side. When this ritual drew to a close, he would stow the bodies under floorboards, before eventually dismembering and disposing of their remains by burning on a bonfire or flushing down a lavatory.

What sort of man could perpetuate such violent perversive crimes? Would his handwriting reveal the true depths of such a dysfunctional and inhumane, dark nature? If so, what might you expect to see in his inky pen strokes? Were there any warning signs? Can we learn anything at all about the rationale of the killer – to understand the 'whys' behind his violent killings? This handwritten essay by Dennis Nilsen was drafted during the latter part of his stay in prison (in the early 2000s). We shall see that the potency of his invasive, depraved and violent nature should not go unrecorded.

Initially I was excited, because the moment I released the hard copy from the non-descript, innocent brown paper envelope, I could instantly see that the handwriting was dripping with clues and it would not be long before Nilsen's secrets came tumbling out. The writing also affected me surprisingly emotionally,

30 Tomorrows Shocks (an essay) by Des Nilsen 31

"Fantasy is a killer and it is in prison where such half dreams can be incubated. When a man is shackled to the artifical, controlled regime with its stifling routine, he is thereby removed 32 from a normality of natural relationships and personal development. When he is denied the power of decision to shape 34 a life style peculiar to himself then 35 he has to invent one by resorting to fantasy. A prisoner has virtually NO power. He has virtually NO rewards for honest effort. He has virtually NO freedom to initiate and/or sustain relationships. His self esteem is only allowed to grow to the stature of that of a 'model prisoner'. The Home Office idea of a 'model prisoner' is a man who enthusiastically 36 collaborates with prison staff. Informs and spies on fellow convicts and becomes a typical institutionalised grovelled (arse kisser). These are the qualities of character which one should aspire to in order to conform to this model of Home Office perfection. A man so conditioned is of no moral value in or out of prison but he is the kind of men who is adjudged fit to be returned to society. In short he learns to tell the psychologists, psychiatrists, governors and social visitors the sort of thing that they want to hear. Naturally he does not reveal his real inner aspirations. In fact NO prisoner ever reveals his 'inner orientation' to prison officials who he doesn't trust anyway. His thoughts and desires are his secrets and his only privacy in prison.

When a citizen commits a serious violent sexually rooted 37 crime he, as well as his victim, becomes what I shall term 'damaged products in society'. There is little official help provided for the victim who is largely expected to recover with the help of friends and relatives in the community. The award made by the Criminal Injuries Compensation Board is merely a token of regret by the State. A wad of notes can never by itself compensate for the magnitude of personal trauma suffered. Often the result of attack is a lifetime of nightmare. Meanwhile the convicted criminal is removed to a prison where he will serve a term of years as punishment for his offence. The average citizen will not normally commit a violent sexual homicidal offence. Therefore the few who do have brought themselves to an abnormal conclusion. Their personality is malfunctioning through the damaging and/or conditioning experiences pertinent to their particular types of lives. To say that they are simply evil men is a cop out on all fronts. I have met hundreds of inmates serving sentences for murder or serious sexual offences and I have not met one who I would describe as an evil man. It was clear, however, that they all had serious personal problems. It was these problems which resulted in their

Dennis Nilsen's essay, 'Tomorrow's Shocks', page 1, unknown hand

chilling me to the core and making me shiver, so I quickly slipped the original documents into protective see-through plastic covers.

Usually when I begin the process of analysing a sample of handwriting, practice dictates that I stand back and regard the whole piece as if I am appreciating an example of artwork, observing and then synthesising all the main components or dominant features. I have been known to analyse samples without even reading the content. Quite often, I have to remind myself to go back and digest the writing on the page, if only out of curiosity. The reason for this is not because there may be the temptation to allow the content to influence me in any way, even at a subconscious level – everything I say is based on objective appraisal and then backed-up empirically with the appropriate handwriting movements – it is because I never want my client to accuse me of having been swayed by extracts of content. On the basis that you (Reader) are my client, this occasion is no different.

So let us begin by looking at the symbols expressed on the page and the unique pattern of Nilsen's psychology, and then we will deconstruct and decipher his handwriting.

The public face Nilsen presents to the world is chillingly 'together', outwardly friendly and superficially polite. 'Togetherness' is seen in the *straight* (albeit progressively *widening*) *left margin* and 'friendliness' is perceived in the sloping forwards of the script and many *rounded* letters. However, if we want to understand how Nilsen was able to navigate the world without detection – if we want to find out more about his social appearance – we would need to consider the structure of his letter formations (particularly observing the letters n and m) and how he joined all these letters together. Does he use people-pleasing garlands or kick-arse angles? Perhaps they are indefinably wavy or loose catch-me-if-you-can style of thready life lines, or arched shapes symbolic of formality, tradition and also secrecy? There is undeniably a preponderance of aggressive *angles*, but Nilsen also embraces a great number of *arcades* and some *garlands*, which provide the strongest clue as to how he was able to hide his extreme behaviour and go about his business in a normal world. Any attempts at being civil, well-behaved and ingratiating can be viewed in the arched formations of some of the individual letters.

However, if we look behind the formal veneer, another picture emerges.

Surveying the *gestalt* – the outline holistic picture – we can see that it is mechanical and unforgiving, and the overwhelming first impression is one of *compactness*. Graphologically, Nilsen is in your face. The writing seems to absorb the scene, leaving no room to breathe. Handwriting outweighs white space, irrespective of the fact that it has been written on pre-lined paper.

Compact writing can be attributed to the *virtually non-existent left-hand margin* combined with *very close word* and *line spacing*. This format inevitably creates *tangling* between the lines, where sentences bump into each other and occasionally overlap. This combination tells of someone with an overwhelming need for company, and someone who was effectively stewing in his own juices. It discloses a writer who had become blinded by personal feelings and was inclined to cling to a point, long after it was relevant. The drive behind this desire (seen in the *very heavy* and *variable pressure*) was equally acute and powerful, revealing that he would stop at nothing – not even forcibly by violence, if necessary – to achieve his craving ends.

However, Nilsen had a dilemma. On the one hand, the crowded, *invasive layout* tells us that he could not bear to be alone. On the other hand, he was contemptuous of people. There was a lack of respect and consideration for others. Nilsen was the sort of man who would impose himself on others for his own selfish ends. We know all this because the writing is not only *compact*, it is also unrefined with a potent mix of *angles*, *very heavy pressure*, *rigidity* and *over-connectedness*.

Furthermore, if we throw another detail into the mix – namely the multiple *supported arcade starting strokes* (*covering strokes* in the *middle zone* letters, where the upstroke draws over the downstroke, e.g. 'c' of 'crime' in essay, page 1, line 26[37], and 'chance' in essay, page 3, line 6[46]) – we also know that Nilsen felt uncomfortable in social situations. In such a scenario he was inhibited, fearful and tense, with a disinclination to get involved with people socially.

However, he loved to talk (his *ovals* are wide open and gaping) and hated being interrupted. He had a self-centred brash desire to communicate at all costs. It is not at all surprising that he confessed. Nilsen always felt he had so much to say and never enough time to do so, even if his perceptions were flawed, unrealistic and deluded, and his judgement was fantastical and spiritually bankrupt. The relentlessly *over-connected* (or joined-up), *marked right slanting* cursive writing with *wide-open ovals* reinforces this need for oral expression. The *abrupt end strokes* meant that he did not sugar-coat his words. Nilsen was incredibly blunt and opinionated, but he needed to vent his spleen without interruption.

So, he did not much like people and felt uncomfortable in social situations, but he needed to talk and did not want to be interrupted. And he just could not bear to

Tomorrows Shocks (an essay continued) by Des Nilsen FIRST DRAFT.

63

offences in the first place. A man is thrown into prison with these problems still very much alive and kicking. If he were a capital offender his problems would be terminated at the end of a rope (and the sin of homicide is absorbed by each and every citizen collectively) Or put another way — everyone has a hand on the lever which springs the trap. Today, judicial homicide is not legally acceptable to a majority of intellectual and political representatives. The alternative (for capital offences) is long terms of imprisonment for offenders. The great tragedy is that prison not only fails to cure a felons problems but programs and conditions them by such expensive concentrations that they become 'worse' and 'fixed' in him. In short — the longer one is subjected to the present type of prison regime the more 'incurable' he becomes. What passes for treatment constitutes nothing more elaborate than solitary confinement, strip cells, punishment cells, fines, loss of privileges etc. supplementary to this in the wholesale giving of the liquid cosh in its many and varied forms. The massive expense of prison is gobbled by an almost obsessional concentration on 'good order, discipline and control' Men in a prison such as Wakefield are seen primarily as very dangerous monkeys who have to be closely watched, directed and supervised whilst they are loose from cells. Consequently a man spends the greater part of his life in this cell. It is the only place where he can relax and be himself. Even then the jail guards still look in at regular intervals.

A heterosexual has only a fleeting contact with a woman on his official visit which (if he is very fortunate) occur every fortnight. In his cell he has no stimulation save for memory, mirrors and his imagination in order to sublimate his sexual drives in masturbation. His memory is diffused by the passage of time and one naturally becomes fixed by masturbation to the (now) jaded excitement of a colour photo of a raped girl. Despite whatever efforts he may make (being weak in his isolation) he can also seek refuge in the arms of the intense memory of the very sexual aberration central to his crime. His other source of stimulation is the twice weekly video-film which becomes a kind of tutor (& carrier) of new ideas. Create a lot of new videos (ordinary films which are seen at the local cinema) depict sex and violence in related proximity. These are the only 'living' 'real' moving women he sees. Ordinarily, outside of prison one can handle these movies within the world perspective of having plenty of real women around. But in prison these movies are mesmerizing, stimuli like oasis in an arid wasteland. He takes these images of women back to the solitude of his cell. He has lost contact with

Dennis Nilsen's essay, 'Tomorrow's Shocks', page 2, unknown hand

be alone. Not even if entertaining guests amounted to nothing more than a 'grotesque illusion of intimacy'.

How could Nilsen get round these various issues?

The *small size* bandwidth of the writing only serves to illustrate Nilsen's dedication and ability to focus intensely. It tells us that he was happy to act covertly, flying under the radar, out of the limelight and without a care in the world for what other people thought. He did not need a fanfare. *Small size* writers often invest most of their energy into thinking rather than doing, so you would be looking for other clues in the handwriting to indicate that there was enough impetus to convert thoughts into action after a period of concentration. Nilsen's sample provides ample proof, with particular evidence hinging on the *strong horizontal t-bars*, the *very heavy pressure* and the copious or prolific *angles* seen both within and without the letter formations.

There is some *diminishing word size* too ('dreams' in essay, page 1, line 1[31], and 'elaborating' in essay, page 3, line 8[47]), revealing his shrewd understanding of people and ability to influence them. Nilsen was an inspired speaker and astonishingly articulate, so it would have been relatively easy for him to use guile and persuade men to come back to his flat, once he had made up his mind and decided on a course of action.

Deeper investigation uncovered a *shark's tooth*. These are usually seen in the letters n or m, but here we can see the x joined to the i in 'proximity', highlighted in essay, page 2, line 39[42]. Normally a graphologist will never take any one handwriting movement in isolation and apply an interpretation without some back-up supporting movements. There is one exception to this rule. Whenever you see a *shark's tooth*, even a solitary one, it an extremely strong sign of an exploitative individual. Here was someone whose courteous exterior hid exceedingly cunning and manipulative behaviour – exposing acts that often involved a sadistic element. Nilsen exceled at taking emotional advantage of other people for his own selfish ends. He was shrewd, clever and crafty, often hypocritical, and good at tricking people. You could expect Nilsen to say one thing and do another. No wonder he could entice unsuspecting men into his lair.

Part of Nilsen's trouble was his *rigid rhythm* screaming inflexibility. He would not have been able to tolerate any deviation from the masterplan and ritual, which he would have followed obsessively and compulsively. Put simply, Nilsen's stiff penmanship (together with his *over-connected* writing with the extreme *right slant*) reflects the behaviour of an unfettered man on a mission. This was a man who did not like being obstructed or cut short when he was in the middle of doing or saying something. Nothing could have stopped him doing what he wanted to do once he had set the wheels in motion. Once he had embarked on a course of action, he was utterly compelled to finish what he had begun. Nilsen was not in control of his behaviour or his actions, and perhaps this goes some way to explaining why his behaviour was so impetuous. We know he would have acted on impulsive whims, because the *word spacing* is so close and the forward slant tilts so obliquely.

As I bravely retrieved the sample from the plastic covers and examined the back of the paper, looking for the tell-tale indentations which would reveal the exact *pressure* patterns used by Nilsen, I could immediately clearly see some patches of ink coming through on the reverse side. Turning back the paper to see why this was happening, I gasped. Nilsen's full stops were not always performed in the right place (i.e. at the end of sentences) and these *resting dots* or momentary pauses were *ground* so deeply into the paper that ink had discharged and come through on the back of the page.

The overly large and heavy dots which bore into the paper, are known as *dot grinding*. Even a single *ground* full stop has meaning (e.g. 'wasteland.' in essay, page 2, penultimate line[44] and 'sees.' four lines above[43]). *Dot grinding* is a sign of immense inner tension which inevitably erupts in its mildest form as irritability or an irrational temper, or at worse, as aggression, reinforcing the intensity of Nilsen's focus and frustration, and further highlighting his overbearing nature. These *dots* emphasised Nilsen's ongoing emotional stress, his fixations and obsessional thoughts, and an underlying current of resentment. Nilsen was clearly the type of man to hold a grudge. As a theatrical image, it brings to mind a brooding silence.

Sometimes these *dots* could be seen *within* the pen strokes, also leaving 'muddy puddles' of ink discharges on both sides of the paper, telling a similar story. This flooding of ink results in dark spots, blobs, ink blotches or excessive deposits of ink either within letters, or infilled circles or loops (e.g. 'gorged' in essay, page 2, line 18[40], 'anxiety' in essay, page 3, line 37[48], 'Prisons' in essay, page 4, line 26[53] and 'hardly' in essay, page 4, line 6 from end[54]). It is graphic illustration of an uncontrollable, compulsive indulgence of sensual and libidinal urges, and the distinct possibility of an impending explosion, which is eventually guaranteed to detonate either inwardly or outwardly.

When *mud* or ink blotches are seen in the *personal pronoun I* and within the *signature*, a disturbed self-concept is revealed. *Muddiness* in the *lower zone* indicates emotional blocks that affect relationships. When you see this feature in the *upper zone*, it shows intrusive, corrupt, unclean thoughts and dubious morals affecting the writing form, strongly suggesting immorality and morbid fantasies. So these *black inky flooding* pauses and *blockages* single-handedly uncovered Nilsen's dark fantasy life and sadistic face too.

The overall *pressure* was deemed to be so *very heavy* (on the *horizontal* as well as the *vertical*) that I could almost read his words by braille, just by touching the back of the page. I say 'almost', because the absolute lack of definition and clarity was due to some variation in the *pressure*. Technically, I could term the handwriting *pressure* as *very heavy* and *variable*. This irregularity was also clearly observed *after* I had scanned the original document, and copies were reproduced and printed.

The *very heavy pressurised* handwriting uncovered an intense personality with a brutal streak, in the hand of someone who found it virtually impossible to forget or forgive, and the *dot grinding* was simply back-up, reinforcing the idea of profound rumination. Nilsen would have been inclined to zoom in and hang on to past hurts and injustices, steeling himself by trying to diminish some of his hurt and pain by retaliating in a way that would be perceived as quarrelsome and highly contentious.

Uneven pressure always contributes substantially and negatively to frail and unregulated emotion. Unusually, in this case, the *variable pressure* could also be distinguished in the individual zonal areas. It is in the *lower zone*, that *pressure* is distinctly much heavier (and darker) still. This means that the amount of energy he invested in his deeply personal life – a life which disproportionally reflected his primal instincts, subconscious drives, sexual appetites and sexuality – was far in excess of what he showed the outside world during the course of everyday activity. It strongly suggests erratic, desultory impulses and uncontrolled emotional responses and violent urges. Sudden bursts of energy (often with a sexual bias) could be expected to occur, according to the amount of pressure fluctuation, reflecting the poor inner emotional functioning of his brain.

Abraham Maslow stipulated that we are all motivated by unsatisfied needs, so pinpointing what these are is critical if we ever want to begin to understand what drives a person's behaviour. The *tension* in Nilsen's writing was a precursor, telling us that unsatisfied needs exist, and if we turn these inside out, we can see which cravings permeated his core. The *dominant* or *largest zone* is the best indicator of

Tomorrow's Shocks by Des Nilsen

65

real life' therefore 'real life's void is gradually filled by a fantasy life which, in time becomes more essential to his expressive drives. His fantasy life becomes his real life. Naturally when he is interviewed by the various prison 'experts' he covers up his fantasy life because if he dares to 'expose' himself he knows his chance of release will be less. A convict has NO power of decision except in his fantasy life which at the root of all his gradually elaborating complexes to his power achieves fulfilment in orgasm. He cannot express love or any normal human relationship with an idea or an unresponsive inanimate (but sexually stimulating) object of a film or a photograph. The attitude of the media and the authorities tends to help reinforce the image of the convict as an evil beast and for this he gets his own back in his fantasies. He can't go to jail or be punished for his fantasies. He graduates from simple fantasies on into more complex ones where the semi conscious drive is for 'realism'. In a few years a convict prefers to be 'banged up' in the world of his cell than face for too long the dull drabness of prison life. He comes to depend on the security of his isolation and his wonderful fantasy world. If he is imagining a tape murder once a week he thus maybe become an incurable 'fantasy' rapist whose only development is towards a real rape as the ultimate realisation of such a fantasy. He becomes two people — the ordinary well disciplined progressing convict going about his prison work and the vengeful irredeemable pervert with a smouldering desire within. Whilst in prison his practical equilibrium is kept in check by generally stressless routine life. He is a potentially dangerous 'melt down' kept safe by twenty foot thick concrete. He has become conditioned to his prison environment and within it he feels 'safe' and secure. He doesn't have to really fend for himself or make any kind of real effort. He has practically no decisions to make. If he is released after (say) fifteen years he can retreat from the world into a quiet unobtrusive solitary personable existence outside wherein he can continue to indulge his sexual + power fantasies as before. He will feel great anxiety at being left to fend for himself and could well crave for the security of his former lifestyle in jail. He might commit a crime because he is unable to cope with any pressure outside and subconsciously wishes to return to prison. If sexual stimuli (in human form) comes his way he can see no evidence (there and then) of any restraints to him as he fulfils his long subdued fantasies. He might only be an ex convict who has been in prison for a non-sexual offence and has acquired his sexual aberration through his prison fantasies.

Dennis Nilsen's essay, 'Tomorrow's Shocks', page 3, unknown hand

where we will find the answers, particularly if the size is out of proportion, skewing the balance of the overall writing. In Nilsen's case, we do have a *large* and *dominant lower zone*, so we can instantly see the considerable amount of energy and lust that Nilsen invested into achieving his sexual ambitions, and this simultaneously tells us that his physiological and carnal needs were not being met. The *size* of the *lower zone* may show the value and strength of desire he placed on his physical needs and personal yearnings, but it would be the accompanying nuances found in the *lower zone* letters that would give up more finite answers.

Depending on other supporting clues identified, you might expect to see ruthless, cruel and vicious behaviour, and acts of physical violence. Here this *irregularity* can be seen in the lower zonal sections of the words 'development' in essay, page 1, line 5[34]; 'capital' in essay, page 2, line 3[38]; and 'images' in the penultimate line.[45] The letter g in 'images' is not only disjointed but also shows an inconsistency of *pressure*. *Segmented* letters offer strong signs that the writer is a law unto themselves. The cumulative graphic evidence witnesses and reveals subversive underground violent tendencies that Nilsen was disinclined to control. *And what this also tells us is that his dark side was hidden from everyone*.

Interestingly, the *lower zone* also relates to material acquisition and practical considerations, so by murdering men, he was able to keep them – it was a macabre form of possession.

By contrast, we see Nilsen's lack of energy and investment in the *upper zone*. Continuing with the theme of *pressure*, we can observe the letter f, which is the only trizonal letter in the English alphabet that covers the whole of the person. It is therefore a good indication of balance. If we look at the word 'from' – the first word in essay, page 1, line 4[32] – the top of the letter f is a lighter shade than the balance of the downstroke, which extends beneath the baseline.

What other sort of behaviour or character traits might we expect to see?

There was a plethora of clues shedding light on the inner workings of his psyche. When I began to look more closely under magnification, it became clear that many *letter parts* were missing. This uncovered Nilsen's internal conflict and tells us that he was in denial – it is dishonesty to self – so he was inclined to gloss over the truth. Nilsen may have had a lot to say, but it was not necessarily truthful.

Now, there is a particular anomaly in Dennis Nilsen's handwriting. It is the unnecessary addition of *superfluous loops* or *balloons*, which are effectively contrived *elaborations* in the *upper zonal* area. (See 'then' in essay, page 1, line 6[35])

– this is the first insertion of an imagination loop after the letter h of
'then' has been written ... then again, the letter l in 'closely' in essay,
page 2, line 21[41] and 'them to be locked away' in essay, page 4,
lines 5-6,[50,51] These accoutrements are a conscious attempt by the
writer to correct or embellish, touch up, garnish and overwork what
has already been produced naturally. This usually means that the writer
is a fixer or perfectionist and finds it hard to be satisfied with things as they are. (And
the more repairing is done, the more this interpretation applies.) It is an indication or
desire to make himself look more interesting and, in this instance, more imaginative
than he really is. It is imagination by design. Nilsen is out to impress, but in reality
these accessories merely expose the fantasist in him. That is because he creates a
distorted upper zone, revealing how his strange thinking patterns and morals were
wildly creative (but not in a good way). Nilsen would have been adept at blagging
and twisting ideas to suit his proclivities and justify his foul actions.

As well as *mended* letters at the tops of tall stems, another of his party tricks was
to do occasional *soldering* (see again 'images' in essay, page 2, penultimate line[45]
– clearer under magnification – he adds the *heavy downstroke* afterwards). This is
where parts of letters are spliced together to create a whole identifiable letter. It tells
us that there is a lot going on under the surface, particularly revolving around bad
feelings inside, and reveals an attempt to patch things up and hide all signs of what
has gone on before. Nilsen was trying to push unpalatable truths under the carpet.

The height and length of our *t-bars* illustrates projection of will and gives clues to
the strength of our self-image. Many of Nilsen's *t-bars* are long and high and
occasionally slashing, revealing the take-charge know-it-all. He was a forceful
personality who did not want to be told what to do, since he was wilful,
domineering and bossy. Nilsen enjoyed being powerful and imposing his ideas on
others; he got off on weaponising his skilful way with words. The *sharp* endings on
some of his *t-bars* show how easily irritated and woundingly critical and sarcastic he
could turn, at the flick of a switch, sometimes to the point of mental cruelty. The
heavy pressure and random *triangular shapes* in this area uncovers yet more
evidence of Nilsen's inner frustration and reveals how he was forced to switch his
sexual energies and desires by sublimating them into this single-minded,
aggressive rant that we see before us today.

Nilsen's emotions were festering and caustic, inevitably affecting his reactions
towards other people – his fellow inmates and the prison officers – when all he

wanted to do was punish. Mental cruelty and sarcasm would no doubt have replaced his earlier ability to enable and fulfil his physical desires. I suspect he would have much preferred, at the time of writing this missive, to have been using pervasive brute force and dabbling with weapons and sharp instruments instead of pen and paper. Nilsen loathed not being in control of his life or being able to make his own decisions.

The *heavy crossings out* also expose suppressed anger. Here it is a sign of passive-aggressive behaviour. This means that Nilsen could not bear making mistakes and had a propensity to evade problems by blaming other people for his actions. Nothing was ever his fault. Making excuses are all emblematic or typical of this type of disorder. There are some examples in essay, page 2, line 13[39], and on page 4, end of line 17.[52]

Starting strokes are like little springboards to action. They tell how the writer consciously and cautiously prepares to unwind before launching into new situations. They reveal the degree of spontaneity, directness and readiness to initiate actions. So all those little *starting strokes* may look innocuous enough, but the preponderance and variety of shapes is very revealing. Nilsen had plenty of time to think about things in prison. There was time to ruminate. And Nilsen's script exhibits the range of ways he pondered.

The predominance of initial braced *straight* and *inflexible, angular starting strokes* (of varying lengths) attest to enduring feelings of deep anger and resentment and grudges about things that happened to him in the past, and which he continued to hold on to. They are complicit in revealing that Nilsen saw himself as a victim, rather than someone who was powerful in his own right. Others are *small arcade* arched shapes located higher, in the *upper zone* area. These illustrate how conscious attention was being paid to outward appearances, and the extent to which emotion was being controlled and displayed rather than truly felt. It tells us that Nilsen was hiding his feelings, with social approval being the underlying motive. *Arcades* that start in the *upper zone* also reveal how much he wanted to show off his intelligence. He begins his missive with a *small wavy starting stroke* on the upper case F of 'Fantasy' (in essay, page 1, line 1[30]). This implies that he wanted to give the impression of being friendly, but in truth he was demonstrating manipulative behaviour, and together with the tight, *rigid tension*, this was a portrait of a man who truly lacked warmth. These tiny details are a reminder that confinement in prison repressed his individuality and freedom.

As we have explored, the *lower zone* is of particular relevance to this analysis, so let us revisit and dig deeper still. There are a few things going on in Nilsen's *lower zone*. We have seen how the *heavy pressure* shows the strength of his unsatisfied needs, and how the *heavy, full* and *very large size* gives strong clues to the value he placed on his subconscious physical drives and need for release of these drives. So we know that Nilsen had an unconscious desire to focus more than the normal amount of attention on sexual interests, and there was a lot of imagination in this area. The thing is, he over-emphasises and dramatizes his needs to a point where he becomes overly zealous and not believable. The *very large* and *inflated LZ* with *heavy pressure* and *angles* is an indication of someone who is sexually active, but has little consideration for people's feelings. Forcing his will would have been a priority. The *pointed* or *angular zones*, at the tips of the greatly fluctuating stems, hint at Nilsen's susceptibility to frustration and explain his aggression in his search for a satisfactory release. The disproportionately long and fluctuating tails also tells us that he needed change and new experiences (and new partners) in his life, since he was inwardly restless, moody and unpredictable, unable to settle exclusively to anything or anyone, but also revealing an inability to curb his restlessness. *Clubbed strokes* (seen visually as abrupt thick endings) tell us that he could not release his sexual needs, so there was inevitably excess energy swimming around clandestinely and unfulfilled.

The clear graphological sign we are rewarded with is this. *Dissatisfaction is plain and palpable, and irrational violent acts can be expected.* To be clear, Nilsen's only means of satisfaction would have been by compensating and making other people suffer.

If we needed any more cogent evidence, there is one more thing. Nilsen has a letter that unexpectedly drops beneath the baseline (see the y in 'enthusiastically' in essay, page 1, line 12[36]). This is a clue to his emotional heaviness and depression. It was a significant sign and ingrained sense of foreboding. *Letters that extend or fall just beneath the baseline* reveal hidden aggression or sneaky, behind-the-scenes activities. These people are often covert. This graphological movement shows an understanding of unconscious motivations, which can be used either positively or negatively, depending on what else is going on in the handwriting and whether there are any other dangerous signs. It can be seen in the script of detectives, vice squad, therapists and

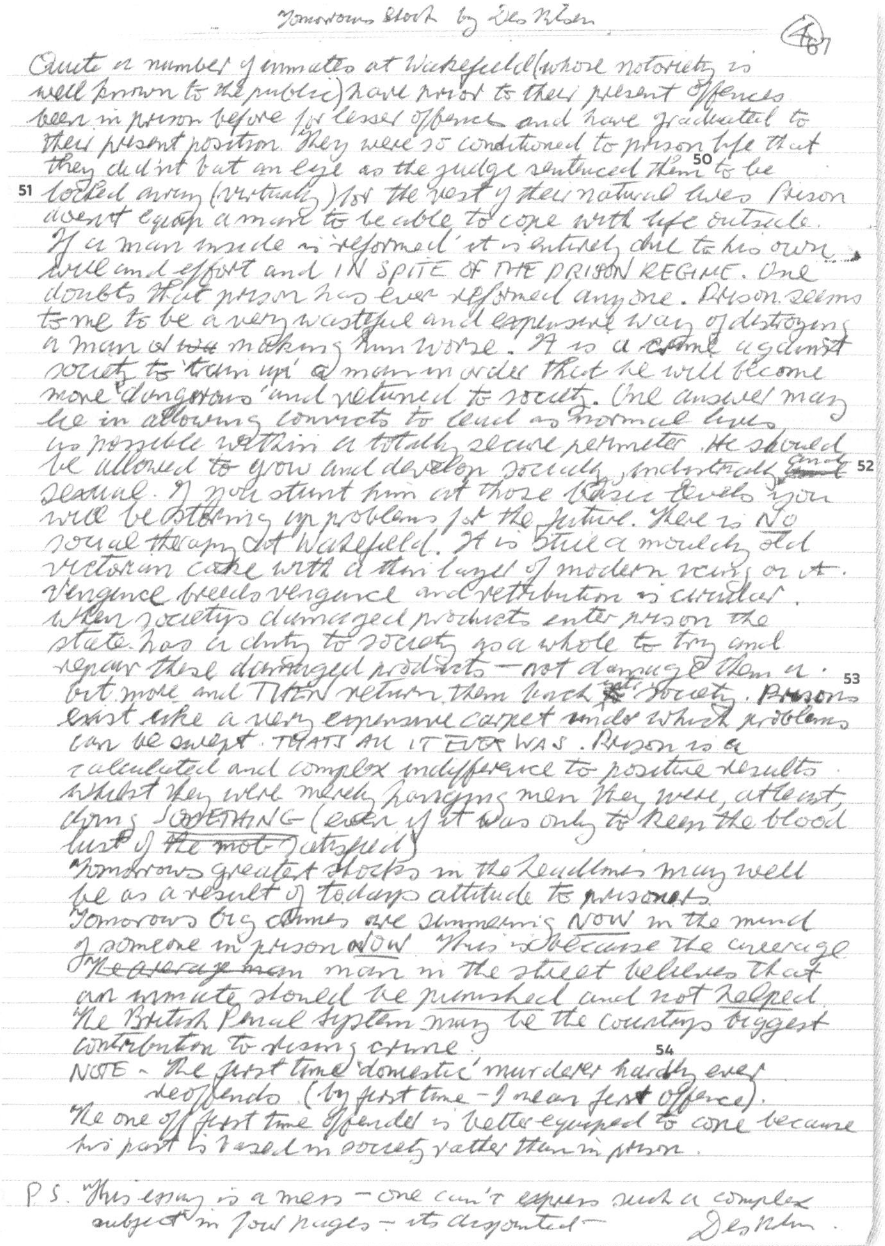

Dennis Nilsen's essay, 'Tomorrow's Shocks', page 4, unknown hand

psychiatrists, as well as criminals. Where a *whole* letter drops beneath the baseline, this is an indication of unpleasant unconscious urges and desires affecting the individual's belief system and behaviour. These compulsions are unlikely to be expressed openly, so they are tucked away, hidden out of plain sight.

Nilsen's emotionality is seen in the *greatly fluctuating middle zone* (varying to the extent that there was clearly an issue in this area of his social everyday existence/life). The *marked right slant*, combined with all three *greatly fluctuating zones*, expose a frenzied personality that, even though he was safely locked up behind maximum security bars, still reminds us that he remained a threat, affected by impulsive excitability and potentially out of control.

Finally, I considered whether the extreme confines of prison, which had eliminated all possibility of being able to release and satisfy his unhealthy appetites, would mean he imploded inwardly instead? There is certainly evidence that Nilsen's physical health was impaired at the time of writing. Anxiety, tension and stress are all seen to be taking their toll in the almost imperceptible weaving of *random scatter dots* and *ink trails* that bear no connection to the script. A superfluous trail of *ink resting dots* has been randomly dropped on to the page (of the bottom right-hand corner of essay page 3,[49] and after 'relationship' in essay, page 1, line 4[33]), and the significance of this unconscious movement should not be underestimated.

It means that the writer is in a serious state of mental exhaustion, too weary even to lift the pen off the paper. This often happens at an early stage of an illness before the writer is even aware something is wrong. We have seen how his *resting ink dots* also occur during the transmission of a pen stroke movement, indicating that something is causing Nilsen to feel extremely tense and anxious. However, now we know that these stress levels had risen to an unacceptably high level and were very likely to have an impact on his physical health, potentially causing something along the lines of cardiac deficiency or respiratory trouble. It is also a sign of obsessional behaviour, which we have already probed in other corners of this chapter.

When we observe, untangle and identify all the facets of the handwriting, then interpret the confluence of clues and finally slot them all together, like a human jigsaw puzzle, we can see how a whole portrait emerges. All the components of Nilsen's handwriting combined held the key that conspired to trip him up, by unlocking the core of his character. Any thoughts of regret or rehabilitation are simultaneously dispelled, as we are given rare insight into his ugly personality and the dangerous elements that resided within his shell. Nilsen had the outward appearance of a man, but inside he was a monster, and his internal machinations were pure evil and demonic. Through the prism of handwriting analysis, we have proved that Nilsen was an emotional con man who effectively conceived and executed dark and violent sexual fantasies. His nefarious acts were laced with obsessive-compulsive tendencies, and he was ultimately addicted to murder in an attempt to satisfy his own unfulfilled sexual needs and an inordinate desire for company, without needing to socialise in the usual conventional way.

Only now do I go back and begin to read the content of the sample and perhaps, unsurprisingly, I discover it is fascinating. The *small size* and *compact layout* prohibit easy reading in many places, contributing to some *illegibility*, so I am forced to slowly decipher Nilsen's words. One wonders if there is any value or truth in his claims and personal experience in prison. Or are we to dismiss his comments out of hand on the basis that we have uncovered his dishonesty and inability to take ownership for his actions, and the fact that he committed a string of heinous crimes, and because his judgement and views on life were clearly and irreparably distorted and twisted?

It would be easy to dismiss this essay as the ramblings of a mad man, but, if nothing else, the dialogue reminds us that an analysis of a piece of handwriting is merely an insight into a brief snapshot moment in time. So we have to ask ourselves: How much of his penmanship has been affected by his lengthy prison term and the physiological and psychological conditions he was under at the time, and how much reflects his core character?

Who could say for certain if Nilsen's fantasy world had always been a part of his life, or if his experiences in prison exacerbated this aspect of his personality? In my analysis I reveal how Nilsen was a fantasist and purposefully devised his own delusions to justify his depraved, murderous actions (by adding the *little balloon loops* to some of his *upper zone stems*, as a later addition or amendment). Having read the content, I wondered if perhaps he had resorted to inventing his own reverie in prison, as a way of coping with what he describes as an 'unnatural environment'.

Pertinently, there is some *avoidance of the right-hand margin*, which means that unconsciously, in his heart of hearts, Nilsen must have had an inkling that his story was never going to end well, and for this reason he was afraid of what the future held in store for him.

So the question is, did Nilsen write in exactly the same way *before* he committed the crimes and went to prison, or did his handwriting subsequently change *after*? Did he always have a good imagination, or did he create and incubate an enhanced fantasy world that could potentially have been even more dangerous had he been released? Although we can clearly see his feelings at the time he penned the essay, without having sight of an earlier sample of handwriting we shall never know the full truth. You could argue that Nilsen's behaviour and feelings whilst he was in prison did not necessarily reflect the whole picture of who he was *before* he was convicted. We know that behaviour is fluid, depending on circumstances, but did his core character change? Does a leopard ever change its spots?

The imposed conditions of prison must have rankled with Nilsen enormously, because he was a take-charge sort of man who wanted to be in control of his life. To have this liberty taken away from him would have caused immense frustration and sorrow. Unbelievably, Nilsen complains that prisoners have *no* power, seemingly unable to understand that that is the whole point. If you become a danger to society by committing violent acts, you are forfeiting the right to live freely, and therefore cannot expect to wield any power over any aspect of your life (or others) any longer.

Whatever the truth, it cannot be denied that there are many dominant movements in excess (primarily the *spacing*, the *pressure*, the *slant*), and as we have seen excess is *always* a source of negativity. What is more, there are many *secondary* and *miscellaneous movements* with further negative interpretations that litter the handwriting throughout. An accumulation of all these graphic features confirms that Nilsen was seriously unhinged. Whether by nature or nurture, Dennis Nilsen was a violent man who was unable to control his perverted sexual impulses.

Betty Soldi – An original illustration of calligraphy

In her search for magical transformation, Betty throws out the rule book, embraces her natural instincts and recognises the value of imperfections. The graphic beauty is seen in the simplicity and movement, and Betty's beautiful 'swooshes' manage to achieve a unique, uncontrived and soulful calligraphic style of rhythm.

Betty is an Italian-based wordsmith and highly acclaimed calligrapher, author of 'Inkspired', and graphic designer working with the world's leading retail brands and luxury labels. Betty heads up a creative studio in Florence and founded three boutique hotels in the quirky artistic Oltrarno district. In 2018 Betty commissioned me to analyse her inky penmanship from a graphological perspective.

CHAPTER 12

Good mental health

Positive mental well-being

Having good mental health means feeling positive about yourself and others, being able to form good relationships and having the resilience to overcome challenges – but how many people have a harmonised, well-adjusted and integrated personality? How many of us have found inner peace and feel comfortable within our own skin? How many of us are fortunate enough to go through life with a clean bill of mental health, without meeting any obstacles or difficulties along the way? And how many people can bounce back easily following problems or setbacks? We all have our inner worries, anxieties and doubts, however hard we may try to reconcile or hide them.

The *rhythm* of our handwriting mirrors the rhythm of our lives. Therefore the best indicator for recognising positive mental well-being can be seen in *rhythmic* handwriting. However, perhaps unsurprisingly, *rhythmic* writing is very rare. So, what does *rhythm* look like on paper? What would you be looking for?

Rhythmic handwriting is a succession of fluid pen strokes which manage to flow harmoniously and fluently without becoming too mechanically repetitive. Somehow the whole script – taking in the holistic vertical and horizontal picture – adheres to a natural consistency from beginning to end, without showing any signs of uncomfortable jarring, ornamental, exaggerated, rigid or hesitant movements. Any disturbance in the progression of the writing across the page is one of the first indicators of emotional imbalance. The overall appearance should be one of individual spontaneity and beauty.

You can intuitively sense *rhythm* if you let yourself be receptive to the pattern the handwriting makes on the paper. However, this can only be achieved if you refrain from reading the content and let your eyes relax into holistic or gestalt mode again.

You could say that a piece of handwriting, performed perfectly, is a sort of 'blueprint' for the perfect human being, but how many of us can write perfectly? Most of my clients come to me because they have a problem: *'Should I hook up*

with them?' 'Should I hire them?' 'Can I trust them?' 'Why do they always behave
like that?' So the closest sample I could find (although you could argue that even
this piece of handwriting verges slightly on the repetitive) is this anonymous sample
penned by a middle-aged man:

Anonymous male, 60s, unknown hand

Jean-Hippolyte Michon

Jean-Hippolyte Michon is known in graphological circles as the French abbot who
coined the term *graphology* from the Greek – *graph* meaning 'to write' or 'I write'
and *logos* meaning 'doctrine' or 'theory' – and he is subsequently remembered as
the founder of graphology. However, to leave out any reference to the other things
he did during his lifetime would be to do him a disservice. Michon (who was born in
France in 1806) had a full and chequered life, achieving many things. Most notably,
he was a Catholic priest, teacher, preacher, archaeologist and author. The following
piece of writing belongs to his hand and was sourced from an original signed copy
of his book entitled *Système de Graphologie*, which was published in Paris in 1875,
just six years before his death. The book is the culmination of thirty years spent
collecting handwriting samples and conducting research.

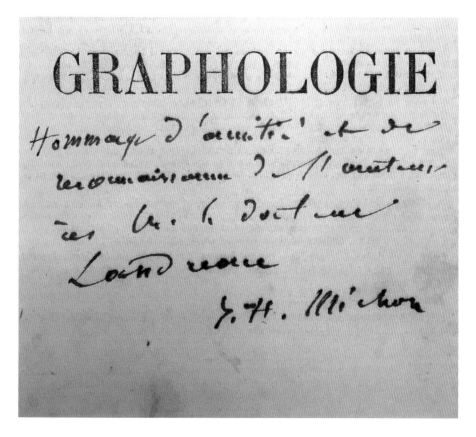

Jean-Hippolyte Michon, age 69, unknown hand

The integrity, intelligence and resolve in Michon's script is indisputable and beautiful to behold, and yet even he struggles to deliver perfect harmony and *rhythm*. This is because the handwriting is partially *illegible* and compromised by too many inconsistencies and flaws (seen particularly in the *variable letter spacing*, some hesitations and occasional sudden *leftward movements*). This discord all reflects (and echoes) the path of his own life which did not run smoothly, so the Frenchman was not without his own personal issues and difficulties that no doubt kept him awake at night.

Staying on a positive note, let us observe another indomitable spirit, and reveal some more aspects of what constitutes better mental health.

Lord Denning's indomitable spirit

Lord Tom Denning (1899–1999) was the most celebrated and outstanding English judge and Master of the Rolls of the twentieth century. He was known as the 'people's judge' and as a 'fearless champion of the rights of the common man', although he could be quite controversial at times.

I first came across Lord Denning's handwriting a few years ago when a close friend of my father, knowing my passion for graphology, presented me with a file full to the brim with cherished condolences letters from a hodgepodge of friends, relatives, the rich and the famous, following the sad and untimely passing of his beloved wife Iris Freeman (Iris wrote *Lord Denning: A Life*, in 1994). David gave me access to this treasure trove of characters on paper and my trained eagle eye immediately alighted on Lord Denning's handwriting. The two-page letter (on pages 191-192) was produced at the age of ninety-seven, three years before his death.

Denning's scrawly handwriting was replete with all the wobbles and jerks you might expect in the script of a very elderly man. The *rhythm* could best be described as *arrhythmic. Arrhythm* in handwriting is commonly seen and characterised by fleeting loses of hand control. These translate into sudden unexpected inharmonious movements, which briefly interrupt the natural free flow and progression of the pen strokes across the page. It is graphic affirmation that the writer experiences some undercurrents of uncertainty and anxiety. Here, however, we can upgrade that interpretation (because of Denning's *high form standard* and the overall quality of the script), which means the final meaning takes on a much more positive guise. So, in spite of Lord Denning's advanced years and deterioration in health, this reinforces that he managed to maintain a realistic approach and continued to be interested in everything going on around him, tackling things in his own inimitable style and looking well beyond traditional methods. Denning did not allow any personal issues to cloud his thoughts or affect his capacity to get on and you could still see his innate personality, the rich character and his indomitable spirit shining through.

Lord Denning's devotion to justice was rooted in his strong faith. His intelligence and quick, powerful, practical mind excelled in reducing issues to their bare essentials. His style, whether in his judgements or in his books, was always simple, clear, vigorous and direct. He was a puritan concerned only with what was fair and just, and his invincible – some may say obstinate – spirit was evident. Lord Denning was undoubtedly controversial, since he was unafraid to speak his exceptional and unconventional mind, but he was also inspirational and influential in society. We shall see how his handwriting supports these opinions and roles. This is his writing:

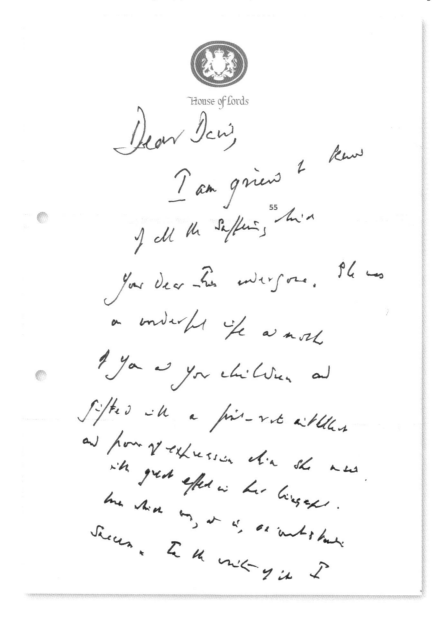

Lord Denning, 'the controversial people's judge', aged 97, unknown hand

This is a transcript of the handwriting:

> *Dear David,*
>
> *I am grieved to know of all the suffering which your dear Iris undergone. She was a wonderful wife and mother of you and your children and gifted with a first-rate intellect and form of expression which she used with great effect in her biography ... which was, and is, an outstanding success.*
>
> *In the writing of it I saw much of her and we became the best of friends. Our friendship continued after its publication and she rang me every month or so and wrote often to tell me of your holidays with her and her joy at the children and ... coming to stay in the country with you.*
>
> *She was very proud of you and ... so much. I can ...*
>
> *Yours most sincerely,*
>
> *Tom Denning.*

The gaps (in red dots) are unknown words, due to the fast speed of the writer's handwriting, some deterioration due to age and the overall illegibility.

Lord Denning's huge intellect can be seen in the *high form standard (FS)*, which is the overall combined qualification of *originality*, *layout* and *speed*, revealing the calibre of personality and also the high level of intelligence at which he was operating and expressing himself. His sincerity is seen in his *signature*, which matches the text in size, shape and style. Not only is he genuine, but also the full stop at the end of his name is a warning that he will always want to have the last word, and is an implicit barrier to people taking liberties with his generosity. The final full stop says: 'Don't mess with me!'

Lord Denning's writing slopes obliquely (the technical term for this is *marked right slanting*), telling of limitless courage and passion. He was 'out there!' restless and enthusiastic, rarely holding back, highly proactive, busy being compassionate, impulsive, emotional and generally responding to everything swiftly. No wonder he was known as being 'fearless' as the 'people's judge!' The *large size* of the writing reveals his ability to see the bigger picture, and the tall, spiky church spires of *upper zonal* stems tells more about his conscientious ways, his spiritual attitude, his ambitious desires and his devotion to implementing his beliefs. He had very high standards and strove to achieve things in life. The *large lower zone* long stems beneath the baseline also emphasise his practical motivation. Denning's inner critic can be seen in the sharp *angular* ticks at the end of his y downstrokes. And some (but not all of the *lower zone downstrokes*) are also *right tending* (this is where the bottom of the stick or loop of the letter y turns rightwards, instead of shooting to the left, which is the usual direction). This means that Lord Denning had altruistic tendencies and was community spirited. All his energies would have gone into the public sphere.

The style of the writing is *simplified* – copybook shapes are reduced down to the bare essentials – stripped back to their simplest, most elementary forms, like sticks and circles, to the extent that some letters are missing or malformed, making it quite difficult to read, virtually illegible scrawl in places, and forcing the reader to concentrate on the whole piece in order to make sense of individual letters and words. *Simplification* is where the writer has developed a more efficient way of composing individual letters, which speeds up the writing by taking shortcuts and eliminating unessential parts, usually whilst retaining legibility. Generally, if there were any neglected strokes, then you would apply a slightly different interpretation. However, here any neglect can be attributed to old age.

Simplified handwriting shows that the writer has matured by experience. The behaviour is natural and life is lived simply and purposefully. There is clear judgment (backed up here by the *clear line spacing*) with a sense of proportion, which means the writer is quick to get to the root of a problem swiftly and without wasting time on unnecessary details. These people are shrewd with uncluttered agile minds, and have the ability to decide quickly which issues are relevant and which are not. They are analytical and objective and have a clever way of making the best of things, arriving at a practical, workable solution. They are able to apply an efficient, succinct and direct approach that cuts across any nonsense and gets straight to the point. Everyone knows where they stand with these writers. *Sharp thrusting upstrokes* (seen, for example, in the word 'which' – w joined to h – in line 2 on the first page of his letter[55]) corroborate and ratify Denning's keen mind.

There is *primary thread - a mixed form of connection* (the way individual letters are shaped), which particularly features a combination of *angles* and *thready* letters (see, for example, the word 'much' on line 1 of letter page 2 of the letter[56]: the *angles* are in the sharp points of the m, and the *thread* is seen in the h hump, which is flattened in appearance, like a piece of knitting that is unravelling). Whenever you see this potent mix (of *angle* and *thread form of connection* – also known as *FOC)*, there will be no questioning the writer's intellect – he or she will be extraordinarily intelligent and sharp in their perceptions – so you know you are dealing with a very clever operator; someone who wants to do what they want to do, in their own way and their own style.

However, Lord Denning was selfless. It was never about him; he was interested in issues outside himself. He did not need or care about popularity for acceptance. We know this, because his *middle zone* letters are distinctly diminished in size – small compared with the other *zones*. The smattering of *potlids* supports this theory (this is where the start of the downstrokes – above the letter p construction – extend upwards, so that it appears to be sticking right up into the upper zone – these are seen in letter page 2, in the letter p in the words 'published' and 'proud'[57,58]), telling us that the writer needs to get at all the facts through questions and answers, because he is determined to be right. These people can be quite antagonistic and argumentative. And where you see an *angular connecting stroke*, you know you are dealing with someone who can potentially be rebellious with other figures of authority.

Further defiance can be seen in the lower case, yet oversized, letter K (known as a *defiant k*), which highlights how much people want to get their own way and follow their own path in life, without interference. Lord Denning was resourceful, audacious and obstinate, and he certainly did not like being told what to do! His *open ovals* reveal his eloquence and determination to speak his mind, but the *simplification* and *fast speed* implies he was not one for small talk.

The writing is also fairly *connected* throughout (with just occasional breaks), which is another feature of an articulate communicator. This is someone who is apt to be quite opinionated, in their single-minded ambitious drive to be purposefully strategic. Cursive writers need constant stimulation. They are inclined to become obsessive about things and follow their passions unremittingly. They think rapidly and logically, quickly grasping all the facts, linking concepts and ideas along the way, whilst calculating the potential risks at the same time. You could call this intellectual logic. Lord Denning was impatient to move forwards, persevering to the point of fanaticism and although he was always prepared to listen, once he was in full flow, he did not appreciate being interrupted!

Lord Denning's big-hearted, open-minded, non-judgmental, undiscriminating, generous spirit is seen in the broad width of the *middle zone* letters n and m. That is, the horizontal width of these letters is rectangular shaped and hence broad (draw little imaginary boxes around these letters, and you will see what I mean). *Broad primary width* is the technical term used, and indicates people who are generally self-confident in all situations. They are people who express themselves naturally and frankly. Used in this context, we can also see that Lord Denning was not only a gentleman who spoke his mind and said what he thought in an influential way, but at the same time he was able to make certain concessions, because he was generally considerate towards other people.

The *wide left margin* is a display of formality – a sense of propriety and courtesy – as well as reflecting his unprejudiced nature. In fact, the margins are wide on both sides, as well as at the top of the page. Lord Denning knew he had not got long for this world, and was becoming more and more withdrawn. Interestingly, the all-round wide margins in this particular sample (given enough other complementary handwriting movements, such as the *large ascenders, broad primary width, angles, high form standard, some right tending lower zone*) also bear testament to his philosophical mind, spiritual independence and conviction of his own value in this world.

The *left tending letter d* (where it bends up, back and over to the left-hand side of the page – in the opposite direction to the rest of the writing) means that he was an intellectual moral freedom seeker. Lord Denning could be contemplative and reflective, and he needed time and space to think.

The writing is *aerated*. Here the words and sentences are all quite widely spaced, so the overall holistic effect is one of pools of white paper (more than words) on the page. If you look closer still, you will see that the *word spacing* is *variable*, sometimes noticeably closer at the beginning of sentence, which tells us that Lord Denning made a conscious effort to be amongst people, although truth be told he was perfectly happy in his own company. *Aerated* writing reveals that ethics and truth are important to the writer. It is also a sign of the cultured mind. These people are clear thinking, interested in ideas and thoughts, and often creative and innovative. They are also experts in taking a broad detached view on things, and then making objective judgments. They are succinct in self-expression.

Reader, I make no apology for repeating myself in some of these interpretations. The point is, meanings are enhanced when they are seen repeatedly in different congruent (or compatible) handwriting movements (with similar interpretations).

Confidence, firm self-esteem and positive self-image are all seen in the *very large personal pronoun I's*, and the *top convex hat* on his *personal pronoun I* (as well as on the *T-bar* hat in the upper case letter of his name 'Tom') leaving us in no doubt that his strong willpower and personal self-discipline made him unimpeachable and a force to be reckoned with. Wherever you see a *convex* hat on the top of a stem (which may be drawn slightly above the stem, so the segments do not touch) you have before you a person with a tendency to curb unruly impulses in order to aim for betterment. It is almost a spiritual sign – always hopeful – revealing the overcoming of what the person considers bad in themselves, and the desire to replace it with good. Margaret Thatcher had a similar T in her handwriting.

Lord Denning's indomitable spirit can be seen in the *baselines dramatically rising*, until they can rise no more, and through pure exhaustion and perhaps some inner sadness they begin to fall just as dramatically, until he can find equilibrium and rally once again (on page 2 of his letter). Clearly he is overcompensating at first, which shows he will not be daunted – he is putting a brave face on his age and deteriorating health. As a complete jigsaw, Lord Denning's portrait is made of stern, stirring stuff. Sadly, no one is invincible, and old age caught up with him in the end.

Can we emulate Lord Denning by taking on some of the positive features in his handwriting and applying them to ours? (I am not suggesting that we all begin scrawling illegibly, but there are other features of his natural script that could help us to practise good mental health.)

Part Three

Looking forwards

CHAPTER 13

Self-help and graphology

Reverse engineering
Can you change your mindset by altering your handwriting?

Let us consider a whole new perspective on handwriting: imagine for just one moment that you could change aspects of your mindset or improve your character, simply by altering or slightly adjusting the way you write. Visualise being able to deconstruct your handwriting movements and then modifying your penmanship to mirror a completely different template – a bespoke made-to-measure personality template – according to the behavioural pattern desired. What if, just by editing one or two handwriting quirks, you could set in motion a personal reformation and begin developing particular attractive traits to which you aspire? Are there any aspects about yourself – any outdated habits, unpalatable traits or areas for development – that you might like to change, if you could?

This idea might sound far-fetched, and the concept disputes the whole premise of graphology, i.e. that *you are what you write* – you cannot help how you write – and it is all those spontaneous organic deviations from the way you were originally taught to write in school that makes you who you are now. So the ultimate success of 'reverse engineering' is a big ask, because you would effectively be trying to re-programme the brain. It might feel like walking in someone else's shoes for a while. However, would the imitation mean that just by writing artificially you could eventually morph into a different human being? The notion begs some pertinent questions:

1. Which is more powerful, the hand or the brain – the conscious or the subconscious?

2. Is there a two-way circuit between the writing hand and the subconscious mind?

3. If so, is it possible to re-educate the brain to write in a completely different way – in a way that enhances positive aspects of personality and diminishes or disposes of any perceived negative patterns?

4. Is it even possible to alter brain habits and therefore change your life through the medium of handwriting?

5. How deeply entrenched is core personality?

6. Do people – can people – ever really change? Or are you truly what you write?

In a fashion some people have been innocently practising 'reverse engineering' for years, just by honing the art of handwriting, otherwise known as *calligraphy* (see page 186). Calligraphers have their own artistic copybook models that are based purely on the beautiful appearance of a piece of script. Yet the skill is often contrived; stylistic flourishes are out to impress. So, it is only skin deep. The method does not induce a complete personality rehabilitation, although the very act of penmanship in itself is still powerful and therapeutic for our mental health.

The hand and the pen it holds are merely the conduit, and the brain is hardwired to send out the impulses, so if you wanted to take a more radical approach and make changes that affect a deeper place in the soul – a place where core character traits are rolled out – it would require a huge dose of self-discipline, perseverance and dedication to re-teach the brain to change, by re-imagining the way we put pen to paper. It would also be a time-consuming procedure, and ultimately may only be temporary and ephemeral, simply because it would be so easy to slip back into old habits and styles of writing.

The process would also depend on one more vital ingredient, namely a prescribed menu of suitable symbols reflecting the characteristics sought. Every writer is unique, hence individuality echoes in handwriting. As always, it is difficult to be too prescriptive, without zooming in on each piece of personal script first. So in order to prescribe a 'template', a bespoke programme of ideal character traits and behavioural patterns would need to be created and drawn up. A doctor rarely writes a prescription for his patient before seeing them, and in much the same way a graphologist would not be able to finely tune a handwriting formula and devise a remedy without having first had sight of the writer's natural organic expression on paper.

Just a word of warning before we leap into a menu of potential aspirations. There ought to be a caveat in place. It is vital that you do not upset the delicate balance of your core character – by inadvertently triggering changes to undesirable aspects of your personality – which could simultaneously set up an imbalance or other unacceptable traits in other areas instead. You could end up exchanging one set of behaviours for another equally unpalatable set of attitudes and behavioural patterns. So *do* try this at home, but approach cautiously, remembering that moderation in all things is key. Begin by making sure you are sitting comfortably, with your favourite pen in hand. Then cherry-pick the handwriting movements you desire and distil into your penmanship. Consider *gently tweaking* small details and transient patterns only to create the modifications you aspire to. (If in doubt, consult a professional graphologist.)

☞ *Shapes. Circles* represent emotion, love and belonging. They are sociable, kind, empathetic and sincere. *Squares* represent practicalities. *Triangles* represent ambition.

☞ *Slant vertically* for objectivity, self-assurance, poise and composure.

☞ *Slant slightly to the right* for more extroversion (*slant* helps emotional expression – but a stronger *right slant* will encourage impulsive behaviour).

☞ *Write with much more regularity* to help improve self-control and personal discipline.

☞ *Write words closer together* to overcome feelings of isolation and to mitigate fears of abandonment.

☞ *Widen/stretch* the letters horizontally (particularly the letters n and m) to embrace generosity of mind and spirit, and simultaneously reduce inhibition.

☞ *Concertina letters* (trim the horizonal width of letters n and m, so they become narrower) to become more discriminating in your relationships.

☞ *Increase the volume or absolute size* to boost the outward appearance of confidence.

☞ *Reduce size* to enhance concentration and eliminate distractions.

☞ *Maintain and balance the zones* to regulate inner harmony.

☞ *Raise the t-bars* to encourage self-assertion and challenge the fear of failure.

☞ *Join up/connect* the letters to think more logically.

☞ *Disconnect a few letters* to allow intuition and creativity to seep in.

☞ *Join some letters* and *disconnect* others to improve listening skills.

☞ *Press harder* on the page to strengthen commitment and endurance.

☞ *Press lighter* to promote resilience and reduce tension.

☞ *Complete the y loops* to build up productivity.

☞ *Close the loops in the letters d and t* to reduce sensitivity to criticism.

☞ *Draw more garlands* (or saucer-shaped letter structures) to create or promote an easy-going, compassionate, friendly nature.

☞ *Raise the ends of baselines* to cultivate optimism.

☞ *Widen the sentence baseline spacing* (so they do not bump into each other and tangle) to improve organisational abilities and enhance perspective on life.

☞ *Explore irregularity* in writing to help ease emotional constraints and obsessive-compulsive behaviour.

☞ *Improve your signature and personal pronoun I* to enhance self-esteem and feelings of self-worth.

☞ *Eliminate starting strokes and lagging t-bars* (placed to the left of the stems) to fight back against procrastination.

☞ *Focus on the rhythm* and spontaneity of your handwriting – the pulse and flow of the script – to arouse feelings of well-being deep down inside and help you attain your full potential in life.

The list goes on.

FROM AUNT HILDA &
GREAT GRANDAD
FOR A NEW ARRIVAL
To MISS TRACEY JOSEPH.

TRACEY WAS MY
MOTHERS SURNAME
EMILY TRACEY

Congratulations
on your
New
Little Girl

FOR THE NEW
ARRIVAL
JUST A LITTLE SILVER THIMBLE
FOR A LITTLE FINGER NIMBLE
WITH COTTON & NEEDLE & THREAD
& WITH FINGER NIMBLE
AND THIS SILVER THIMBLE
SO MUCH CAN BE DONE IT IS SAID
FOR MUM & DAD
FROM GREAT GRANDAD
TURNER

**Great Grandad Turner's
handwritten card**

*In memory of my grandmother's
father who died when I was a
baby. This card was received by
my parents on the occasion of
my birth in 1961. I may not
remember my Great Grandad,
but this treasured card offers
a poignant insight into his
character long after his death.*

CHAPTER 14

The power of handwriting

The humanity of handwriting
And why we should continue to handwrite

There is a corner of my office that is given up for boxes of handwriting samples. Rummaging around in these is like delving into people's souls, evoking memories of folks past and present – friends and relatives I have known so well and people I have in my mind's eye but have never met. Every piece of handwriting is naturally different, reflecting the unique identity and individual character of the writer, some inextricably linked to my history.

The Proustian power of handwriting cannot be underestimated. Writing is like a sixth sense that immediately awakens a memory, like a time machine transporting you back to another era in the blink of an eye. A portal to my childhood and an invisible trail to my grandmother's essence – the *sound* of her voice, cajoling, teasing, soothing; the *feel* of her dry kiss on my cheek and her hands *touching* and gently embracing my neck; the unmistakable sweet *smell* of her cheap perfume tainted by a whiff of John Player cigarettes, triggering a memory of how she skilfully balanced an inch of ash, defying gravity, whilst puffing down to the very last dreg. What if I lost all that?

What is more unique and evocative than a piece of handwriting? Writing by hand sets us apart as human from the uniform-regularity, artificially manufactured fonts and robotic equipment in this fast-paced world of computerised gadgets where the emphasis is on disposable, often transient information that rubber-stamps our society. All that typing just looks the same.

People seek to find meaning in the hectic environment we inhabit and so the handmade word will continue to resonate with the sensibility of human beings. There is something beautiful, traditional and romantic about receiving a personalised handwritten letter – something that can be treasured always. How many people keep their emails or feel the same affection for digital notes and text? Letters can become a part of history – a memory of our individuality and presence, long after we have gone, ensuring in such simplicity that we do not disappear forever.

Aside from this shameless emotive mooting, there are other more prosaic reasons why we should never lose the art of handwriting – why we should continue to write – and why handwriting is so beneficial and relevant to mankind. Not least because writing is a basic human form of expression, like speaking, so if the ability to write is allowed to atrophy, then the loss is likely to be far greater than we realise.

Given that handwriting is one of humanity's foundational achievements, the dwindling of writing has gone largely unremarked. Recent national statistics* have shown that there has been a resurgence of all things handwritten, particularly since the Covid-19 pandemic, which indicates that the emotional relevance is important (and that handwriting will never be outdated, even with the rise in technology). A whopping 70 per cent of people have handwritten shopping lists, cards, messages and to-do lists in the last twelve months, and more males than females have penned love notes and wish lists! Does that make men the more romantic genus of the human species?

To put things into perspective, electronic technology is the newcomer. The first typewriter was manufactured in 1873, the first home computer in the 1970s, whereas handwriting in some shape or form has been around since 3400 BC, nearly 6,000 years ago.

Writing by hand is a craft we should continue, for many reasons:

☞ Handwriting is a crucial skill that promotes creativity and enhances imagination, with ideas flowing more freely. You may have noticed that writing – mediated by hand rather than a machine – engages the brain differently. This means your thinking is different when you write, more measured and richer. So whilst you may find that typed documents can be composed quickly, it still pays to switch to handwriting for deep thinking and note-taking.

☞ The process of handwriting imprints knowledge in the mind more effectively than using a keyboard and computer screen. This is because handwriting activates

---

* Conducted in August 2021 by Ancestry® – the global leader in family history and consumer genomics.

neural pathways known as the Broca's area of the brain – the area most often linked to speech production. Students studying for exams find that by writing notes they have better memory retention and gain a higher degree of comprehension or understanding when they are confronted with an exam paper. This recall serves them well for years to come and often lasts long into adulthood. These same pathways created by the brain are also used for other tasks, such as problem-solving. So if these neural pathways are not used (or worse still are not laid down in the first place) then problem-solving will become more difficult.

☛ Handwriting is synonymous with general development and growth. The importance of handwriting in child development cannot be underestimated or ignored. Handwriting has unique cognitive properties that help to shape how children learn to read, write and talk. When children learn to write, they are simultaneously building other developmental skills, such as sequential memory and fine motor ability.

☛ Children delight in spontaneous motor play – otherwise known as scribbling. It gives them a sense of self, a means of expressing themselves, from a very young age. The art of learning to write helps children develop a sense of balance, symmetry and rhythmic movement (as well as the appreciation of creating something personal and artistic on paper). In fact, when children practise writing and perfecting their signature, it is a very personal statement – a form of identity, their public image – underpinning feelings of self-worth, self-esteem and self-confidence.

☛ People in the midst of depression or experiencing some type of trauma may not be able to articulate exactly what they are thinking and feeling. This is certainly true for children, who do not yet have the education or maturity to understand what is going on inside their heads. So writing and drawing is also a vital channel for children at times when words are inadequate. It is known that children were so traumatised by the Grenfell Tower fire incident in London in June 2017, that in the aftermath all they wanted to do was draw. They could not talk about their experiences and feelings, and desperately needed to find their voices, but were unable to articulate the horror in words. For these children, their only means of processing emotion was through pencil and pen.

☞ There are several diseases and conditions that can affect the brain and, in turn, the motor skills required to write. Neurologists are able to tell a great deal about what is happening inside the brain by looking at the changes that occur in handwriting. As we have seen, writing by hand is also important for mental health.

☞ Handwriting prevents brain decay in old age, and has been proven to arrest Alzheimer's by continuing to stimulate nourishing blood flows to the brain. So you could say that the art of writing is an insurance policy for life.

☞ Recognising and pinpointing what is going on in someone's mind – to have an insight into how they are thinking and feeling, and therefore an ability to understand their behavioural patterns synchronously with their core personality – will not only help raise awareness of the exact difficulties the writer is experiencing, but will also give onlookers an indication of how they can be helped or supported going forwards.

Our society's tendency to take the writing process for granted is leaving our children disadvantaged. Most adults are able to quickly jot down notes, write messages, etc. when necessary, but children cannot do this and need to practise writing regularly in order to learn to do so. Adults see the use of computer technology as a way of improving their adult lives. However, by teaching this philosophy to children, we are forgetting the skills we have already learnt and acquired when we first used a computer keyboard, and which have greatly added to our overall thinking and communication abilities.

There are still many people in the world (older people, people in developing countries) who do not have easy access to electricity, let alone computers, who are not contactable by email, or even telephone. These people still want to communicate, and so how do we continue to connect with them? And what happens if the power dies or a battery breaks?

These days we are drawn to digital methods of memory preservation – blogs and tweets and status updates – but handwritten diaries endure, especially during wartime. Diaries and journals do not need electricity or to be handled with care, and they carry a unique form of literary DNA. Each stroke of the pen is a highly individualised signature giving insight into the writer's emotional state at the time.

Remember: it is not just handwriting, it is someone's whole psychological profile on paper, and will continue to be an important skill that holds relevance in many different areas of our daily lives.

The way we write is the result of brain transmission through the medium of the hand – the pen we hold is merely the conduit. The tactile experience of the handwritten stroke and the freedom of expression this elicits allows the writer to draw upon the deepest recesses of the heart and mind, so the psyche flows on to the page uninhibited. What other channel allows us to literally make our personal mark today and take our place in history tomorrow?

How will communication fare without it?

It is an important choice that reflects the unique story of each writer.

Handwriting is the shape of humanity.

Part Four

Appendix

CHAPTER 15

Tell-tales

This section is an addendum to the case studies. Each 'tell-tale' references significant aspects of personality investigated in this book and drills down to the nitty-gritty nutshell of character, decoding the shortcuts of generic traits in handwriting.

Can you hide your true character?

1. People who write in *upper case letters throughout* may think they are hiding their true identity, but they are already revealing that they lack confidence and have underlying feelings of inadequacy (see page 145, Daniel's suicide letter). Upper case letters are all in the *middle zone*, so we also know that daily affairs and relationships take priority in their world, as well as everything that impinges on the ego. Upper case letter writers are egocentric, although interpreted more positively they also uncover the type of people who are interested in practical solutions for practical problems.

2. Some people write in *upper case letters* following a trauma or illness, or because they feel guilty or anxious.

Some say they write in *upper case letters* throughout because it is easier to read (and this may be perfectly true – upper case letters are, after all, the 'polite letters'), and so they think they will come across as straightforward characters. However, in truth they are revealing that underneath they are just the opposite – quite vulnerable – and do not want other people to know what they are really like. Or they have difficulty facing up to themselves as they really are and want to find a way of holding their true personality in check. The point is that upper case letters represent your *ideal* self and lower case letters represent your *real* self. So what does that tell you about people who choose to write in *upper case letters throughout*? Are they simply polite and considerate individuals, or do they have something to hide? Are they genuine, or is it just artifice?

3. In much the same way, writers who develop a fake or manufactured *persona* or *stylised* type of elaborate writing are posers who are concerned with projecting an image, and are therefore motivated to present themselves in the best possible light (see page 18, Wendy's handwriting). They are often introverts with excellent social graces and the masters of smoke screens. This is either because they desire to be different and special and want to stand apart from the crowd, or they simply want to be liked. Either way, they are attempting to conceal deep insecurities, arising from earlier experiences in life. These types are rattled by sudden, unexpected change. They lack spontaneity, so everything is planned to the nth degree.

4. Narcissism is often disguised and difficult to detect, and yet narcissistic behaviour is toxic and has an impact on people, often leaving permanent damage and scars. It can be found in many strata of society. Hamlet said: *'The devil can assume a pleasing shape.'* However, where you see a simulated style of handwriting, you may be uncovering a narcissist. This is because manipulators are always concerned with appearances. Narcissism is a vast overestimation of self (or exaggerated self-love), superiority, chronic insensitivity, lack of empathy, clear entitlement. In short, it is all about them.

5. Exaggerations, wherever they are found, uncover compensation for a perceived lack within the personality. Hence, an overdeveloped *persona* or paradigm equals an underdeveloped personality, and perhaps that is all you need to know.

Do you give out mixed messages?

Human beings are complex creatures and are frequently difficult to understand, and these complexities are seen visually in handwriting movements that appear to be incompatible, contradicting one another on first sight. However, if you can remember that *one meaning never cancels out the other* and you are able to amalgamate the conflicting information so they complement rather than clash, you will get a deep insight into what makes that person tick. A list is never finite, but here are some commonly seen antagonistic mixtures and a couple of rarer combinations:

1. You may see the extrovert's *marked right slant* together with *narrow width* of the letters. This means that the writer enjoys socialising but will not get personally involved. This is because they are private people and may be a little scared of letting anyone get too close. So although they give out the vibe that they are friendly and outgoing, they often have very selective friendships. These writers are surprisingly self-protective inhibited types, who are terrified of getting carried away by their emotions and impulses. This *counter-dominant* will be enhanced if the *word spacing is wide* too, illustrating how powerfully the writer unconsciously needs their own space and keeps people socially distanced.

2. Or, you may have a *large and dominant middle zone* with a *left slant*. This is commonly seen in a young girl's handwriting. This combination of movements uncovers a strong dependency on emotional contact, but if anyone gets too close, they run a mile. These types can be a bit of a tease and everything will be a great drama.

3. A *wavy line* or *thready* writer may be shifty and evasive, adept at circumventing problems. They may come across as totally politically correct, but when this *form of connection* is combined with *heavy pressure*, this tells you that underneath the sweetness and light front, the writer will be as competitive as hell. This is someone who invariably Gets. What. They. Want. Like slippery eels, they see which way the prevailing wind blows and go with it, forever changing their tune and playing up to circumstances. These types are super-effective in sales or on a political platform.

4. *Angles* and *thready forms of connection* (seen in the same script) are another potentially dodgy combination, but everything can be turned to a positive or a negative depending on circumstances and the individual's way of handling things. In a more positive content, it can mean that the writer is brilliant, with lots of non-partisan, aggressive energies at play.

5. Where you have *angles* and *garlands* in the same script, this reflects the typical iron fist in velvet glove. They may seem all smiley, sweet and gentle, but underneath they are much more forceful and determined than you realise.

6. *Heavy pressure* with an absence of the *lower zone* is sometimes seen in the script of sports people whose powerful energies are being diverted away from the bedroom.

7. *Small sized* writing penned with a much larger signature reveals a truly modest and unassuming person who chooses to present themselves in a 'bigger' way.

8. A *right slant* penned with letters that are *disconnected* or unjoined reveals someone who is ambitious but potentially gets easily distracted. However, this meaning will be mitigated if there are movements that show how hard the writer is trying to control any negative impulses. For example, the script may be *regular*, *angular*, *rigid* and *stilted*, with self-discipline identified by *firm pressure* and *crucifix* and/or *convex style of t-bars*.

What motivates you in life? What is key to your happiness?

Let us take another peek at the *zones*, because this is where you will find the best clues for revealing people's core values and motivation. The *zones* will not only tell you where the writer's interests can be found, but will also uncover what they tend to spend most of their time and energy on, brilliantly pinpointing motivation. However, it is important to consider what is going on in *all three zones* (not just the *largest* one) and how they interact with each other, because they are all interrelated.

1. The *dominant zone*, which will be disproportionately large compared with the other *zones*, skewing or fudging the balance, is where the writer focuses most attention, desire and drive. So, if, for example, the *lower zone* is clearly dominant – larger than the *upper* or *middle zones* – you will know that practical considerations inevitably headline the writer's world.

2. The *smallest* or weakest *zone* will be less important (to the writer), giving insight into which aspect of their life and personality has been neglected. So if you are interested in personal development, this is the area that reveals potential for growth.

3. People who are reliable and hard-working and motivated by deserved recognition for their efforts will exhibit *zonal balance* (i.e. where all three *zones* are equally sized).

4. The *middle zone* focuses on everyday life – social connections and communication – reflecting the writer's self-esteem, and the value placed on satisfying ego needs.

5. *Large* and *dominant middle zone* writers can be seductive and demanding! They like to impress and have the ability to sell themselves, personalising whatever they do so people take notice of them. At the other end of the continuum, people with disproportionately *small* and *weak middle zones* lack self-confidence and compensate for this with aggressive drives.

6. City businesswomen or 'geezer-birds' often have *small middle zone* writing with *heavy pressure*. This has a different meaning and uncovers a strong father influence.

7. *Small* and *carefully executed middle zone* (with *light pressure*) is often seen in the writing of first-rate research workers.

8. A *large* and *dominant upper zone* underlines the achievement motive. All aspirations and ambitions reside in the upper zone, so developing ideas and achieving goals will be more important to these people than having security or material possessions. If the *upper zone* fluctuates, this reveals that the writer is dissatisfied at an academic or career level, and wants to achieve success, but in reality is over-reaching themselves by having dreams beyond their ability. An underdeveloped *upper zone* means the writer is pragmatic.

9. A *widening left margin* reveals someone who is results-orientated.

10. *High-crossed t-bars* belong to take-charge types who excel at making decisions and delegating, although they can be bossy!

11. Overly *rising baselines* may reveal unrealistic expectations.

Can you trust your partner? How can you tell if someone is dishonest or hiding something from you?

The chances are you will see some of these indicators in their handwriting. Just remember that there is a fine line between being reticent in sharing your thoughts and feelings and being downright dishonest. There are also varying degrees of dishonesty, ranging from a propensity to be economical with the truth, to telling little white lies, to deliberate and compulsive lying. And from small deceptions to disingenuity and lack of integrity, to fully blown adultery and betrayal. So it is only when the handwriting movements appear in significant numbers – you will need to see a combination of at least five of the movements below – that you can safely say that someone is untrustworthy.

1. If the griffonage is purposefully illegible – where letters are ambiguous or neglected, where there are *missing letter parts*, where there are *elaborations* or *exaggerations* and *distortions*, or where there is compulsive *retouching*, these are all warning bells that things might not be quite as they seem.

2. If the *pressure* is *very light*, your partner may suddenly disappear without a trace. It may not be because they are dishonest. It is more likely that they are trying to avoid confrontation or conflict at all costs.

3. The tall *upper zone* stems have an upward *starting stroke* that covers the same trajectory as the downward stroke, revealing that the writer is unlikely to say what is on their mind. These are known graphically as *covering strokes*.

4. There may be *wide word spacing* if the writer values their privacy.

5. The letters n and m may look *very narrow* or squeezed if the writer is constrained and inhibited and keeps their thoughts to themselves.

6. If the handwriting is *disconnected*, the writer may not be intentionally withholding information. It is more likely that they are not very good at bonding.

7. The *oval* letters are a giveaway when it comes to revealing what pops out of people's mouths. Look to see if they have *superfluous loops* and *knots* (these people are as good at kidding themselves, as they are at deceiving other people), or if they are *stabbed* inside (denoting evasiveness) or *contaminated* (and filled with ink – the writer tells tales or makes up stories) or have *inner spirals* (insincerity) or have been *drawn clockwise* (flouts convention). If an *oval* is open at the bottom (i.e. on the baseline, for example the letter b would look like an h), this is strong sign that the writer's standards have dropped, and they are not as honest or sincere as they may appear.* If the *ovals* are open at the top, this is much more common and simply reveals a propensity to indiscretion

---

An open 'b' on the baseline is not always about dishonesty. It can reveal someone who examines their own feelings and draws on their primary instincts to understand who they really are. This writer is trying to hide their weaknesses. They may act contrary to convention. They may also provoke others, without meaning to – they are the types who will cut off their nose to spite their face! So it is very important that you apply the correct interpretation, and this is why you need to see clusters of movements rather than isolated symbols.

– your partner is likely to be a gasbag!

8. *Rhythm* is the prime evaluator of honesty, so it follows that the *rhythm* will be poor. This means the *speed* of the writing will be very slow, uncomfortable and artificial, and all attempts to write naturally will be blighted.

9. Manipulative types may exhibit the infamous *shark's tooth*. You only need to see one of these movements to know that you are dealing with a shrewd and cunning individual – someone who takes advantage of others either emotionally or financially. These people are likely to say one thing and do another. They will smile sweetly whilst stabbing you in the back.

10. A *lower zone* loop that wriggles up the stem (i.e. it goes to the right and crosses backwards) also reveals manipulation. These people are brilliant bluffers and have the ability to play a situation to suit themselves. There is also a sense of defiance, so you never know what they are going to do next! They excel in the sales arena. (Sir Winston Churchill and Samuel Pepys both exhibit this movement in their handwriting.)

11. There are other clues revealing potential devious behaviour: artificial or *stylised* handwriting (known as *persona*), *printing* in upper case letters throughout, strong *mixed slant* (within a word), *erratic baselines*, *thready* formations seen together with *angles*, flattened, shallow or *creeping arcades* or arched shaped letters, and a large collection of *pseudo garlands* and *pseudo arcades*. *Pseudo garlands* and *arcades* are loops that occur in the *middle zone* letters, where the copybook states a single or covering stroke should be. The *pseudo garland* goes in an anti-clockwise direction, and the *pseudo-arcade* in a clockwise direction. *Pseudo garlands* show someone in the habit of embellishing the emotional content of what they are saying in order to appear more captivating and alluring. *Pseudo arcades* reveal someone who gives the impression of being something they are not, so there will be some sort of pretence or concealment. Also, they can be astute in their handling of people in order to win them over or get what they want from them. There is another interpretation: I have frequently found *pseudo arcades* in the handwriting of people who tend to worry a lot.

12. *Split letters* are associated with anti-social personality disorders. *Split letters* in the *middle zone* are to do with someone who has an over-reactive sensitivity that prevents them from relating emotionally, and may break with what is orthodox, i.e. by having affairs.

Are you hoping your partner will make a commitment? How is your sex life?

Perhaps you think your partner is having an affair? These clues will help you to dig deep and flag up some warning signs.

1. A *greatly fluctuating slant* peels back the layer of unpredictability. You will never know where you stand with these types because they are forever moving the goal posts.

2. Is the *word spacing* very wide? These individuals will freeze you out rather than getting involved. And they will find it hard to talk about what is bothering them. On the other hand, if the *word spacing* is close and the overall appearance of the script is compact, this unveils someone who fears abandonment or being jilted. If the *letter spacing* is so close that letters are touching or *mingling*, this is a warning that the writer will be needy.

3. Do the tall *upper zonal* letters fluctuate greatly? These people cannot make up their minds, so they keep

changing them. And if the long *lower zone* stems are *slanting to the left* (or pulling to the right – it is the same thing), they will never tell you what they are feeling deep down inside, creating even more confusion.

4. Is your partner procrastinating or dithering? If so, you would expect to see lots of *starting strokes*, and the *t-bars* may be executed on the left side of the stems. The *speed* of the writing will probably be *slow* too, and the letters may also be *narrow* and *disconnected*.

5. If the handwriting *pressure* is *light*, the writer may be affectionate and sensitive, but they will hate rowing and confrontations and will be unlikely to commit easily.

6. If the *pressure* is *heavy or very heavy*, your partner will be emotionally intense and will not get over upsets easily. They may still be brooding long after you have gone to bed.

7. *Pasty* strokes reveal a warm nature that is partial to sensual pleasures. These types are tactile and sometimes hedonistic.

8. If the writing looks *muddy* and there is excessive ink flow with ink-filled letters, this is eroticism gone wild. Your partner's sexuality may be linked to all sorts of unconventional practices, and they will make little effort to curb these impulses. Guilt or anxiety is often a part of the bigger picture, or there may be a secret that is literally choking the writer inside. At best, their emotions are so intense, they are likely to have a bad or even uncontrollable temper. They simply cannot help themselves.

9. Is the *last letter g disconnected* from the rest of the word? If so, the writer is capable of 'ghosting'. This means they can abruptly cut off all contact with you without any warning or explanation for doing so. Even if you try to reach out and gain closure, you will be met with a wall of silence. These types are commitment-phobes who have trouble connecting emotionally in intimate relationships and will often get cold feet at the eleventh hour. Sometimes causing arguments can be symptomatic of this condition. Even married people may feel compelled to withhold a small part of themselves. The reason for it specifically being the g is because that letter is believed to contain the family circle in the *middle zone*. The shape of that circle tells a lot about the writer's family relationships – for example, someone who makes the figure 8 g leaves the circle open and is likely to have incomplete family relationships.

10. *Small loops* at the start of the letter m are a sign of jealousy.

11. Whenever you see a *potlid* (this is where the p stem extends above the circular part), you will spot an argumentative streak. Also, an *upward diagonal stroke on the letter t or T is a sign of someone who enjoys disagreeing for the sake of it.*

12. If the second downstroke of the letter n hovers above the baseline (i.e. it stops short of touching the baseline – this is known as *suspendu*), the writer is likely to be non-committal and indecisive, and may refrain from any sort of commitment. These writers can have second thoughts and back off at the last minute, potentially pulling out of an agreement. It shows a fear of trusting someone else.

13. A *tee-pee d* uncovers the stubborn individual. They frequently do not allow others to get close and can end up feeling disconnected from people.

14. A collapsed or *concave t-bar* reveals a person who is a soft touch and potentially submissive.

15. A small letter t followed by a larger or taller letter h is the sign of a risk taker.

16. *Regularity* in a script is a sign that the writer likes routine. Here, familiarity does not breed contempt.

17. Spoiler alert: The *lower zone* is a deeply personal, private area. People with *large lower zones* have deep subconscious drives and primal instincts. The *size/length*, *fullness* and *pressure of the lower zone stems* give away the strength of their sex drive. They may have personal desires that they like to keep hidden from other people. So if you do not want to know what it all means, avert your eyes from beneath the *baseline*!

a. A *heavy, full and large lower zone* reveals a strong appetite for sex.

b. *Cradle lower zones* are gentle, caring and affectionate. They can also indicate sexual passiveness and immaturity.

c. *Single strokes* or *lean lower zone sticks* uncover a lack of empathy. These people may have good business sense, but they are inhibited emotionally. They are matter-of-fact and practical – they can take people or leave them – and they do not always think about the consequences of their words or actions.

d. Compressed (or overly *narrow loops* in the) *lower zone* indicate repression and bottling of feelings. These people are sexually inhibited. They may need a big hug.

e. *Lower zone loops* atrophied or *crossed low*, beneath the *baseline*, is a clear indication of disappointment in life. There is often a feeling of impotence of some kind, and a desire to be appreciated. There can be an overcompensation resulting in promiscuity.

f. *Triangles in the lower zone* represent the domestic tyrant. This is repressed aggression that manifests itself in the alpha male – the 'wham-bam' type.

g. *Long, angular lower zones* tell of resentment and frustration. These people are loving, but hungry for sex.

h. *Claws* or *felon claws* can reveal greed. They also mean contrariness and unexpected, rebellious social behaviour. These people tend to provoke others and are difficult to get along with for any length of time. *Clawed lower zones* can also uncover a fear of looking at emotion, symbolising feelings of guilt. There will be a deprivation of some kind – financially, emotionally or sexually – that the writer has chosen to suppress in their subconscious, rather than face truthfully. They can be defensive about their security needs but will deny that they have a problem. It may be difficult to help these people, because they have put up such a strong block. Sometimes they enjoy being a martyr and put themselves in a position where they become a victim – expert at self-destruction. The 'claw' keeps the writer holding on to frustration, embarrassment and past grievances.*

i. Extremely wide *lower zone* loops show that the writer is romantic and adventurous, but in danger of fantasy overtaking reality. They may brag about their sexual prowess, yet be unable to perform.

j. Someone with a greatly fluctuating *lower zone* will be fidgety and restless, and may lack self-control. Boredom is not an option for these people – they like lots of variety and spice in their sex lives! A disproportionately *long, fluctuating* and *tangling lower zone* (where sentences bump into each other) tells of a need to search for many sexual partners.

k. A *hooked* (or shepherd's crook) style of *lower zone* loop unearths a loyal, family person.

l. The *lower zone* is not just about sex. It also tells of practical considerations, such as the writer's need for material possessions, money and security.

Are you compatible in the workplace?

With whom do you work? Are you part of a team? Do you have a difficult line manager? Do you work in an open-plan office that relies on everyone being on the same page and having mutual respect? Do you share similar characteristics, values and skillsets? Are your personalities complementary, or are there difficulties in communication, resulting in clashes? The seamless compatibility of interpersonal dynamics in the workplace can be fraught with potholes, and should not be underestimated. So let us examine a few matches that may or may not get along in the workplace.

---

* There can also be a positive meaning for *claws*, depending on what else is going on in the handwriting. This is why you have to look at handwriting holistically, as well as dissecting and scrutinising. It can also reveal someone who strongly attaches themselves to a person or a cause they believe is worthy, and they will hang on in there even if the going gets tough.

1. *Rounded letters with angles.* A potentially highly compatible mix. The warmth, sociability, tact and support of the people-minded *rounded* letter writer works well with the hard-working, confident, energetic *angular* writer. *Angles* provide the purpose and the backbone, and get the job done, whilst the *round* letter writer keeps the love flowing. The *rounded* type needs the *angles* deadlines to work effectively, provided the *angular* type is not too critical, tough and aggressive towards the gentler soul. *Angles* need to lead, and *rounded* types are happy just to support and be involved.

2. *Heavy pressure with light pressure.* These two writers do not understand each other, so it is a potentially frustrating and unhappy mix. Initially, a *heavy pressure* writer admires the *light pressure* writer's breezy approach to life – nothing seems to bother or phase them - but it will not last long. *Heavy pressure* writers work physically hard – investing 100 per cent and tackling problems head on. *Light pressure* writers tend to apply mental energy – working smart rather than hard – and managing to avoid confrontation at all costs. *Heavy pressure* writers will think their light pressure peers do not care, and will be frustrated by their refusal to face up to issues. *Light pressure* writers

will remove themselves from the problem and recover from any upsets much quicker than *heavy pressure* writers, who will be worrying late into the night. *Light pressure* writers will find their *heavy pressure* colleagues too intense and controlling.

3. *Large size with small size.* This is potentially a complementary mix. It is the showroom and the backroom combined. The *large size* writer excels at delegating and the *small size* writer is only too happy to oblige and be hands-on. The *large size* may be restless and undisciplined, giving it large, but the *small size* is concentrating and effectively organising the minutiae. The *small size* is busy thinking, whilst the *large size* gets on with doing. The modest *small size* is happy to keep a low profile, whilst the *larger size* enjoys all the attention, so all in all they should get along famously.

4. *Two dominant middle zonal types together.* These two could potentially be great friends in the office, although they might not get any work done. They will treat the workplace as an opportunity to socialise and may be too busy chatting and sorting out each other's problems. On the other hand, they may both be too needy and selfish, lacking the maturity and conscience to realise that they cannot both hog the limelight.

5. *Connected with disconnected.* This can throw up some difficulties. Cursive writers are logical and work methodically, whereas *disconnected* writing is attributed to people who are inventive, intuitive and forever scanning randomly for new information and data. *Connected* writers usually have a plan and hate being interrupted when they are in the middle of working or saying something, whereas *disconnected* types rarely know what they will be doing next – they are in the moment, thinking on their feet, flitting from one thing to another and excelling at multi-tasking. So there would not be an easy rapport, and they are unlikely to collaborate easily. The *disconnected* writer may drive the cursive writer mad!

6. *Arcade with thread.* The *form of connection* represents people's attitude and behaviour and tells how they adapt to their surroundings. *Arcade* writers tend to be polite and formal and loyal to the cause. They can be slow to assimilate information initially and very much like to do things by the book. *Thready* writers, on the other hand, are spontaneous, enterprising rule-breakers with a strong tendency to avoid heavily loaded emotional situations and conflicts. They need personal space without constraints to work effectively. Interestingly, both types can be quite

the perfectionists and highly creative. They are also both inclined to secrecy. Their roles in the workplace will dictate if this combination blends or clashes, and positively or negatively. Ideally, there would be a mixture of letter structures in each individual, which tells of a more mature ability to get on well with everyone.

7. *Close word spacing with wide word spacing.* This can be an uncomfortable union, because the *close word* spacer will suffocate the *wide word* writer. People whose words are *closely spaced* crave company and are often needy and dependent on others. Whereas the writer who leave *wide spaces* between their words will feel overwhelmed by other people invading their space. They need room to breathe and operate effectively. They enjoy social distancing and cannot bear to be crowded.

Does it matter if your child does not carry on writing the way they were taught?

There are no hard and fast rules for analysing children's handwriting. Children, like adults, all develop and mature at their own pace. So it is impossible to set an age at which the character begins to show, and writers will therefore need to be assessed on their own individual merits. These are the ways you might expect a child's handwriting to develop at different stages of maturity.

1. As a rough guide, in later childhood (between eight and twelve years of age), and once a child gains some skill with writing, a rhythm will emerge without the need for copybook guidelines. Size normally decreases in proportion to maturation, as does realism, objectivity and conformity. There is also improved (usually increased) *spacing* and arrangement between letters and words, as well as more emphasis on *connecting* letters together.

2. The process of handwriting imprints knowledge in in the brain more effectively than using a keyboard and computer screen, because it activates the Broca's area of the brain. The motor functions and cognitive development involved in writing, speaking and reading are all able to converge in a co-ordinated and integrated way – a process identified with thinking.

3. *Quality of pressure* is an affirmation of personality – a good indication of dynamism and vitality.

4. *Slant* shows the child's attitude to connecting with other children and grown-ups.

5. *Rising baselines* reveal enthusiasm, and falling baselines indicate tiredness or disappointment.

6. *Garland forms* uncover an openhearted and adaptable child. *Arcade* shapes reveal more closed characters, but possibly constructive types. *Angles* show energy, but sometimes also aggression and frustration.

7. Cursive writing is the same as joined-up thinking. These children will have some continuity of thought, ideas and action.

8. *Disconnected* writers may have difficulty relating to other children.

9. Children who *print* may feel lonely. They may also be spending too much time surfing the Internet, scanning for information to stimulate and flood their minds.

10. *Irregularity* is normal in children's writing, although excessive *irregularities* can indicate nervousness and possible lying (usually driven by fear).

11. The *zones* offer up insight into a child's desires. So dominance in the *middle zone* reveals an affectionate child – one who is conscious of their own personality and their environment. A large *upper zone* indicates imagination and a taste for intellectual things. *Lower zone* dominance uncovers a child who is practical, with instinctive tendencies.

12. The *margins* give a good idea of a child's need for security or for adventurousness. The wider or widening the left margin, the keener the child will be to get out in the world.

Are you concerned about your child's progress?

Every child is different and will need assessing individually, so it would be irresponsible to try to shoe-horn a child to 'fit' pre-conceived ideas. However, here are some tips on what you *might* expect to see in the handwriting of children with issues.

1. Temper tantrums can be seen in writing with *angles, narrowness* and *rigidity*.

2. Shyness can be seen in *small size, left slanted writing, wide word spacing, arcade formations, narrowness* and a *small middle zone*.

3. Disruptive behaviour can be exhibited in *large, heavy writing that is very irregular and over-connected*. The *rhythm* is likely to be erratic. *Angles* reveal that the child needs to channel their energy into something productive, otherwise they can quickly become disruptive and/or aggressive. *Rounded* handwriting may seem to be less problematic or physically demanding, but can create issues in other ways through constant attention-seeking behaviour.

4. Fears and phobias are uncovered where you have *very wide margins* and *very wide spacing between words and lines, light pressure* and *small* writing with lots of tight *starting strokes*.

5. Depression can be seen in strongly *falling baselines* and/or *very light* or *variable pressure* patterns. The *signature* may also be crossed out (through the middle) revealing a sense of personal dissatisfaction underneath, and feelings of self-doubt.

What is going on inside my teenage daughter's head?

Adolescence is a difficult time. So between the ages of twelve and fifteen, the successful resolution of self-identify, self-image and self-esteem are a vital precursor to intimacy in personal relationships. In leaving behind their childish roles, adolescents need to know who they are and what they stand for. (This is the reason why there is so much experimentation with signatures.) So, it would be perfectly normal to see the following handwriting movements.

1. Low self-esteem can be observed in greatly fluctuating *middle zone* letters and a *small personal pronoun I*.

2. An *irregular or variable slant* that flip-flops forwards and backwards reveals exaggerated emotional responses due to inner insecurities, uncertainties and immaturity.

3. A *strong (marked) left slant* can be expected at a time when teenagers are withdrawn, defiant and rebellious, self-conscious, self-centred and self-absorbed, selfish and very emotional, but trying hard to bottle things up.

4. *Blotchy, smeary writing* in a teenager can signify the onset of puberty with all the emotional tension and emerging sexual urges.

5. Note that handwriting *distortions* are perfectly natural during adolescence. It is to do with normal glandular changes associated with puberty.

6. At the end of puberty, there may be a brief break in *pressure* – it becomes *light* – reflecting the sudden release in tension. However, usually within a year, this returns to the writer's natural level.

7. Huge *exaggerations in size* reflect the adolescent's opinion of themselves and the role they believe they have to play in life.

8. *Round, broad letters* reflect ego amplification, whereas *narrowness* exposes inhibition.

9. *Elliptical* (broad and flattened) *ovals* tell of emotion and anxiety – an uncertainty about who they are and where they are going in life. *Elliptical ovals* can be more serious in adults, because they reveal a grave uncertainty that the writer feels they have not been able to reach their full potential (for whatever reason) and do not know what they ought to be doing going forwards. There is likely to be quite a lot of soul-searching going on.

Are you stressed? Or is someone you know behaving out of character?

The list of stress factors is never finite, but here are some good indicators.

1. *Heavy pressure* writers are most likely to become victims of stress. They feel very strongly about things and invest so much energy and emotion into everything they do, plus they have such a low tolerance for frustration.

2. If the *small letters on the baseline are fluctuating greatly* – i.e. they are all different sizes – this is symptomatic of stress. A variable *middle zone* height uncovers emotion on a continuum from touchiness to grumpiness to erratic mood swings. This is all because the writer's inner contentment and self-confidence varies.

3. Tense, stressed writers are more likely to write from the wrist and bend their forefinger towards the pen, creating (often small and neat) letters, which show signs of cramp. The tension impedes the natural flow and *rhythm*, and shows how hard a person is trying to control and concentrate their energies. The technical term for this is *contraction*, which is the opposite of *release*, and suggests left brain

dominance. Other signs of *contracted* (or cramped) writing are *distorted letters forms, pointed zonal loops, disconnected, lean and narrow letters, angles* and *vertical emphasis*. These people are incapable of relaxing and become easily aggravated under stress. It is all because underneath they are worried about not doing well, and this fear often stems from childhood. They believe they have something to prove in life and put themselves under huge pressure to achieve.

4. Consistently *falling baselines* is usually a sign of despondency, depression, exhaustion and temporary negativity. In children's handwriting, this is more likely to be a sign of disappointment and a feeling that there is no point in making any effort because they will only fail anyway.

5. *Jerky, shaky, hesitant* or *tremulous* handwriting, lacking in fluency, can reveal that the writer is in a state of anxious stress at the time of writing, provided they are not elderly or potentially suffering from some sort of illness, such as Parkinson's.

6. Unexplained, unprescribed *scatter dots* (like misplaced full stops) seen within the whole text, tell of a person who is worried about something.

7. Unexplained *resting dots* within or during pen strokes and letters are an indication that something is causing the writer to feel very stressed. They need to stop, unwind and relax. *Resting dots* in the *middle zone* are also commonly seen in women's handwriting (usually between the ages of forty-five and fifty-five years of age), if they are going through the menopause. This is because the reduction of oestrogen receptors in the brain produces anxiety and 'brain fog', which is naturally reflected in the handwriting.

8. *Dot grinding* uncovers inner tension, obsessive thinking patterns and resentful silences. When you see this movement, it is likely that irritable, tempestuous behaviour will follow.

9. *Ink trails* lead you to discover that the writer is in a serious state of stress and exhaustion. Note that this can appear at an early stage of illness before the writer is even aware that anything is wrong. If you see this movement, it would be time to visit your doctor for a physical or mental health check-up.

10. If the *baselines are rigidly straight*, as if they have been written on a ruler, it is the sign of a control freak – someone who cannot cope with any change. Personal discipline marks the personality, which is all very admirable, but this restricts natural spontaneity and puts the writer under huge pressure, simultaneously diminishing their inability to deal with hassles. So, when they are affected by anything stressful, they tend to really let go – explosively.

11. Where you see a *claw* (this looks like an upside down or inside out loop in the long tail of a downstroke y), this means that the writer is suppressing their fears. These people may not want to face whatever is stressing them out, but nevertheless their worries may keep them awake at night, tossing and turning. Whatever is bothering them will be unacknowledged and hidden from public view.

12. Anxious people sometimes doodle to release their stress and resolve their problems. This is because the very act of putting pen to paper releases repressed feelings like activating a personal safety release valve. Doodles are nothing more than subconscious thoughts and repressed emotions spilling out of the back of your mind. *Shading-in* reveals worries and uncovers tension, anxiety and stress. The *heavier* the shading, the deeper the issue. In handwriting, this *shading* can be seen in *retraced* strokes. These are deliberate movements where the pen stroke or word is redrawn. This is a sign of compulsion in order to reduce anxiety. For example, you may see the individual making a ritual out of trivial things. This approach is not a rational attempt to reach a solution, but it is perceived to be a way of reducing anxiety by making a constant effort.

How do you recognise violent indicators in handwriting?

We have seen what triggered Dennis Nilsen's predilection for depravity and violence. And we all have a propensity and ability to behave in ways that may seem out of character, depending on circumstance. On the anger spectrum, these can range from mild irritability to impatience and frustration at one end, to clear signs of inherent violence that may be triggered more easily at the other. Handwriting gives an indication of how dangerous a person can be at any given time.

1. *Angles with light pressure* uncover someone who grumbles, whines and verbally criticises.

2. *Angles with heavy pressure* reveal an aggressive, intolerant, domineering personality, someone who insists on doing things their way, and will do so forcefully if necessary. *Angles* are despotic and dictatorial, so they can be cruel.

3. *Lower zone angularity* means potential angry outbursts, but these people will probably pull themselves together and calm down quickly, because the anger is unconscious, so it flares up suddenly from out of the blue.

4. *Very heavy pressure and/or variable pressure* is an excellent indicator of pent-up aggression.

5. *Very heavy vertical or downstroke pressure* is seen in the writing of people who are tough, uncompromising and potentially ruthless and aggressive.

6. *Very heavy horizontal pressure on (long) t-bars* reveals someone who is demonstrably angry and argumentative, inclined to shake their fist and harangue people. It is all part of a power complex.

7. *Strong, smeary, maybe flooded pen strokes* uncover an obstinate nature that is consumed with anger, but with no release. These people can be anti-social and disorderly.

8. *Thick pressure or clubbed strokes* reveal brutality or cruelty (particularly with poor quality writing). These people's default setting will be to strike or hit first and ask questions after.

9. *Ink-filled ovals* reveal a sensual nature with intense emotion that needs expression. They also signify a nasty temper and the possibility of an inner combustion or an outer explosion.

10. *Small ticks* on letters reveal impatience.

11. *Stabbed ovals* belong to someone who can be spiteful.

12. A *large defiant buckle letter k* reveals someone who can be bolshy and awkward.

13. *Potlid p's* are argumentative and contentious.

14. *Misplaced upper case letters* is a sign of inappropriate behaviour and sudden temper.

15. *Strong underlinings and/or crossings-out* reveal dogmatism (with others) and anger (with self).

16. *Distorted letters* (particularly in the tall stems of the UZ) reveal a disturbed mind that may be capable of anything.

17. *Over or totally connected* cursive style uncovers the fanatical thinker who is trapped inside their (often psychotic) thoughts.

18. *Split letters* are associated with anti-social personality disorders. These writers may be spiritually bankrupt and a law unto themselves. There *may* be violent tendencies, resulting from a lack of personal cohesion and self-understanding. *Split letters* are also associated with a less dangerous connotation – they can also be indicative of a speech impediment, such as stammering.

Glossary

A catalogue of graphological and psychological technical jargon (or terms) and their meanings, listed in alphabetical order

Absolute size   The vertical height or dimension of a word – the sum of all three *zones* – determined by measuring the distance between the tips of the upper stems (or loops) to the base of the lower tails (or loops). The conventional or *medium size* is approximately 9mm.

Aerated   A combination of *wide word* and *wide line spacing*.

Angles or Angular (FOC)   Sharp-tipped, jagged or spiky tops of *middle zone* letters. Also seen where curves are replaced with direct/straight lines in the connections between any letters.

Angular garlands   A *garland FOC*, instead of having a smooth rounded bottom and upstroke, has an *angular* form to this part of the *garland* on the *baseline*, which may turn inward or outward.

Anima   The unconscious feminine, feeling side of a man's soul.

Animus   The unconscious assertive, masculine side of a woman's soul.

Anxiety   A vague, unpleasant emotional state with qualities of apprehension, dread, distress and general uneasiness

Arabesques   Flying curves, usually seen in the initial strokes of *capital letters*, often covering (like an umbrella) or underlining the following word.

Arcade (FOC)   Arched, rounded shapes at the top of *middle zone* letters.

Archetypes   In Jungian theory, primitive mental images inherited from our earliest human ancestors, still present in our unconscious.

Arrogance arcades   *Arcade* strokes (*connecting* or *starting strokes*) of any size, which elevate from the *MZ* into the *UZ*.

Arrhythmic writing   Imperfect, discordant, or cacophonous rhythm. This is seen where sudden, unexpected movements (such as fleeting loses of hand control) briefly interrupt the tempo of the writing, affecting the natural free flow and harmony. Most of us have some *arrhythm* in our handwriting, but the degree to which this happens will vary.

Baselines   The imaginary line (on unlined paper) the writer writes upon.

Broad   Seen in *middle zone* letters, where the height is less than the width.

Broken or split   Where letters are constructed in two separate strokes instead of one fluid movement.

Claws   Seen in *lower zone* loops where *left tending* anti-clockwise *arcade* shapes replace normal clockwise loops.

Clubbed   The progressive thickening of an *end stroke*, so the end of the stroke appears thicker than the start.

Columning or 'Chimneys'   Where an invisible gap runs down through the handwritten text, so the page looks like it has been split into two vertical halves. This can happen at any point in the text – not necessarily in the middle.

Concave baseline   A baseline which dips, sags or is indented.

Connected or cursive   Joined-up letters.

Connecting strokes   The shape of strokes that join letters together.

Conscience   A coherent set of internalised moral principles that provide evaluations of right and wrong.

Conscious   The aspect of mind that encompasses actions and emotions of which people are aware.

Contracted   Cramped letters seen in tense handwriting. The letters may be underdeveloped and deprived of completion.

Convex baseline   A baseline which is arched, curving outward or bulging.

Copybook model   The style or system of handwriting taught in schools.

Counter dominants   Featured or stand out handwriting movements whose collective presence is incompatible and therefore whose interpretations inevitably clash.

Covering strokes   Where the writer draws a downstroke or upstroke directly over its previous stroke, so that the two strokes overlap and appear as one.

Cradles   Incomplete *concave* curved loops of *lower zone* stems, giving the appearance of a cradle.

Crucifix t-bars   Centrally crossed t-bars, without a curve at the bottom of the t-stem.

Currency   The quality of the handwriting, as seen in the smoothness and fluency of the pen strokes where there are no deteriorations or impediments.

Defence mechanisms   Enduring patterns of protective behaviour designed to safeguard the ego against anxiety.

Disproportionate zones   A lack of symmetry in the *zones*.

Disconnected   Letters that are unjoined and separated, therefore not linked.

Distinct pen strokes   A type of pen stroke that is thicker on the downstroke and thinner on the upstroke.

Dominants   The stand out feature/s of prevalent handwriting movements.

Dot grinding   Heavy dots that bore into the paper, often visible on the reverse side.

Double walling   Single loops within ovals, cutting them in half.

Ego   The real self and the nucleus or centre of the *conscious mind*.

Elaboration   A style of imaginatively composed handwriting, which is decorated by making more movements than necessary.

Elliptical ovals   Stretched out, elongated, oblong or ovoid shaped ovals in *middle zone* letters.

End strokes   The final or last stroke the pen makes before it is lifted from the page, (seen at the ends of letters and words).

Extroversion   A person who draws energy from being around others, and directs their energy towards people and the outside world.

Flooding   This occurs when the ink of the ductus floods a letter part, usually an oval.

Fluctuation   Refers to the varying ratio of a handwriting movement.

Forms of connection (FOC)   The blanket term for the shape of letter structures, particularly looking *within* letters n and m.

Form standard (FS)   The overall quality of a piece of handwriting, in terms of how positively movements should be interpreted (assessed from speed, originality and layout).

Fullness   Curved letter parts that are noticeably inflated, plump or full.

Garland (FOC)   Concave or cup-shaped tops of *middle zone* letters (often observed where the letters n and m look like u and w).

Horizontal emphasis   An emphasis on rightward movement, usually seen synchronously with *broad width*.

Horizontal tension (HT)   The tautness in the pull of the baseline.

Identification   This is where a person copies the characteristics of another person (this may be done either consciously or unconsciously).

Illegible   Unintelligible scrawl which cannot be read, even in context.

Inferiority complex   This occurs when a collection of repressed fears stemming from an exaggerated sense of inadequacy, give rise to feelings of imperfection.

Interlinear tangling   Parts of letters (usually in the *lower* or *upper zones*) that overlap between lines.

Introversion   A person who directs their energy inwards to their own internal, private world and their inner thoughts and feelings.

Irregular   A variety or variation in letter *size*, shapes and *spatial arrangement*.

Layout or Spatial arrangement   The distribution, organisation, symmetry and clarity of how text is arranged on the page.

Lean   Curved letter parts made straight, and appearing meagre, thin or lean.

Left tends or tendencies   Where parts of letters, loops or *start/end strokes* are pulled, turned or extended towards the left.

Left slant   Writing that reclines or leans backwards, forming an obtuse angle with the baseline.

Legible   Where every letter can be read and understood, without any guesswork involved, even out of context.

Letter spacing   The space left between letters.

Line spacing   The distance between the *baselines*.

Lower case   Small alphabet, or any letters that are not written in capitals.

Lower zone (LZ)   The section of any letters containing downstrokes (such as y and g).

Margins   These refer to the space left on both sides of the page, in relation to the size of paper (on A4 paper an average left margin would be approximately 1in).

Middle zone (MZ)   The central section of letters (such as the a, e, m and r).

Mingling   Letters that touch each other.

Miscellaneous movements   Handwriting movements that only occur once or twice or very occasionally in the script.

Mixed form of connection (FOC)   A combination of several different types of letter structures.

Mixed slant   Writing that alternates between a *right* and *left slant*, forming both acute and obtuse angles with the baseline.

Muddy writing   Ink blotches.

Narrow   Seen in *middle zone* letters, where the height is greater than the width.

Neglect   Poorly formed letters often with parts missing, causing illegibility.

Originality   Handwriting that deviates substantially from the copybook model taught in school, but is still clear, legible and aesthetically-pleasing without ornamentation.

Overcompensation   Behaviour that is OTT or excessive and surplus to requirements, to offset feelings of inferiority.

Overconnected   All letters are joined excessively, without any breaks, and sometimes words are linked too.

Part connected (50/50)   A balance where letters are partially joined or linked together.

Pasty   A well-nourished pen stroke that is thick and broad (so the upstrokes look the same as the downstrokes).

Persona   A superficial, affected handwriting style, which is consciously designed to show what we would like people to think we are, rather than what we really are. It can therefore be compared with the public image of our *signature*.

Potlids   The initial downstroke of the letter p extends upwards, invading the *upper zone* space.

PPI   *Personal pronoun I* (assessed in relation to other capital letters).

Prescribed   According to the copybook model taught in schools.

Pressure   The weight of the pen exerted on the page, and the depth, groove or indentation mark produced (on the reverse side of the paper).

Primary thread   An amalgamation of at least three types of *forms of connection (FOC)*.

Pseudo arcades   Where there are *unprescribed* clockwise loops within the middle downstroke of the letter m.

Psyche   The human mind.

Ragged   Irregular, uneven, disorganised or frayed.

Regularity   Uniformity and consistency in letter *size*, shapes and *spatial arrangement*.

Repression   An unconscious form of self-protection. This operates by blocking, controlling, censoring or banishing unpleasant or undesirable feelings into the unconscious, thereby protecting the individual from ideas and influences that would produce anxiety, apprehension or guilt were they likely to become conscious.

Resting dots   Inadvertent, unconsciously formed dots, that occurs when the pen stops suddenly mid stroke.

Rhythm   Fluent, harmonious tempo of handwriting. This cannot be measured empirically; it can only be observed.

Right slant   Writing that inclines or leans forwards, forming an acute angle with the baseline.

Right tends or tendencies   Parts of letters or end strokes pulled, turned or extended towards the right.

Rigidity   Stiff, inflexible handwriting showing an unyielding clockwork *regularity*.

Rounded Curved pen strokes where the copybook prescribes angles.

Scatter dots Random dots that appear in the body of the script, but seem unrelated to it, being neither punctuation marks nor i dots.

Secondary movements Handwriting movements that exist, but are not stand out features seen consistently or frequently in the script.

Sharp A type of pen stroke that is thin or fine.

Signature A conscious projection of identity.

Simple A child-like style comprising copybook shapes reduced down to their most elementary form, but without any clever shortcuts.

Simplification A style of writing that uses intelligent shortcuts to strip back letter forms to the bare essentials.

Slant The direction and angle of handwriting.

Spatial arrangement *Layout* of text on the page.

Speed How quickly or slowly a piece of handwriting is executed, depending on movements that either accelerate or impede the progression of script.

Starting stroke A preparatory stroke penned as a lead-in to the first letter of a word.

Stilted Where the *rhythm* of the writing is restrained from flowing naturally.

Suspendu Where the final downstroke of the letters n, m and h stop short of the *baseline* and hover above it, so the letter looks incomplete.

Thread FOC Minimal, neglected, flattened, often illegible *middle zone* letters.

Trizonal dynamics The delicate balance, interplay and cohesion between all three zones.

Unconscious The part of the psyche of which the individual is not aware, encompassing repressed primitive impulses and desires that are too anxiety-provoking to be accepted into consciousness.

Upper case *Capital letters* (related to our social image, reflecting what others think of us, and not what we feel inside).

Upper zone (UZ) The section of any letters containing tall stems or loops (such as b, d, f and l).

Vanity loop Inflated loops on the lower case stems of letters t and d only.

Vertical or Upright slant Handwriting formed at a right angle to the baseline, with minimal variation.

Vertical emphasis An emphasis on up and down movements, usually seen synchronously with *narrow width*.

Wavy line FOC Unstructured letters n and m appearing like double-curved horizontal s shapes.

Word spacing The distance between words.

Zonal balance Where the *middle, upper* and *lower zones* are matching or equal sizes.

Zones Three individual sections of letter parts, seen within the *absolute size*. (It is important that the *zones* are regarded *proportionately*, i.e. in relation to each other.)

Acknowledgements and credits

I am indebted to Elaine Quigley for introducing me to graphology, hooking me into the magic of the subject and challenging me to change the course of my life; to Mary Black for teaching me everything she knows about graphology, and then generously helping to give my work direction; to my mother for her kind patronage; to my husband Paul, for his unstinting background support; and to my two daughters Emma and Maddie Yuille, who were my bedrocks and salvation through all the hard times and the difficult years.

I would also like to offer grateful thanks to the following people for giving me permission to use their handwriting samples: Catherine Jamet-Kerman (for permitting the reproduction of her husband and mother-in-law's letters and allowing me to unpick their characters and explore the familial relationship so intimately and publicly); the Freeman children for Lord Denning's letter sourced from their parents' estate; Diane Simpson for Dennis Nilsen's original notes, and Betty Soldi for an original sample of her 'inkspired' penmanship.

Heartfelt thanks also to the brave people who gave me access to this precious part of their intrinsic DNA and allowing me to dissect them publicly: Lily Alexander, Jonny Benjamin MBE, Wendy Haxton, Jessica Martin, Molly Martin, James Pout, Amanda Wigzell, Rosalind Wyatt and not forgetting all those who requested complete anonymity!

BRITANNIA BRIGHT'S BEWILDERMENT IN THE WILDERNESS OF WESTMINSTER